MORE THAN MEETS THE EYE

MORE THAN MEETS THE EYE

Watching Television Watching Us

John J. Pungente, S. J., and Martin O'Malley

M&S

Harry Beale's soliloquy from the film *Network* reprinted in the Introduction is from the Applause Publication, *The Collected Screenplays of Paddy Chayefsky*, 1995/Network © 1976 Metro-Goldwyn Mayer and United Artists Corporation. Excerpts from Len Masterman, *Teaching the Media* (London: Routledge, 1985) and *Teaching the Media: International Perspectives* (London: Lawrence Erlbaum, 1998), reprinted in chapters 1, 6, and Final Thoughts, courtesy of Len Masterman. Excerpt reprinted in chapter 3 from *Honey, I'm Home: Sitcoms* ©copyright 1992 by Gerard Jones with permission of Grove/Atlantic, Inc. Excerpt reprinted in chapter 5 from *Beyond Blame: Challenging Violence in the Media* with permission of the Center for Media Literacy, Los Angeles. Barry Duncan quoted with permission of Barry Duncan.

Canadian Cataloguing in Publication Data

Pungente, John J.
     More than meets the eye : watching television watching us

Includes bibliographical references.
ISBN 0-7710-7100-0

1. Television criticism.   2. Television programs.   3. Television broadcasting.
I. O'Malley, Martin.   II. Title.

PN1992.8.C7P86 1999   791.45   C99-930261-2

We acknowledge the financial support of the Government of Canada through the Book Publishing Industry Development Program for our publishing activities. We further acknowledge the support of the Canada Council for the Arts and the Ontario Arts Council for our publishing program.

Typeset in Minion by M&S, Toronto

Printed and bound in Canada

McClelland & Stewart Inc.
The Canadian Publishers
481 University Avenue
Toronto, Ontario
M5G 2E9

1 2 3 4 5 6   04 03 02 01 00 99

For my parents, Mary and John Pungente, with love and gratitude.
– J. J. P.

For my sister, Margaret, my first mentor.
– M. O'M.

Contents

Introduction: Ignatius, Meet Buffy! Buffy, Meet Ignatius!

～

It's just hard not to listen to TV – it's spent so much more time raising us than you have.

　　　　　　　　　　– Bart Simpson to his dad, Homer, on *The Simpsons*

M y day begins at four-thirty when the streets are quiet and the city is at peace. After a gentle predawn run, I shave and shower, say mass in my apartment, then walk across the street to my office where I teach people how to watch television.

Media education has become my life's work and I enjoy it more than I ever could have imagined when I started teaching as a young man. Media education did not exist when I was a student in high school. The media was just the media, no message there. The best we could expect in the 1950s was a break from classes to watch a scratchy version of *A Tale of Two Cities* on a roll-down screen. *The Honeymooners? I Love Lucy?* We watched, of course, but they had nothing to do with school.

When I get to my tenth-floor office, chances are there will be e-mail from some of my colleagues, perhaps about last night's *Ally McBeal*, the hit series from Fox Network about a charming if ditzy Harvard-trained lawyer with a penchant for miniskirts. In my field, media education, we take *Ally McBeal* seriously.

In Canada, we tend to call this field "media literacy," but it is known as "media education" in most other countries. By the time the average Canadian child graduates from high school he or she will have spent twice as much time in front of the television set as in the classroom. The only occupation that engages more of his or her time is sleep.

It is important for children – for all of us – to understand exactly what television is and how it affects us. Television is too pervasive, powerful, and influential to be viewed passively. We teach people how to read critically, how to interpret history, how to solve problems, so why not teach them how to watch television? We teach people to be literate about print. Why not about the media?

In *More Than Meets the Eye: Watching Television Watching Us,* my co-author, Martin O'Malley, and I want to assist television viewers – and consumers of all media – to understand more about the media that has become an integral part of our lives, no matter how much we watch or don't watch TV, or go to movies, or read newspapers and magazines, or listen to the radio, or connect on the Internet.

We live in a mediated society. Our culture and our business are formed by the mass media. Whether we think this is a good thing or a bad thing matters not: what does matter is that we develop an informed and critical understanding of the nature of the media, their impact, and the techniques they use.

Polls consistently report that people regard television as their most trustworthy source of news. We hear it with our own ears, see it with our own eyes; it *must* be real. And yet, the 1998 movie *Wag the Dog* shows how mischievous television can be. People who saw the movie will recall the vivid image of the frightened girl clutching the cat, running from the enemy, dodging bullets in the war-torn village – an image created in a television studio. There were no bullets, the girl wasn't frightened, there was no war-torn village; there was no war.

I use the term "well-watched" as others have used "well-read." I first heard it used by Moses Znaimer, founder and President of Citytv in Toronto. To be "well-read" is not enough these days. We are no longer well-educated, knowledgeable, or learned if we are ignorant about media. Media education, of course, involves newspapers, magazines, radio, film, video games, advertising, even music videos and the Internet – everything that makes up popular culture. This book will concentrate on television because of the impact it has on our lives and our fascination with it.

Media education is not television-bashing. Television is neither good nor bad itself. It is just a medium. We want to give people the tools to look at television critically so they can make their own informed decisions about what they watch.

Ninety per cent of TV may be junk but the other 10 per cent can be educational, entertaining, and worth watching. We should work on that excellent 10 per cent, encourage it, and do what needs to be done to make the 90 per cent worthwhile. What I hope for – it may take decades – is that we can build an audience whose critical sense is such that it demands better programs. And that some of these media-educated people will go on to produce and create excellent TV programs in the future.

I love television, but often am saddened and distressed by how it can be used and misused, at the wonderful opportunities missed, at the stubborn resistance to it by people who should know better. At the same time, as an educator, I appreciate the splendid "teachable moments" that occur on just about any TV program, from *Masterpiece Theater* to *3rd Rock from the Sun*, even *The Jerry Springer Show*.

Harry Beale and the American Way

"Commercial television makes so much money doing its worst," said Fred Friendly when he was head of CBS News, "it can't afford to do its best." Alas, Friendly's remark still holds true, especially in the United States, which produces the bulk of the world's popular television.

What is the problem with media education in the United States? There were hopeful signs in the 1960s and there are still encouraging pockets of enlightenment, but media education in the United States remains primarily defensive. Television generally is considered harmful to children, thus children must be "inoculated" against it. Television, according to this view, encourages children to smoke, do drugs, act violently and immorally, and so the message too often is don't watch, don't try to learn from television. Run, hide, ban, censor! No wonder media professionals in the United States distrust media education.

There are the I-refuse-to-watch-television people. Nothing new here. There were the I-refuse-to-read-books people when movable type was invented, then the I-refuse-to-watch-movies people when movies started (and the I-refuse-to-watch-talkies people when sound came along). I come across it in the most surprising places, often from people I admire. Russell Banks, the superb American writer of books such as *The Sweet Hereafter* and *Cloudsplitter* tells a *Globe and Mail* interviewer (April 25, 1998): "The adults in our society have abandoned their children. We've put them in the custody of the amoral free-market economy and turned them into consumers. That's what's hurting them . . ."

I agree with Banks, he's nailed it. So far, so good, but he can't resist adding: "First we kill all the television sets and then the lawyers."

Clever, but why do Americans say these things? Is it a weird tic in the national psyche? A fear, a last stand by a writer-driven, print-biased coterie of Tall Foreheads? John Irving recently wrote an amusing retrospective on his novel *The World According to Garp* in which he reminded us of Garp prowling his neighbourhood at night, depressed by his neighbours' television sets. "There is the faint, trapped warble from some televisions tuned into The Late Show, and the blue-gray glow from the picture tubes throbs from a few of the houses. To Garp this glow looks like cancer, insidious and numbing, putting the world to sleep. Maybe television *causes* cancer, Garp thinks; but his real irritation is a *writer's* irritation: he knows that wherever a TV glows, there sits someone who isn't *reading.*"

Marshall McLuhan didn't bother with "well-read," "well-watched," or "media literacy." He called it all "education." In *Understanding Media: The Extensions of Man*, he writes: "Education is ideally civil defence against media fallout. Yet Western man has had, so far, no education or equipment for meeting any of the new media on their own terms. Literate man is not only numb and vague in the presence of film or photo, but he intensifies his ineptness by a defensive arrogance and condescension to 'pop kulch' and 'mass entertainment.' It was in this spirit of bulldog opacity that the scholastic philosophers failed to meet the challenge of the printed word in the sixteenth century. The vested interests of acquired knowledge and conventional wisdom have always been bypassed and engulfed by new media."

From McLuhan to – Harry Beale. Beale, "the mad prophet of the air waves" in the movie *Network*. He was mad as hell and wasn't going to take it any more. That's what people remember about Harry Beale, but he said more than that.

You and 62 million other Americans are watching me right now, that's why! Because less than 3 per cent of you read books. Because less than 15 per cent of you read newspapers. Because the only truth you know is what you get over this tube!

There is a whole and entire generation right now who never knew anything that didn't come out of this tube. This tube is the gospel. This tube is the ultimate revelation. This tube can make or break presidents, popes, prime ministers. This tube is the most awesome, goddamned force in the whole godless world. And woe is us if it ever falls into the hands of the wrong people ...

So, listen to me! Television is not the truth! Television is a goddamned amusement park. Television is a circus, a carnival, a travelling troupe of acrobats and story-tellers, singers and dancers, jugglers, side-show freaks, lion-tamers and football players. We're in the boredom-killing business ...

We deal in illusions, man! None of it is true. But you people sit there – all of you – day after day, night after night, all ages, colors, creeds. We're all you know. You're beginning to think that the tube is reality and your own lives are unreal. You do whatever the tube tells you. You dress like the tube, you eat like the tube, you raise your children like the tube, you think like the tube. This is mass madness, you maniacs! In God's name, you people are the real thing! We're the illusions. So, turn off this goddamn set! Turn it off and leave it off. Turn it off right now, right in the middle of this very sentence I'm speaking now ...

As with Russell Banks, I agree with Beale – until he tells us to turn off our television sets. Americans seem to be fixated on this. What a breakthrough it would be if instead of turning off their TV sets, the television-reformers started watching TV critically. All that American energy, technological savvy, all those American television sets . . .

There was a terrific horror movie in the mid-1950s called *Invasion of the Body Snatchers*, about a small-town doctor who discovers his town is being taken over by aliens. It really was scary – spooky. One by one, friends and neighbours turned into zombies, but they looked the same, so you couldn't tell for sure. The weapons were gigantic, gelatinous pods, which the aliens sneaked into your house. You were okay as long as you stayed awake, but if you fell asleep your external body was remade into an emotionless zombie, gurgling in the pod. It may have been one of those creative happenstances, but it was the mid-1950s and nothing can convince me that those pods were not meant to symbolize television sets. It's typical of the attitude of many Americans (and not only Americans) to look on television with horror.

Interesting to note that explicit sexuality disturbs American viewers more than viewers in other countries, even their clean and chummy neighbour Canada. Interesting, too, how the reverse is true with explicit violence. Not surprising, then, that the third week of April in the United States has been designated "TV Turnoff Week" by a group known as "TV-Free America." I find this menacing, as it can be reduced to: *if it scares you, kill it.*

Could it be that many people in North America, having been immersed in the culture of television for so long, and so passively, have come to believe the myths, fantasies, and dreams of television more than they believe in themselves?

The only way to get better television is to learn how television works, show the seams, learn to watch carefully and think critically. We are smarter than our television sets.

A Career of Media-Watching

Television has turned out to be one of the most phenomenal of all human inventions. It touches lives more immediately and pervasively than anything that predates it, with the possible exception of the discovery of fire.

– Ellen de Franco, *TV ON/OFF*, 1980

I am a Jesuit priest, a member of the religious order founded more than four hundred years ago by Ignatius of Loyola, whose writings urge us "to praise, reverence and serve God our Lord and by this means save our souls." He also urges us "to make use of all the things on the earth insofar as they help us to the attainment of our goal and to get rid of them insofar as they prove a hindrance to our goal." Ignatius was a soldier, a scholar, and an educator, but he also liked to dance.

Ignatius would have been thrilled by television. While some of the language, violence, soap-opera situations, and the depiction of people might have made him shudder, he would have seen the potential of television as educator and entertainer. How could he not? A medium this powerful, this pervasive, this *global* – a household item as common as a table or a chair.

I wonder what he would think of *Buffy the Vampire Slayer*, *The X-Files*, and *Two Fat Ladies*, three of my favourite television shows. Ignatius would not much care for *The Jerry Springer Show*, all that punching, kicking, hair-pulling, profanity, sex. More likely, he'd frown at the way it panders to such a low level, the way it's just, well, stupid. I suspect he would get a kick out of *Due South*, the Canadian series that chuckles at its polite Canadianness as it pokes fun at our well-intentioned, hyperventilating American cousins. Don't think he'd care much for the V-chip, which allows big people to program television so as not to corrupt little people. No, he would see the V-chip for what it is: censorship, which is antithetical to education.

Back in the seventeenth century, Jesuit Athanasius Kircher discovered the principle on which the projection of images is based, which makes him the father – literally and figuratively, you could say – of the movie projector. In the early, formative years of Hollywood, Jesuit Daniel Lord played a key role in developing The Hollywood Code, a guideline for standards of good taste in movies. And at the 1998 Academy Awards, Jesuit Chris Donahue won an Oscar for *Visas and Virtues* in the category of best live-action short film.

For thirty-five years I have been teaching students about the media, teaching their teachers, travelling the world to see how media education is done in other countries. We have indeed become the global village Marshall McLuhan predicted in the 1960s when he became the most popular exponent of what we now call media education.

I grew up in the 1950s when television was still new. "Watch too much and you'll get hypnotized," we were warned. The first television I ever saw was when I was about eleven years old and on a motor trip with my parents heading to California. At some motel by some highway I watched parts of the political convention that selected Dwight Eisenhower as the Republican candidate for President of the United States. At another motel on another day I watched *Howdy Doody*. What I remember is that, no, it did not hit me like a ton of bricks. And I wasn't mesmerized by it. I preferred to be outside in the clear fresh air.

Television didn't really have a significant effect on my life until I was in my early twenties. We didn't watch much television at the Winnipeg high school where I was a boarder. And when I joined the Jesuits, the first two years were known as the "novitiate," when we were not allowed to read newspapers, listen to radio, or watch movies or television. We could speak English only after the main meal, for half an hour; at all other times conversations had to be in Latin, even for kids who had never studied Latin. We were allowed to write our parents only once a month. There were to be no outside influences. The idea was to be like Christ in the desert while we decided if this was what we wanted to do with our lives. This all seems ancient history now: Jesuit training has been drastically changed.

After two years of novitiate, followed by two years of "juniorate" – devoted to studying the classics and modern languages – it was time for three years of philosophy at Gonzaga University in Spokane, where I also earned a master's degree in English. I was now ready to teach English and my first assignment was at St. Paul's High School in Winnipeg. In addition to my regular curriculum teaching, the Jesuit principal, St. Clair Monaghan, asked me to conduct a non-credit film course. The first year I taught a Sunday afternoon film course for students from Grade 9 to Grade 12. We studied films such as *Dr. Strangelove, Lord of the Flies,* and *Citizen Kane.*

I enjoyed teaching film studies. One summer I took a four-week course in film studies at Columbia University, after which I returned to St. Paul's eager to involve myself in a more structured program. For my Grade 9 class, I started with the films of Charlie Chaplin, knowing that a pie in the face always gets attention. By the end of that school year I had brought them along to *The Birth of a Nation.* By this time my students knew enough about silent films to appreciate the D. W. Griffith masterpiece.

They were enthralled.

The Jesuits do things in a strict and logical progression. After studying philosophy, we spent a few years teaching, then we did "special studies." It was like choosing a major, only more so, as it invariably meant choosing your life's work. I was studying in Spokane when I was given the opportunity to "volunteer" for media education. I leapt at the chance as a grunt at boot camp might leap at the chance to serve on the French Riviera. Then – I waited. As the order was then administered, these decisions were made for us. Each July 31, the feast of St. Ignatius, we found out what we would do the next year. I got my wish and moved to California to pursue film studies.

I arrived in San Francisco in the fall of 1967, the height of the hippie era. I was twenty-seven years old, a few years from being ordained. I lived with the Jesuits at the University of San Francisco, down the street from the fabled Haight-Ashbury intersection. Every morning I got a ride to class at San Francisco State University on the back of a Harley-Davidson, a roaring hog driven by a huge young filmmaker from Denver with a tangled beard and granny glasses, a really nice guy. I got into the spirit of the times by allowing my frizzled black hair to grow into a modest afro. I got teargassed once, when I happened to be in the wrong place at the wrong time during a campus riot.

There was the wonderful live music at the Fillmore and the Avalon: Janis Joplin with Big Brother and the Holding Company, Jimi Hendrix, Cream, Jefferson Airplane, Country Joe, the Doors. And there was Marshall McLuhan, the hottest academic in North America, who would later appear in Woody Allen's *Annie Hall*, and give a featured interview in *Playboy*. McLuhan was recognizably, unabashedly Canadian. In my master's program there was a seminar on McLuhan, so guess who got called upon to be the spokesperson for the future of television, the global village and "the medium is the message"? I crammed *The Gutenberg Galaxy* and *Understanding Media: The Extensions of Man* every night in my room, staying a few pages ahead of my classmates. Merely being a Canadian in the field of media education was to be a part of the legacy of Marshall McLuhan.

Thirty years later, same thing. Being Canadian, from the land of McLuhan (and Harold Innis, the brilliant theorist who preceded and inspired him) colleagues around the world expect me to know a little more about media than most people, just as they expect me to know a little more about ice hockey. Well, I still don't know much about hockey.

Church and the State of Media Education

It was in 1939 that one of the first functional prototypes of the television set appeared prominently at the New York World's Fair. It was considered something of a gimmick then. The great philosopher Bertrand Russell displayed an uncommon lapse in prescience – but reflected conventional wisdom at that time – when he declared: "Television will be of no importance in your lifetime or mine." Russell died in 1970 at the age of ninety-eight, when, if he cared to, he could have watched *Mary Tyler Moore* and a man hitting a golf ball on the moon.

The previous year (1938), the Church first recognized the need for serious media education. Pius XI wrote an encyclical on the motion picture and its impact on the young, urging that the church take seriously all aspects of the new media by instituting the formal study of media in schools. At the time, movies were uppermost in his mind, but television was on its way. For an institution often regarded as hidebound and slow – yes, it took a long time to accept that Galileo was right – this was remarkably farsighted.

Three decades later Pope John XXIII inaugurated an era of openness in Church affairs. Media education may not have been the hottest item on the agenda, but it was there. The Vatican II document *Communio et Progressio* said: "Catholic schools and organizations cannot ignore the urgent duty they have in this field. It is never too early to start encouraging in children artistic taste, a keen critical faculty, and a sense of personal responsibility based on sound morality. This sort of training must be given a regular place in school curricula. It must be given, and systematically, at every stage of education."

When they returned home from Rome, the Australian bishops immediately pushed for mandatory inclusion of media education in Catholic schools in Australia. In 1972, they issued a document titled *A Bounden Moral Duty*, in which they declared: "Very special attention must be given by all parents and all educators to the right formation of the young in relation to those all-pervading media of communications. This is a bounden moral duty. It cannot be put aside without very grave consequences and qualms of conscience."

While the English led the way, introducing a form of media education when they introduced film education in the 1920s, Australian schools, both

Catholic and public, gave the movement a big boost in the 1970s. Canada now is regarded as the third-most enlightened country in the world in media education after Australia and the United Kingdom. In May 1998, the World Council for Media Education, meeting in Brazil, recognized the Ontario Association for Media Literacy as "the most important media education body in North America."

After Sweeney Todd

I was teaching in Winnipeg on a bitterly cold morning in November 1982, when I received a call from England. Would I like to travel around the world and investigate how media education was being taught in schools? And could I fly to London the next week to discuss this?

I was in my early forties. I had never been outside North America. November is always a busy time at high school, with examinations approaching, and a pressing item on my agenda was *Sweeney Todd*, a student production I was directing. We were well underway, rehearsals had started, and the play was scheduled to open in less than a month.

They wanted me in London in a week.

"I'm teaching, you know. I'm the principal. I can't just do what I want. It's not the way with the Jesuits. There's the Provincial to consult . . ."

"We'll take care of that."

"But, *Sweeney Todd* . . ."

"We'll arrange the plane tickets. No reason you shouldn't be free to go to the theatre while you're in London."

I arrived in London the next week. My career in media education slipped into high gear. In 1984, over a period of nine months I visited sixty-two cities in twenty-nine countries, covering 53,219 miles by plane, bus, truck, car, boat, train, and the occasional rickshaw. My mission was to examine how media education was being taught in schools around the world. The trip was sponsored by the Centre for Communication and Culture in London, a Jesuit institution. The end of that trip marked the beginning of a new direction for my work in media education, work that would include training teachers, acting as a consultant for the media, writing text books, and speaking at conferences worldwide.

A Dialogue on Family Values

To prepare for this book and to get my thoughts in order I met with Martin O'Malley most Friday mornings in my office throughout the winter of 1997–98. Martin and I attended the same high school in Winnipeg, then he went on to a career in journalism at *The Globe and Mail*.

Martin is a self-admitted television Luddite. When we first sat down across his tape recorder he confessed he had never heard of *Ally McBeal* or *Two Fat Ladies*. He said he likes watching televised baseball games, a sport I find incredibly boring, but he redeemed himself somewhat by saying he is a fan of *Frasier*.

In a typical morning session, early on, when we were discussing the ways and wherefores of media education, the subject of values emerged. The evening before, I had watched an episode of *Union Square*, which was about a woman in her forties who had a sexual liaison with a young college student. "The older woman worried whether she should have done this," I said to Martin. "She was with the kids in a coffee shop and the young people said to her, 'It doesn't matter.' The message was, 'If it feels good do it.' If that's the message presented in every program, eventually that kind of value becomes a value that you accept."

O'MALLEY: So what? Why interfere with that?

PUNGENTE: You don't *interfere* with it. You're accepting it without being aware of it. Once you're aware that values are being put across by the media you can accept them or reject them as you wish. Just be aware that this is being done to you consciously by the people who make the media.

O'MALLEY: But who is benefiting? Whose vested interests are being served? The advertisers?

PUNGENTE: Oh, most certainly.

O'MALLEY: Promiscuity is not a product.

PUNGENTE: No, no. The advertisers are benefiting if the message is appealing to young people, who will therefore watch the show. And if they watch the show they will therefore buy the product. We're buying into a way of life. I took the promiscuity thing as a very obvious example. There are better ones, such as the example of family. What is a family? Where do you learn what family values are? From watching *Roseanne, Home Improvement, Seinfeld?* Which is the family?

O'MALLEY: Good question. What is a family today? Work as family? Friends as family?

PUNGENTE: The families on *ER* and on *Seinfeld* are as viable a family as the family in *Home Improvement.* They're all important because they're all putting values on what kind of family you have. If you hate the values, at least be aware that they're there, then you might decide not to watch the program. Rick Salutin did a wonderful column in *The Globe and Mail* on the religious show *Nothing Sacred*, about priests in a rectory in an inner-city parish. He said the priests are too pretty, the problems too predictable, the endings too neat. Hollywood does that to everything. When it comes to values conveyed on TV, like the *Union Square* example, the problem is, what do we do about it? Do we say no, no, no? Or do we give the kids the tools to watch it, so they'll know that this value is being put across? As a parent or a teacher you might then say these are values you don't uphold, you don't think are right.

O'MALLEY: The underside might be that someone might totally agree with you that something should be done about it. Wouldn't you get suspicious if that someone was a religion-based, evangelical type who believes promiscuity is evil? Isn't this the old and departing "imparting knowledge" pedagogy, as opposed to the "critical autonomy" you people in media education are supposed to be espousing?

PUNGENTE: Yes, all we want to do is make people think. In order to make them think, make them critically autonomous, we have to give them the tools to do it. That's what media education does. It says, "Look, there's an ideology here." This week, for my television program *Scanning the Movies*, I used *The Postman*, the Kevin Costner movie. I chose to do it from the point of view of ideology because the movie is just American jingoism. It's an epic movie, beautifully photographed, even well acted by many of the cast.

There is a message in this movie. It's not just about a postman who delivers mail. It's showing us that the American way of life is the right way of life and anybody who goes against it is evil.

Therefore, if they try to destroy our way of life we must destroy them, so we can rule forever. You might not realize you are being given a whole way of life, a whole ideology. That's what we want to make people aware of. Is it a good ideology? Is it a bad ideology? You make that decision.

O'MALLEY: Let's consider the matter of the passive, accepting television audience. Is it easier to sell them stuff if they are uncritical?

PUNGENTE: Of course it is. This is why media education for the most part is not working in the United States. There is a group of people who say media is bad. These are the "inoculationists" who want to protect children from the evil media.

O'MALLEY: Latter-day book-burners?

PUNGENTE: Their grasp of media is that it's all bad and media education is the only protection against this evil.

O'MALLEY: What about the elitists who say they don't watch television, who say we'd all be better off if we didn't have television sets in our houses?

PUNGENTE: It's much better for advertisers to have a Pablum-fed audience that just doesn't care. That's what we have in much of North America, but in countries like England and Australia you don't. They have better quality products – better film, better TV.

O'MALLEY: Is there anyone on the other side leading an anti-media education movement?

PUNGENTE: People who make the media are terrified of media education because they think it is going to say bad things about them, force people not to watch television. And there are the groups that think they are doing media education and are opposed to real media education. They think they are protecting the children, they're not trying to give them any skills, not teaching them to be critical thinkers. God help them if the kids become critically autonomous because they'll realize that what they're being fed by these so-called media educators is wrong.

O'MALLEY: These inoculationists, they would be supporters of the V-chip to control what children watch on television at home?

PUNGENTE: Yes. Most countries go through this phase, but they go through it quickly, within a year or so. The United States has not gone through this phase quickly; it's been mired in it for about fifteen years.

O'MALLEY: Returning to the pedagogy of media education, and considering what Marshall McLuhan had to say in *Understanding Media*, wasn't this the case in the sixteenth century when the pedagogical establishment looked in horror at the rise of new literature, when the establishment considered the new literature subversive because it was popular?

PUNGENTE: Yes. McLuhan talks of the "defensive arrogance and condescension" of the literary establishment, the status quo, in the sixteenth century. And he encountered it in the 1960s – the pop culture, the mass entertainment, they were something to be defended against. McLuhan said, "The vested interests of acquired knowledge and conventional wisdom have always been bypassed and engulfed by the new media." But media go ahead and do what they do. Only people who are intelligent enough to grasp the new media get anything out of them.

Answering Back

Educator Neil Postman ends his book *Amusing Ourselves to Death: Public Discourse in the Age of Show Business* on a note of sceptical optimism when he suggests that the best way to improve television is to encourage people to talk back to their sets. "No medium is excessively dangerous if its users understand what its dangers are," he says. "To ask is to break the spell."

How best to do this?

"The desperate answer," Postman suggests, "is to rely on the only mass medium of communication that, in theory, is capable of addressing the problem: our schools."

So, let's go into a classroom.

I once began a session for media education teachers in England by showing a music video of an androgynous-looking person singing "So in Love." This was years ago, when the singer was not yet famous. I chose this music video to illustrate another of the "key concepts" we use in media education: Audiences negotiate meaning in media. When we look at any media text – a movie, a situation comedy, a music video – each of us finds or "negotiates" meaning in various ways. We come to it with our personal needs and anxieties, the pleasures or troubles of the day, racial and sexual attitudes, family and cultural backgrounds. All these factors affect how we process information received from whatever we are watching.

In the "So in Love" video, a forlorn figure appears doing laundry, wearing yellow rubber gloves, slowly walking from room to room. A drop of water becomes a tear. The words, plaintive, haunting, describe the singer's despair after, seemingly, having been deserted.

(My remarks are in italics.)

So, what did you see there?

"A lonely man doing household chores, missing someone . . ."

"Maybe the man's wife left him. He's depressed . . ."

"It isn't a man, it's k. d. lang . . ."

If you had to put a narrative to it, tell us the story. All music videos have a story.

"She's grieving, there's been a loss. There is an empty baby's chair."

"She's had an abortion."

"k. d. lang's gay!"

"She is?"

Do you know why the video was made?

"I know the song, 'So in Love.'"

"The words speak of loss . . . hurt . . . yet, 'So in love . . .'"

Who wrote it?

"Cole Porter."

Why is k. d. lang singing a Cole Porter song?

"I dunno."

"Wasn't Cole Porter gay?"

It was for Cole Porter's one-hundredth birthday, if he had lived that long. It was part of a compilation album of Cole Porter songs performed by various artists, called "Red, Hot and Blue." It was produced to raise awareness of AIDS. It shows a woman, alone, hanging up a woman's nightgown, doing dishes.

"There's a shower stall, but it's not a baby's chair, it's one of those toilets sick people use. Is her partner dying of AIDS?"

Do you know where the song's from?
>"Broadway musical . . . not *Carousel*, just a sec . . ."
>"*Kiss Me Kate!*"
>*Where does* Kiss Me Kate *come from?*
>"The Taming of the Shrew."

(Things are starting to cook.)

The song as originally written has nothing to do with AIDS, *nothing to do with the gay life. It was the essential love song sung by Howard Keel to Kathryn Grayson when they're finally expressing their love in* Kiss Me Kate, *an exquisite moment between a man and a woman, written by a man who was gay.*

(Then: a connection, a sudden flight of thought, like geese overhead, coming home.)

>"Erica Jong says in *Fear of Fifty* that whenever she has seen *Carousel* and hears the song 'If I Loved You' she hears crying around her and it's always men who are crying."
>"A male lament about missed opportunities, lost loves."
>*You brought that to the video. I love it!*
>"If I watched that video again I'd watch it entirely differently." [this from a teacher.]
>*Because you'd be bringing to it what you didn't have twenty minutes ago. Kids bring to television what they didn't have twenty minutes ago. It's enriching, empowering. It's like cleaning your glasses when they're dirty. Don't tell them what they should be enjoying. Let them find out themselves.*
>*Ask questions. Break the spell.*

A Toolkit for Television Watchers

Different chapters of *More Than Meets the Eye* focus on different topics, providing background, explaining the pros and cons of such topics as the situation comedy, consumerism, the portrayal of the family on television, as well as values, news, violence on television, the phenomenon of the talk show and the soap opera, how television "gives good grief."

Our intention is not to judge but to provide the tools, so people can make their own evaluations. We are not television critics.

You will find few examples from Canadian television. There are two reasons for this. First, Canadians have access on basic cable to the four American networks as well as to their own three major English-language ones. Second, out of a possible twenty-eight hours a week of prime-time programming, Canadian shows are not that evident on two of the three Canadian networks. At the start of the 1998–99 television season, while CBC ran 26.5 hours of Canadian programming per week, CTV ran only 6 hours a week, and Global, 2.5 hours a week.

In Britain in 1998, the top ten shows were all British. In Canada, only *Hockey Night in Canada* and local news shows made any top-twenty list – and then only in Toronto and Vancouver. The CBC accounts for only a quarter of TV viewing, and private stations have overwhelmingly used U.S. fare. Only a quarter of the prime-time TV we watch is Canadian. Most Canadians watching prime-time television are not watching Canadian shows. Half the shows Canadians watch are dramas, but fewer than 9 per cent of these are Canadian.

In Canada most of what we see on television comes from the United States, some small part of which is brilliant, too much of which is not. When we think of high-profile news programs, we tend to think of *60 Minutes*. When we think of sitcoms, we think of the now defunct *Seinfeld*, perhaps *Frasier* and *3rd Rock from the Sun*. When we think of cop shows and occupational dramas, we think of *NYPD Blue*, *Law & Order*, *Buddy Faro*, and *ER*. My visits to other countries afford me the opportunity to widen my perspective and keep abreast of the developments and trends in media around the world. There are wonderful television programs beyond North America, and the world has much to teach us. But, in *More Than Meets the Eye*, as in our own television watching, we will concentrate on North American television.

Martin O'Malley suggested that I try my hand at writing a general interest book on media education. I balked because I am not a writer nor am I used to explaining the media without the use of video clips, overheads, and plenty of time for discussion. O'Malley offered to help write the book if I would provide the explanations, background, and ideas. Throughout the winter of 1997–98, we sat across a tape recorder in my office, then we rolled up our sleeves and began to put our thoughts on paper. And these thoughts range wide, from vampires to lawyers, from the family to the church, from selling violence to selling out, from the non-stop talkers to the father-figure news anchors. It's all here – inside Plato's cave.

1

Inside Plato's Cave

~

The media are now, arguably, our culture's primary symbolic system. They will certainly be so throughout the next century. Those who do not understand how the media work, how they construct meanings, how they can be used, and how the evidence they present can be weighed and evaluated are, in contemporary cultures, considerably disadvantaged and disempowered.

— Len Masterman, "Media Literacy, Information Technology and the Teaching of English," 1997

In *The Republic*, Plato describes a group of people who have lived in a cave all their lives. They are chained in such a way that they can only look straight ahead. A fire burning behind them throws light at a platform in front of them. Men pass behind a screen on the platform carrying all sorts of figures which they hold above the screen for all to see. These are figures of people and animals and various objects. Sometimes the carriers speak as they go by, sometimes not. The people watching see the shadows of the objects thrown on the wall of the cave. For them, reality is nothing but the shadows of the objects and the voices that accompany them.

Plato meant this as a parable for his time. And, although it could be, it doesn't have to be a parable for our time. It doesn't have to be about the way we watch television. The ability to distinguish between shadow and substance must be part of our lives.

Given television's popularity and economic impact, it was probably inevitable that many individuals would claim to have invented it. But no one person had a sudden flash of inspiration that gave birth to television. The idea for television had been around for a very long time in legend and in fact. St. Clare of Assisi (born 1195), for example, was sick in bed one Christmas eve and could not attend midnight mass. She prayed to God for help and suddenly one wall of her convent cell became, as it were, a screen. She was able to watch and hear midnight mass. St. Clare is the Patron Saint of Television.

Television came about through parallel research and development in many countries, including Britain, the United States, Germany, Japan, France, and the Soviet Union. Two basic systems, the mechanical and the electronic, were developed near the end of the nineteenth century. A mechanical system for television was in use in Britain and Germany by the early 1930s. By 1936 it was replaced by the electronic system and there were broadcasts in Britain, the United States, and Europe.

The beginning of World War II closed down most television transmission. The BBC ceased broadcasting on September 1, 1939, in the middle of a Mickey Mouse film. When they resumed broadcasting after the war in June 1946, they began exactly where they had stopped the film. Germany broadcast in Berlin throughout the war using special public viewing rooms. They recognized the propaganda value of television and continued broadcasting until November 23, 1943, when the transmitter was destroyed by Allied bombers. At the New York World's Fair in 1939, NBC produced a three-and-a-half-hour broadcast of the event and in 1940 was producing some fifteen hours of programming a week. By 1941, CBS and NBC were both broadcasting on a regular basis, but with the bombing of Pearl Harbor on December 7, 1941, America went to war. Though there was no official order to stop broadcasting, no sets were being manufactured, and there seemed little point in continuing without an audience. By 1942 American television all but shut down.

After what some have called a very long commercial break, television came back after the war and soon made up for lost time. It had taken radio thirty-eight years to reach an audience of fifty million, it took television less than fourteen years to reach fifty million viewers. (Worth noting too is that it has taken the Internet only four years to reach fifty million people.)

On May 14, 1996, the Census counted 28,846,761 Canadians living in some 11,580,000 households. Statistics Canada tells us that of these households 11,482,000 have at least one television set (more than half have two or more); 11,425,000 have a radio; 9,808,000 have a video tape recorder (one in five homes has two or more); and 8,539,000 have cable television. As well, 98.6 per cent of our households have telephones and 18.6 per cent have a cellular phone.

Computers? The Internet? These "new" technologies may well be what replaces television. They are here and growing in importance. In 1997 Statistics Canada reported that 45 per cent of homes with children under eighteen (i.e., 1.7 million homes) had computers and that 20 per cent of them were surfing the net. As well, 4,200,000 households have a computer, a number which has doubled in five years. The number of households on the Internet almost doubled between 1996 and 1997 to an estimated 13 per cent. A 1997 Nielsen survey revealed that almost one out of every four people over the age of sixteen in Canada and the U.S.A. uses the Internet. While in 1996, 57 per cent of all users were men, this dropped to 51 per cent in 1997. The biggest on-line group are still the twenty-five to thirty-four-year-olds, but the percentage of users aged fifty-five to sixty-four has increased from 18 per cent in 1996 to 27 per cent in 1997. At 41 per cent, Ontario and British Columbia residents lead in the uses of the Internet.

We watch some 22.8 hours of television a week, compared to the people in the United States who watch about 50.8 hours a week. We spend about 700 hours a year eating, 400 hours a year reading newspapers, magazines, and books, 50 hours a year in church or synagogue, and 1,180 hours a year watching television. By the age of sixty-five, the average Canadian will have seen 3,000 entire days of television, which works out to watching television for nine full years of your life. People in Atlantic Canada tend to watch more news and public affairs programs, westerners tend to watch more sports, and easterners watch a lot of drama.

Canadian children watch television 17.9 hours a week. By the time they graduate from high school, they will have spent 11,000 hours in a class-room, 10,500 hours listening to popular music, and 15,000 hours watching television, during which time they will have seen 350,000 TV commercials. Children spend more time watching TV than they spend in any other activity except sleeping. By 1988, according to Michael Winship, in his book *Television*, "for every child born in the world, a television set is manufactured – a quarter of a million every day."

Another statistic: on September 2, 1997, *Time* reported that in the United States, 342,686 people attended the twelve major-league baseball games played that day; 1.28 million people went to the movies; 10.96 million households watched *Home Improvement* on television; and America Online subscribers logged on 16.7 million times.

The three major television networks (ABC, CBS, and NBC) in the United States can't hang on to their viewers. Their share of viewers has slipped below 60 per cent. Preteens have gone to Nickelodeon while teens are watching MTV and have joined the over-fiftys on cable channels. The networks are trying to hang on to the age group that has the most disposable income – urban, unmarried eighteen-to-thirty-four-year-olds.

As *TV World* pointed out in June 1998: "Canada's television landscape is already fragmented by two distinct language groups, U.S. channel over-spill, 75% penetration of multichannel TV, as well as an explosion of local specialty channels launched in the last three years." Traditionalist broadcasters saw their share of audience drop to 58.9 per cent in 1998 while the specialty channels grew to 31.2 per cent. Canadian viewers have more programming choices than anyone else in the world.

Television, more than other media, is part of our lives. It dominates our cultural and political life. Almost all information which we have, other than what we experience ourselves, comes from the media. And that information is not just presented to us, it is first shaped into a form of reality. Television presents us with model behaviour, beliefs, and values, and does this in such a way that we are not aware of its influence. Television is a passive entertainment – we let it wash over us – but it is entertaining and can make us laugh and cry.

Television is also big business. It sells us products, values, ideologies, life styles, and cultures. The tendency today is toward increased concentration of ownership of media in fewer and fewer hands, as well as integrated ownership patterns across several media. This means that a small number of individuals decide what television programs will be broadcast, what films will be screened, what music will be recorded and make it to the airwaves, and what issues will be investigated and reported by television news.

What can we do? We need to take a passive medium and make it active. We need to understand how we can watch carefully and think critically about television. This does not mean that we have to give up being entertained by the media. Movie critic Pauline Kael could have been discussing television when she wrote for *The New Yorker*: "People go to movies for the various ways they express the experience of our lives, and as a means of avoiding and postponing the pressures we feel. This latter function of art, generally referred to as escapism, may also be considered as refreshment, and in terms of big city life and small town boredom, it may be a big factor in keeping us sane." The more we learn about television, the more tools we have to deal with it, the better able we will be to put our mass-mediated world into perspective.

Peter Weir's 1998 movie *The Truman Show* is not just the story of a man whose life is, and has been since infancy, shown live to the world twenty-four hours a day on commercial television. It is more especially the story of a grown man who is in the process of awakening to this fact. Day by day the man becomes increasingly literate about the media as it affects him. *The Truman Show* is about media education.

The reasons for learning about television have changed over the years. It was in England in the 1980s that I first met Len Masterman, Senior Research Fellow at the University of Liverpool. Two of his works, *Teaching about Television* and *Teaching the Media*, published in the mid 1980s, remain benchmarks for media education. What Masterman wrote was basically for teachers. But the points he makes apply to all of us.

"For hundreds of years," Masterman writes in *Teaching the Media*, "society has valued reading and understanding the meaning of texts. Yet in today's society, the visual image is arguably more important than the printed word. There has been no corresponding focus on reading the meaning of visual images."

And:

"The world economy is fast becoming an information economy. Information is a commodity to be bought and sold. A danger exists that new classes of 'information-rich' and 'information-poor' may result, with the information-poor unable to afford the information they need to better their lives."

Masterman's work has had considerable influence on the way people learn about the media in many countries including Europe, Australia, and

Canada. Masterman explains the background of why people study the media in his introduction to *Teaching the Media: International Perspectives*, published in 1998.

"The earliest answer to the question 'Why study the media?' ran something like this. The mass media are really a kind of disease against which children need to be protected. What the media infect is the culture as a whole. Culture is contaminated by the media's commercial motivations, their manipulation and exploitation of their audiences, their corruption of language, and their offering of easy, low-level appeals and satisfactions . . . If the media were a definite kind of cultural disease, then Media Education was designed to provide protection *against* it . . . That earliest paradigm is now popularly known as the inoculative paradigm."

In the early 1960s, a new generation of teachers who had been influenced by popular culture – especially film – produced a new answer to the question, "Why study the media?" "It was to enable students to discriminate not against the media but within them – that is, to tell the difference between the good and the bad film, the authentic and the shoddy television program, and work within popular culture of some integrity and work that was merely commercial and exploitative. This was the 'popular arts' paradigm."

For many reasons, this paradigm died in the mid 1970s. By the late 1970s, teachers began to approach the understanding of media ". . . as a signifying system that needs to be read critically, rather than windows in to a reality that had to be accepted." Throughout the 1980s an international movement of media teachers gravitated towards another interpretation of media education. It goes something like this: "In contemporary societies the media are self-evidently important creators and mediators of social knowledge. An understanding of the ways in which the media represent reality, the techniques they employ, and the ideologies embedded within their representations ought to be an entitlement for all citizens and future citizens in a democratic society."

As we work through this third paradigm, Masterman says we begin "to answer what is probably the most important question faced by educational systems in the late twentieth century and beyond: What constitutes an effective democratic education for majorities of future citizens?"

Concepts 'R' Us

For school-age children in Canada, media education is a required part of the English language arts curriculum in Grades 1 through 12. However, as an adult, you will have to search diligently to find a night course or a seminar on anything vaguely resembling media education. But the media still has a tremendous impact on us and on our lives and we need to know how to deal with them.

In order to discuss the media and to learn more about it, we need a set of guidelines or concepts which apply to any medium. The following eight key concepts were originally developed by members of Ontario's Association for Media Literacy as part of the Ontario Ministry of Education's Resource Guide for Media Literacy in 1987. They are the main tools we can use to think critically about the media.

1. *All Media Are Constructions*

The media do not present simple reflections of what is around us. Rather, the media present carefully crafted productions that are the result of many decisions and determining factors. These are made by people with specific ends in mind. Technically, these productions are often excellent, and this, coupled with our familiarity with such productions, makes it difficult for us to see such productions as anything other than a seamless extension of reality.

Len Masterman offered an example of this when he wrote about a Nottingham art teacher, Fred Bazler. "Fred held up to a class of eight-year-olds a painting of a horse and asked them what it was. When the kids answered, 'A horse,' Fred said it wasn't. This caused some confusion, but after a little prompting the children began to understand the distinction between a horse and its representation in a painting."

The critical viewer's task is to make these seams visible. We have to learn to take apart these constructions to see how they were made much like we might have taken apart toys when we were younger to see how they were put together.

TV sitcoms like *Sports Night*, *Newsradio*, and *Murphy Brown* are set in television or radio stations. We know that we are watching fiction but we tend to forget that as we get caught up in the story line. By using any number of production techniques – camera angles, editing, sound – the show can be made to present a certain view that may not be the entire truth. The critical viewer needs to be aware of these techniques.

2. The Media Construct Reality

What the media are constructing is a certain representation of reality. We all have our own view of reality. We've been building it since the day we were born. The question is, where do we get it from? Much of it, other than what we experience for ourselves, comes from television, radio, newspapers, film, magazines. The media are responsible for most of the observations and experiences from which we build up our personal understandings of the world and how it works. Thus to a great extent, the media, rather than ourselves, give us our sense of reality.

Much of our view of reality is based on media messages that have been preconstructed and have attitudes, interpretations, and conclusions built in. *The New York Times Magazine* reported on September 20, 1998: "So much information is discerned through it, so much experience formed by it, that television has become as real as anything outside of itself."

There was a frightening illustration of this phenomenon when passengers of a U.S. cruise ship learned that their ship was on fire only when they turned on their television sets to a local Florida news station. The fire was being broadcast live.

There are many shows on TV about doctors but which of these tells us what it is really like to be a doctor? Emergency rooms may (or may not) be the locus of non-stop action such as takes place weekly on *ER*. The health system in the United States may (or may not) be in the terrible shape that *Chicago Hope*, *ER*, *Diagnosis Murder*, and *L.A. Doctors* make it out to be. The images look so real that we can be lulled into thinking that they are real. Jack Solomon points out in his book *The Signs of Our Time*: "Since we see them, we trust them, often failing to realize that, like all signs, they have been constructed with a certain interest behind them."

3. Audiences Negotiate Meaning in Media

Basic to an understanding of media is an awareness of how we interact with media content (TV shows, movies, radio programs, newspapers, the Internet). The second key concept concentrates on the ways in which the media contribute to the construction of reality. But we also have to realize that each of us brings something unique to the media – ourselves. If the media provide us with much of the material upon which we build our picture of reality, each of us finds or "negotiates" meaning according to individual factors: personal needs and anxieties, the pleasures or troubles of the day, racial and sexual attitudes, family and cultural background, moral standpoint, and so forth. All of these will affect our interpretation of what we are watching on television. And because each of us brings with us such different experiences, we have to be open to the fact that different people will experience the same television show in different ways.

Watching a sitcom like *That '70s Show* is a very different experience for someone who grew up in the 1970s than it is for a 1990s teenager. The show is filled with references, styles, and attitudes that are totally foreign to someone who did not live through the period. Both groups may laugh at what they see, but they are probably laughing for different reasons. Or if O'Malley and I – two people the same age – were to watch CTV's hockey drama, *Power Play*, our reactions would be coloured by the simple fact that he enjoys the sport while I have no interest in it. And the way African-Americans react to portrayals of their race on shows like *The Hughleys* is significantly different from the way other races react.

4. Media Messages Have Commercial Implications

Most media production is a business, and must make a profit. The economic basis of television has a very real effect on content, technique, and distribution. Networks look for audiences to be delivered to sponsors. Program content makes viewers targets for advertisers and organizes them into marketable groups.

People who watch soap operas, for example, can also purchase magazines that summarize plots, follow the lives of the actors in the tabloids, and exchange gossip with fans over the Internet. Sports fans can buy memorabilia and star-endorsed products, play fantasy versions of the game on the Internet, or read about their favourite sport in the newspaper. In a real way, such people are constructing their own fantasy universes based on a favourite show such as *Star Trek*, *Baywatch*, or *Monday Night Football*. The question to ask is how much of their own personality is shaped by such commercial forces.

Questions of ownership and control are central since a relatively small number of individuals control what we watch, read, and hear in the media. The companies involved are Time Warner, Disney, Rupert Murdoch's News Corporation, General Electric, Tele-Communications Inc., Viacom, and CBS. This concentration of ownership has far-reaching implications for how we perceive our world and our place in it.

5. Media Messages Contain Ideological and Value Messages

All media products proclaim values and ways of life. And that way of life and those values are usually those of the established social structure. This makes sense when you consider that the media and advertisers are the chief beneficiaries of the established social structure.

The mainstream media convey, explicitly or implicitly, ideological messages about issues such as the nature of the good life and the virtue of consumerism (*King of Queens*), the role of women and men in society (*Veronica's Closet, Everybody Loves Raymond*, and *Suddenly Susan*), the acceptance of authority (*Working*), and unquestioning patriotism (*JAG* or *Pensacola: Wings of Gold*). While the media may not be directly responsible for creating values and attitudes, they legitimize and reinforce them. The critical viewer tries to uncover these ideological messages and value-systems by looking out for clues that reveal the underlying assumptions. What groups are represented and what groups are left out, for example? There are very few older people in the current crop of sitcoms. Why?

Concentration of media ownership is also important in this respect. The ideologies, values, and attitudes portrayed on television are those of the people who decide what to put on television. If they are conservatives (big "C" or small "c"), their messages will be much different than if they were liberals (big "L," small "l").

6. Media Messages Have Social and Political Implications

The media have great influence in politics and in forming social change. Television can affect the election of a national leader on the basis of image. This has been clear since the 1960 Kennedy–Nixon debate. The media also involve us in concerns such as civil rights and social issues, sitcoms bring gay characters out of the closet and make them socially acceptable. Other programs may deal with the effects of global warming, environmental issues, famines in Africa, and the AIDS epidemic. They can give us an intimate sense of national issues and global concerns, making us indeed McLuhan's Global Village.

Political parties use television because this is where the voters are. No campaign rally can attract the number of voters that will see a candidate on the evening news. Politicians speak in sound bites to make the news.

The biggest single cost in political campaigning is for television ads. While the ads reach a great many people, they can also backfire. In the 1993 federal election, the Progressive Conservative party went from being a government with a formidable majority to a defeat that cost them all but two of their parliamentary seats. There were many reasons for this stunning reversal but some observers believe that a critical error was a television spot aired just before the election. As *Maclean's* reported in May 19, 1997, the thirty-second spot "showed unflattering photographs of Liberal leader Jean Chrétien. The images emphasized his contorted mouth, the result of a birth defect, while the ad asked: 'Is this a prime minister?'" The ad provoked immediate outrage from politicians and the public.

In the United States, the Lewinsky scandal was tawdry but, as the *New York Times Magazine* reminded us on September 20, 1998, "it is also an irresistible story of sex and power, and television's unblinking focus on it is playing an active role in Presidential politics and governance."

7. Form and Content Are Closely Related in Media Messages

As Marshall McLuhan noted, "The medium is the message." Each medium has its own grammar and bias and codifies reality in its own particular way. Thus, different media reporting the same event will create different impressions and different messages. For example, television works best with images. Therefore, the evening news will be more likely to show fires, earthquakes, and rioting protesters than the latest round of talks between the nurses' union and the hospital authorities. A newspaper or magazine cannot show live pictures, but they can give you more detailed information about why a fire started or the issues that caused the riot. To see this concept in action read today's paper, listen to today's news on the radio, and watch the evening TV news. They will present, more or less, the same subjects but there will be a great difference in how they present them.

8. Each Medium Has a Unique Aesthetic Form

Media education is not only about understanding media texts and their implications for our culture and society, but also about how to enjoy and produce them. Just as we notice the pleasing rhythms of certain pieces of poetry or prose, so we ought to be able to enjoy the pleasing forms and effects of the different media. Our enjoyment of media can be enhanced by an awareness of how pleasing forms and effects are created. Television is at its best with live events. There is an extra thrill and pleasure in watching a sporting event live on television that cannot be got from reading about it or watching a replay after it is over. And television offers a real sense of sharing and participation in its coverage of world events like the opening of the Olympics or the funeral of Diana, Princess of Wales.

2

Vampires, Lawyers, Aliens, Doctors, and Cops

~

TV, as its most Cromwellian critics never tire of telling us, is debased, popular entertainment out to make the fastest buck by pandering to the most vulgar possible mass tastes. The same charge of whoredom has been brought against Hollywood films, the Victorian novel and Elizabethan drama.

— Frank McConnell in *Commonweal*

E very evening there are hour-long programs on television that have been called "prime-time dramas," "adult programming," and "long sitcoms." The nomenclature varies, as does the style and content of the various programs, but I prefer simply to call them hour-long shows. Sitcoms tend to be short and snappy, confined to thirty minutes. When a sitcom concept is pushed beyond thirty minutes it usually suffers from the law of diminishing returns (or they run out of laugh track). The elbow room of the hour-long drama allows for funny *and* poignant, and a multitude of subplots.

Some hour-long dramas make it, some don't. Some make it for the wrong reasons and some don't make it for the wrong reasons. It is a sad fact of television life that excellent programs too often don't make it through their first season because they *are* excellent. There is no accounting for taste; there should be.

Television has always courted respectability. For whatever reason, television programmers seems to equate respect with drama. In 1928, five years after U.S. television first began broadcasting, the first drama, an adaptation of John Manner's *The Queen's Messenger,* was broadcast – live, of course (there was no other way) – out of New York.

The 1950s have been called the Golden Age of Television Drama. Every week live drama was seen on *Studio One, The U.S. Steel Hour, Playhouse 90, Kraft Television Theater* and many others. Television drama, from the beginning, has offered us examples of the ways media construct reality. *Requiem for a Heavyweight* presented boxing in a light many viewers had never considered. *The Days of Wine and Roses* looked at the effects of alcoholism in a non-flinching manner but ended in a way that many saw as unrealistic. At the same time, these dramas presented some very obvious value-laden messages about boxing and drinking.

TV drama can deal with a wide variety of reality and emotions, including the possibility of death and tragedy – themes usually not explored in sitcoms. Dramas also allow for endings where problems are not resolved. TV dramas present a view of reality that will reinforce whatever ideology or values or social issues are the concern of the programmers. As TV got better at what it did, it was able to present what appeared to be an even more realistic view of life. Studios were abandoned for location settings, which added realism. The depiction of violence became more graphic.

The advent of filmed television series and videotape brought live drama to an end early in the 1960s. The social realism of the 1950s was replaced – and for the most part has remained replaced – by action and adventure. This was the era of the Cold War, a time best represented by the black-and-white morality of good versus evil. It was first reflected in the Western dramas which became a staple of television until the late 1980s. Of the many shows of this time some that are well remembered include *Cheyenne, Maverick, The Rifleman, Bat Masterson, Wyatt Earp, Rawhide, Wanted: Dead or Alive, Gunsmoke,* and *Bonanza.*

But there were other genres as well. There were shows about the law (lawyers, cops, private eyes, spies), about doctors, about fantasy, about families, and about quirky topics. Each of these genres changed over the years. But as they've changed their goal has remained the same – the construction of a certain reality.

The kindly old family doctor of 1955's *Dr. Hudson's Secret Journal* gave way to the young *Dr. Kildare* (1961–66) battling the problems of a city hospital. *Ben Casey* (1961–66) added some controversy by taking on the medical establishment and the issue of doctor–patient romance. *Julia* (1968–71) not only gave the nurse her first show but also broke ground for blacks. One of the big hits was *Marcus Welby, MD* (1969–76), where Robert Young knew best. Perhaps the most famous and best loved of all doctor shows was *M*A*S*H* (1972–83), which cloaked its anti-war message in wonderful humour. And the 1980s saw shows like *Trapper John, MD* (1979–86), the over-the-top *St. Elsewhere* (1982–88), and teen doctor *Doogie Howser, MD.*

The 1990s have brought at least four new doctor shows: the comedy mystery of Dick Van Dyke as Dr. Mark Sloan in *Diagnosis Murder* (1993 to present), the workings of a large urban hospital and the lives of its doctors in *Chicago Hope* (1994 to present), the intelligent and compassionate stories of *ER* (1994 to present), and the new kid on the block, *L.A. Doctors* (1998 to present), about a private clinic.

But there is something missing from the contemporary doctor shows. There always used to be a doctor who was wise and good and who always knew what to do. Now, all the characters seem to struggle with issues on their own. One effect of this is to make the viewer more of a participant in the program, often consciously or unconsciously finding a character with whom to identify. This change may have come about because viewers no longer see TV itself as the "wise father-figure" many once thought it to be.

I wonder what 1950s detectives in *Dragnet* (1951–59, 1967–70) would have thought of the clumsy *Columbo* (1971–78, 1989–90 and continuing with specials) or the colourful 1990s detectives of *Nash Bridges* (1994 to present). And Joe Friday would have been amazed at the variety of detectives, lawyers, and spies who have appeared over the last forty-eight years. We all have our own list of favourites. Each reflects in its way the public morality of its own era.

The Cold War era which painted most foreigners as evil and anti-American was reflected in two shows: *The Man from U.N.C.L.E.* (1964–68), with Napoleon Solo and Ilya Kuriakin doing lighthearted battle against the forces of evil, and *I Spy* (1965–68) with Robert Culp and Bill Cosby as two undercover agents (the first drama series to star a black actor). Never far out of sight beneath the humour was the ideology that the U.S.A. was the only defence against the enemies of the Cold War.

The TV lawyer has changed drastically over the years. There was the solid, incorruptible person always there to help, as seen in *Perry Mason* (1957–66), with Raymond Burr in the title role of the lawyer who never seemed to lose a court case. Perry would not survive one episode as a lawyer today in a show like *The Practice* (1997 to present), where a group of mismatched lawyers both win and lose cases as they battle their own emotional problems. And it is difficult to imagine what Perry Mason would say to Ally McBeal. Television is a commercial venture. Times have changed and shows about lawyers had to change if they were going to sell on television.

TV cop shows have tried for more realism over the years, beginning with *Hill Street Blues* (1981–87), arguably the best cop show on television, blending humour and tragedy through brilliant writing, acting, and technical excellence. The trend has continued with three shows – *NYPD Blue* (1993 to present), the award-winning gritty portrayal of New York cops; *Law & Order* (1990 to present), where detectives catch criminals in the first half and prosecutors try to convict them in the second half; *Homicide: Life on the Street* (1993 to present), an Emmy award-winning cop show set in Baltimore. While these shows depict cops fighting crime, a great deal of time is devoted to their personal lives, which adds another layer to the constructed realism that is presented to the viewer.

Fantasy and science fiction have always been popular on television. Twenty years ago there was *Night Stalker* (1974–75), in which a reporter stalked a mysterious killer each week, and in the 1990s there is the cult hit *The X-Files* (1993 to present) with FBI agents in search of the truth out there somewhere. Such shows span the history of popular North American television.

The *Star Trek* TV series have had a tremendous appeal for over thirty years. *Star Trek* (1966–69) was the cult original about the starship *Enterprise* and its crew, which sparked the spinoffs *Star Trek: The Next Generation* (1987–94), *Star Trek: Deep Space Nine* (1993–99), and *Star Trek: Voyager* (1995 to present). The wonders and adventures these shows offer attract viewers but all of the shows are based on the presentation and defence of American values and ideologies – "To boldly go where no one has gone before."

And there are the fantasy shows, which over the years have presented us with social, political, and commercial messages. *Lois & Clark: The New Adventures of Superman* (1993–97) not only continued Superman's pursuit of "truth, justice, and the American way" but offered a fine portrayal of Lois Lane that went far beyond the stereotype of the "helpless" female there only to be rescued by Superman. *Fantasy Island* (1978–84 and 1998 to present) focused on what happened if people got to live out their fantasies, with the new series being somewhat darker than the original. For the most part, the fantasies were seen as not being "good," and people had to learn this by undergoing some form of unpleasantness; an interesting take on redemption through suffering.

On the darker side of fantasy, there are shows about people who seem to have been given certain powers which cause them a great deal of pain until they use their powers to destroy the evil around them. In *Early Edition* (1996 to present) the main character is given tomorrow's paper today and spends each show preventing the tragedies listed in the paper. *Millennium* (1996 to present) features an ex-FBI agent who can enter into the minds of murderers but suffers terribly for this in his personal life. *Charmed* (1998 to present) tells of three sisters who are witches. They come across as Charlie's Angels with supernatural powers, which they use to destroy the many demons which seem to inhabit San Francisco. The best of this genre may be *Brimstone* (1998 to present), which recounts the dark, almost *film noir* adventures of a man who returns from Hell to recapture 113 escapees from Satan's domain.

Family dramas include *Little House on the Prairies* (1974–83), set during the 1870s, or *The Waltons* (1972–81), about a rural Virginia family who survives the Depression. We've also had *Dallas* (1978–91), the long-running tale of the Texas Ewing family and their oil holdings; *Dynasty* (1981–89), about life in another oil-rich family; and *Trinity* (1998), about the lives and loves of five siblings in the big city.

And in a category all of its own is the world's most watched program, *Baywatch* (1989 to present), also known as "Babewatch," which has music, very fit lifeguards, and very little dialogue.

Youth-oriented shows are a more recent development. They include: *Melrose Place* (1992 to present), about a group of twentysomethings searching for happiness; *Beverly Hills 90210* (1990 to present), in which some very old teens live out the days of their lives in a posh high school; *Dawson's Creek* (1997 to present) brings us rich teens in a Boston suburb who suffer the pangs of growing up (unfortunately, we suffer along with them); *Party of Five* (1994 to present) has five children left without parents who must survive on their own, which they do with much angst each week.

These youth-oriented shows are very closely tied to the fourth key concept: media have commercial implications. This becomes clear when we look at one more show that fits this category. *Felicity* is about a first-year college student who leaves her home in California to follow her love to New York. Introduced with great fanfare at the start of the 1998–99 season, the show is distinguished by the superb acting of lead Keri Russell and the ensemble cast as well as by the excellent writing and direction. By the end of November 1998, the show had some 5.5 million viewers per week – placing it in 99th position just behind *Buffy the Vampire Slayer*.

So, *Felicity* is a not a hit overall. But it is a very big hit with one of the most powerful demographics. As *Entertainment Weekly*, December 11, 1998, reports: "Among all prime-time broadcast network series, it boasts the highest concentration of eighteen- to thirty-four-year-olds in upscale households (people making $75,000 or more). A narrow niche, for sure, but one that has khaki-clad Gap execs swinging from the chandeliers. 'If you're one of the advertisers who want to target young affluent women,' says David Marans, senior partner at ad agency J. Walter Thompson, 'this is your baby. It's a marketer's dream.'"

What is important to the television executive now is not the household ratings – how many people in how many homes are watching a certain show – but what demographic is watching that show. The group that interests the television executive the most is the eighteen- to forty-nine-year-olds. Advertisers believe that this is the group with the most money to spend and the willingness to do so. So the shows that get made are those that appeal to that age group. Of course, the networks will tell you that they want everyone to watch television. We might want to take that with a grain of salt. In fact, if we are over fifty, we might want not to believe it at all.

And then there are some shows that have been described as off-the-wall, or stupid, or well-intentioned failures. I call them quirky and sophisticated. I believe that they are successful and point television in directions where it must go. It is a question of television aesthetics. These quirky shows give us a different type of pleasure than what we get from the other

TV dramas. I believe them to be the North American equivalent of what is best in TV dramas in other countries, such as Britain's *The Singing Detective* or *House of Cards*.

There haven't been many of them in North America, but among the best is *Moonlighting* (1985–89), about an international fashion model and a private detective who become partners. The series depended a great deal on the romantic comedies of the 1940s where the verbal sparring of the couples thinly disguised a hot sexual subtext. Another quirky drama, *Picket Fences* (1992–95), was set in the fictional town of Rome, Wisconsin, and this Emmy-winning series poked at the hottest issues of the day while not taking itself seriously (the mayor dies by spontaneous combustion, nuns perform mercy killings while humming "Killing Me Softly," a woman goes to her death in a dishwasher surrounded by her favourite plates).

Twin Peaks (1990–91) is about thirty-two days in the surrealistic life of a small Washington town, with a dwarf, a lady with a log, an unsolved murder, and an FBI agent who loves cherry pie. It is one of U.S. television's greatest achievements. *Northern Exposure* (1990–95) tells of a young Jewish physician assigned to a rural Alaskan town whose inhabitants include an ex-astronaut mayor; a young native who makes Bergman-like films; a female pilot whose dead lovers return as dogs and bears; a New Age ex-con disc jockey who quotes Kierkegaard, Kant, and Nietzsche along with Def Leppard; and a teenage cheerleader from Saskatoon who marries the oldest man in town. It made for a wonderful mix that was entertaining and enlightening television.

In the summer of 1998, ABC ran seven episodes of *Maximum Bob*. Based on the book by Elmore Leonard, this amazing series tells of Florida Judge Bob Gibbs who sends an underaged drinker to the electric chair, and of his wife, Leanne, a professional mermaid who eats bananas underwater, reads auras, and believes she is possessed by the spirit of a southern slave girl. Told with wonderfully written humour, these stories presented a very different view of the law.

Buddy Faro (1998 to present) is about a legendary 1970s detective who comes off a twenty-year bender/hibernation to greet the 1990s for the first time. The offbeat humour and the unexpected reversal of the television convention that anyone over thirty is corrupt takes us beyond entertainment. And then there's *Ally McBeal* (1997 to present), about whom much more later in this chapter. These shows are escapist, surrealist, post-modern – call them what you will. They make no attempt to create a "believable" reality and because of this probably come closer than any other TV drama to the real world. They have no qualms about presenting values and ideologies which are in-your-face and, on the surface, very much the opposite of traditional values. The fun – and the aesthetic pleasure – for the critical viewer is to use the key concepts to open up these shows and to explore what they are saying.

The Doctor Dramas

I love ER and I'm not ashamed to admit it. It makes me know I did not waste my life after all by not becoming a medical doctor. I might have ended up in an emergency room. You never have sex, no one appreciates you, and it's always raining or snowing outside.

– Ellen Gilchrist, writer

ER is consistently television's top-rated hour-long drama. Between September 1997 and May 1998, an average of 30.2 million people watched *ER* every week. This is a huge audience, second only to that of *Seinfeld*, which was the top-rated show with an average weekly audience of 34 million viewers. (I keep up to date on ratings by reading *Entertainment Weekly*, a publication I recommend to anyone who wishes to take television and other media seriously.)

ER is set in the fictional Cook County General in downtown Chicago. It deals with the minute-to-minute calamities in the Emergency Room, exploring the lives and worries of its staff. The ensemble of doctors is led by Dr. Greene, played by actor Anthony Edwards, and includes Dr. Ross (George Clooney), Dr. Weaver (Laura Innis), Dr. Carter (Noah Wylie), Dr. Benton (Eriq La Salle), Dr. Del Amico (Maria Bello), Dr. Corday (Alex Kingston), and Nurse Hathaway (Julianna Margulies).

In 1994, the two-hour pilot for *ER* told forty-five medical stories and had eighty-seven speaking parts. Of necessity, then, *ER* is about action, motion, speed. This is achieved by the use of many devices, among them the Steadi-Cam (a harness device which allows the cinematographer to "wear" the camera so that it moves as he moves), which captures a lot of motion without the jerkiness you see on, say, *NYPD Blue*. Surprisingly, this constant motion, described as "channel-surfing without the remote," appeals to viewers. Perhaps it keeps the viewer from punching the channel-changer, which would certainly make it appealing to programmers.

ER has been called "a soap opera on speed." Certainly, *ER* shares a number of elements with the soap opera, which may partly account for its sustained popularity (soap operas tend to have large and loyal audiences). It has a great deal of melodrama with an emphasis on romance. There are continuing plots and subplots within each episode. A new crisis, either physical or emotional, is only a few minutes away. The reality that is constructed in soap operas is constructed to appeal to a demographic made up almost entirely of women and teenage girls. It is a demographic that tends to identify with many of the emotional problems of the soap opera characters. Television producers know that female viewers are attracted to medical shows because they do resemble soap operas. The on-again off-again romance between Dr. Ross and Nurse Hathaway could be a story line plucked from the afternoon soap *General Hospital*. However, *ER* differs from a soap opera in significant ways. *ER* has better production values. More importantly, its characters are more fully developed. "*ER* is irresistible," writes *TV Guide*, ". . . an emotionally complex collection of distinct individuals."

Interestingly, television producers know that men watch *ER* too, but they regard it as an action show. A TV action drama focuses on a hero – or heroine – who settles problems through direct action in the course of an hour. (In this respect, action drama is like a sporting event.)

So *ER* effectively hits four hot-buttons: 1) fast-paced enough to give the illusion of channel-surfing without channel-surfing, 2) soap opera appeal, 3) appealing to women for one reason, 4) appealing to men for another. Were the producers of *ER* smart enough to know this before the program began or were they lucky? According to *Newsweek*, in October 1994, *ER* was destined to fail. The magazine's television critic listed these reasons why *ER* should not succeed:

> 1. No big-name stars. Being a celebrity is very important in North American popular culture. TV series are often sold not on the basis of their plot but on which celebrity is connected to the series. This does not

always guarantee success as was clear in Nathan Lane's 1998 failure with *Encore, Encore!* When *ER* began, none of its lead actors were celebrities. That has changed. George Clooney is considered a celebrity and, to a lesser extent, so are Noah Wylie and Julianna Margulies. This is reflected in a very commercial way. A thirty-second ad on *ER* costs $565,000 – the most expensive thirty-second ad on any prime-time series.

2. The camera moves too fast.

3. The story lines do not have neat beginnings, middles, and ends.

4. Too many new characters show up in each episode.

5. It's about doctors, not everybody's favourite people.

6. It takes place in an emergency room, one of the last places most people want to be (unless in dire straits).

7. Health care is "boring," medicine is "scary."

8. There has not been a successful doctor's show since *St. Elsewhere*. (This last point reminds me of the persistent Canadians who invented the board game Trivial Pursuit. They were told that board games are a no-go because there had not been a successful board game since Monopoly came out at the height of the Depression in the 1930s.)

Michael Crichton, Harvard Medical School graduate and best-selling author, produces and writes *ER*. In the *Newsweek* article, Crichton says, "The pace of TV has been artificially slowed. I wanted to crank it up to something resembling reality." Crichton is making an assumption about the speed at which TV programs present reality. Remember the second of the key concepts outlined in Chapter 1: media constructs a version of reality.

What is this "reality" Crichton wants to heighten? Perhaps *ER* confirms preconceptions you have about real emergency rooms and the people who work in them. Dr. Greene may be a typical emergency room doctor. But most of us have little firsthand experience of a real emergency room. Such experiences are generally confined to the make-believe of television.

ER's plots mostly focus on the 1990s crisis zone known as The Family. But there are many different kinds of "family," the nuclear family, the extended family, and the occupational family of the workplace. In an *ER* episode titled "Into the Good Night," a man with a terminal heart condition says a difficult farewell to his wife and daughter. As Dr. Greene observes this he thinks of his own family. He is a workaholic whose long hours at the hospital keep him from his lawyer-wife and young daughter. In a soap opera, Dr. Greene doubtless would change his ways, find a way to bring the family closer, and as the credits roll they would be heading toward the welcome sunset of happily-ever-after. But *ER* doesn't do this. Dr. Greene does decide to change, but there is no welcome sunset. His wife leaves him and moves to another city, which causes Dr. Greene to immerse himself in his "family" of colleagues in the emergency room.

The scripts for *ER* are well written, often superbly written, which brings the characters to life, making it easy for us to identify with them. This is what good writing does, though good writing seldom gets the attention and respect it deserves. Once we have identified with the characters in *ER*, we might find that they have problems similar to ours. Or we might wish that their decisions regarding love, death, career, and family could be ours. Or do we care about them because they seem to be "real" people? Some of this will depend on what the viewer brings to the program. As the third key concept tells us, we add to the TV producer's view of reality all the individual factors that make us who we are. Commenting on the impact of *ER*, David Westin, president of ABC Television Network Groups, says: "People see the U.S. as a grittier place. Good entertainment has to reflect how people are feeling."

Oh?

Is life in the United States in the 1990s really grittier? Perhaps it is television that has become grittier, turning to the surefire lure of blood and guts that has always attracted audiences. Because it is a construction of reality and not reality itself, television can never truly reflect society.

For a comparison, consider another hour-long medical drama, *Chicago Hope*, a straightforward medical drama set in a high-tech research hospital. When *ER* started in 1994 it went head-to-head against *Chicago Hope*. The best *Chicago Hope* ever did was place 45th in audience popularity, which is respectable, but far down the track from number-one-rated *ER*. Many viewers and critics consider *Chicago Hope* better than *ER*. One could argue that the slower pace of *Chicago Hope* is more realistic than the rush-rush, Steadi-Cam pace of *ER*. (The true pace of an emergency room probably is more like baseball – long stretches of boredom punctuated by frantic activity.) Whatever, CBS eventually moved *Chicago Hope* to another evening so it did not compete directly against *ER*.

To start the fourth season of *ER* in 1997, the program went live for its first episode. Using the pretext of a documentary crew filming a typical day in Emergency, four complete camera crews captured action that included gang warfare, people hurt at a rock concert, and maimed children. The show was set in real time. As I watched it, I jotted my questions:

Does using real time make it more real? Not as long as the action is seen from a variety of viewpoints. The director makes the decision as to what we will see and for how long.

How does this episode compare to the "live" drama on Playhouse 90 *years ago?* We knew the *Playhouse 90* performances were plays, yet we willingly suspended disbelief.

How much disbelief did we have to suspend for the "live" version of ER? Or did we find ourselves thinking we were watching an actual documentary, depicting a real emergency room? In the end, *ER*'s faking of a documentary, using documentary techniques, seemed to me merely a clever trick.

At the end of the 1997–98 season, Dr. Ross of *ER* faced censure for his unauthorized use of a medical procedure called "ultrarapid opiate detoxification" on an infant born to a heroin-addicted mother. The episode caused a furore when critics brought attention to an article in *The Wall Street Journal* in April 1998 that showed how some television shows were being successfully lobbied by medical foundations to include specific diseases in their plots. The *Journal* noted that Dr. Neal Baer, an *ER* writer and producer, had been swamped by the Henry J. Kaiser Family Foundation with information about the risk of a particular sexually transmitted disease. This risk was later mentioned on *ER*. Baer denies that he was lobbied to mention either the detoxification procedure or the sexually transmitted disease on the show.

In contrast to *ER, Chicago Hope* – in the third episode of its fourth season – switched from realism to surrealism. This is an unusual step to take. While such a move might indicate either desperation or a sudden burst of creativity, the real reason may be an attempt to raise audience ratings. In the episode, when neurosurgeon Dr. Aaron Shutt (Adam Arkin) suffers an aneurism, he goes into a delirium. He has hallucinations, among them a song-and-dance number depicting his surgery, presided over by Dr. Jeffrey Geiger (Mandy Patinkin, the Broadway singer). This would be quite familiar to television viewers in Britain where writer Dennis Potter used the same technique in many of his television shows, the most famous being *The Singing Detective.*

Though *The Singing Detective* carries this off with style and disturbing grace, *Chicago Hope* did not succeed nearly so brilliantly. In his marvellous *Dictionary of Teleliteracy*, writer David Bianculli says *The Singing Detective* is "quite simply . . . the best dramatic work ever written specifically for television. Ever. No exceptions; no qualifiers." I won't disagree with Bianculli. As good as some of the new hour-long dramas are – cop shows, medical yarns, other-worldly puzzlers – they do not come within shouting distance of *The Singing Detective.*

Over and over TV critics have mentioned the realism and pace of *ER* as reasons for the success of the show. Trevor Cole of *The Globe and Mail* thinks otherwise. In an illuminating piece in *Broadcast Week*, the newspaper's weekend television supplement, Cole argues: "*ER* may be accurate, but viewers are not gathered round the tube because the needle is going in the right vein. As for the pace, look closely at an episode of *ER* and what you notice is not the rush of editing and movement, beyond the occasional gurney dash from ambulance to operating room, but the luxurious time given to moments of private anguish."

This is an interesting insight. Cole holds that *ER* can "slow to a crawl when the emotional occasion demands it: the elderly man who sang a song to his deceased wife; the heart patient who was to realize gradually the imminence of his death; the suicidal transsexual who spoke softly of the disgust she provoked in others' eyes." Cole concludes: "Television loves the adrenalin spike of sudden pain and heartache, but few shows in the history of the medium have given such respect to quiet despair."

What *ER* does is not entirely new, of course. Writers of literature and drama have long understood the necessity of changing pace. Life changes pace too and TV drama uses this fact to build its own version of reality.

Buffy the Vampire Slayer

We like to talk big – vampires do. "I'm going to destroy the world." That's just tough-guy talk. Strutting around with your friends over a pint of blood. The truth is, I like this world. You've got . . . dog-racing, Manchester United.

And you've got people. Billions of people walking around like Happy Meals with legs.

– Spike, a British vampire, speaking to Buffy

Buffy Summers is a young woman who has been chosen to be The Slayer, a tough job but somebody's got to do it. Her job is to eliminate the world's undead who happen to congregate under the town of Sunnyvale where Buffy and her high-school friends live. Her friends include Willow, who is in love with Oz, a teenage werewolf, and Xander, who has a love–hate relationship with Cordelia. Buffy, played by Sarah Michelle Gellar, is directed in her mission by Rupert Giles, the school librarian, played by Anthony Stewart Head, and aided by the mysterious Angel (David Boreanz), who began the series as a reformed – at least temporarily – vampire.

Derek Boles, a high-school English teacher in Toronto, once was asked why teachers should teach about the media. "Two reasons," he replied. "First, it's important. Second, it's fun." If popular TV fare demonstrates that teaching about television can be fun, none does it better than *Buffy the Vampire Slayer*.

"I told him that I loved him and I kissed him and I killed him." This sounds like something Lauren Bacall would have confessed to Humphrey Bogart in one of their *film noir* movies. Actually it's the way Buffy explains how she killed the vampire she loved. As Ken Tucker writes in the November 6, 1998 edition of *Entertainment Weekly*: "It was an example of an unguarded, unironic emotionalism in a slam-bang series that prides itself on its blithe knowingness and sarcasm and just keeps getting better at juggling hilarity, gothic romance and horror."

Based on a popular horror movie, *Buffy* premiered in 1996–97, and finished 133rd at the end of its second season, winning Emmys for make-up and music. But it has a strong following among the young audience important to advertisers. In its second season, *Buffy* increased its audience 19 per cent to 6 million viewers per week – the fifth-greatest growth of any returning show.

Buffy is about teenagers. But it is possibly meant more for adults than teens. It may be impossible to create a "real" TV show about "real" teens – I realize this as a former high-school principal – but there have been some worthwhile attempts. There was the well-made Canadian series *Degrassi High*, and the short-lived *My So-Called Life*. Then *Beverly Hills 90210* vainly tried to depict teens by using superannuated twentysomething actors (with even older writers, directors, and producers).

Buffy comes closest to depicting the reality of teenage life than anything else on television. Don't be fooled by the weekly dose of vampires and monsters. The vampires and monsters *are* the point. This is, metaphorically, teenage reality. The obvious joke, as Ken Tucker pointed out, "has always been that vampirism and lycanthropy are metaphors for *really* raging hormones." The series explores the serious side of this joke.

Buffy could be a role model for all teenage girls. She is smart, willing to learn about herself and live with who she is, even if she happens to be a vampire-slayer. She is independent, reliable, maybe too much a Type-A personality, but still an entirely credible 1990s teenager. Other shows deal with teenage problems – love, sex, peer pressure, school work, family problems, body image, dreams, insecurity, self-esteem – but *Buffy* adapts a literary and film genre for television. The Vampire myth and the sexuality it evokes speak powerfully to today's teenagers.

And parents recognize this as well. Speaking of Angel, a vampire with redeeming qualities, Pat Kipping, the mother of two teenagers, told me: "Is Angel not the epitome of the 'toxic male' which most young girls need to learn about?"

The most popular teen show in the United States during the 1997–98 season was *Dawson's Creek*. Four white, upper-middle-class, beautiful teenagers living in an affluent Boston suburb appear to have everything money can buy. They are all fifteen years old, though they look much older. This becomes glaringly apparent in classroom scenes where they could easily be mistaken for the teachers as they mingle with actual fifteen-year-old extras.

Consider the dialogue in *Dawson's Creek*:

"You're such a sphincter."

"My emerging hormones are destined to alter our relationship and I'm trying to limit the fallout."

The first is meant to be funny, the second serious. Or is it the other way around? Or are they trying to make normally inarticulate teens precociously erudite? Are they attempting to give vent to inchoate teenage frustration and confusion? The dialogue is a stretch and the producers can't resist injecting the soap-opera scenario of a fifteen-year-old male student embarking on a love affair with his thirty-nine-year-old female English teacher.

Questions that emerge after a few episodes of *Dawson's Creek*:

Will Joey (a girl) ever make it with Dawson (her childhood chum)?

Will Dawson realize that Joey loves him?

Will Jen (the new girl in town) and Dawson find true love?

Who will Pacey (the randy fifteen-year-old boy in love/lust with his English teacher) sleep with next?

These questions could be pre-credit or end-credit voiceovers for any afternoon soap opera.

Dawson's Creek followed *Buffy the Vampire Slayer* on the Warner Brothers network, which determined that the two shows would be a perfect match, throwing a wide net over the teenage audience. In the 1997–98 season, it seemed to work, as *Dawson's Creek* turned out to be one of the top teen shows on television. Teen viewers are attracted to a constructed reality that will likely never be theirs. This is their soap opera, complete with teenagers who have the wealth and looks they desire.

Dawson's Creek does do some things rather well. The production values are excellent (and expensive). And the writing and situations sometimes are clever and witty, but only sometimes. Basically, it is a world of surfaces with little depth.

Entertainment Weekly says of the two shows: "*Buffy* revs up its fans with wise-cracking, full-blooded, vivacious teens; they make the *Creek* crew seem a little pokey. The Net has said it welcomes whatever viewing-luring controversy its sexual themes attract; in that case, it might have done better to pair *Creek* with its other family drama, the moralistic-in-a-different-way *7th Heaven*. In any case, *Dawson's Creek* needs less cleverness and more emotional spark. As the sixteen-year-old in my house said after watching three episodes: 'It's like *My So-Called Life* without the life.'"

The appeal of *Buffy the Vampire Slayer* is in smart writing and dark, anything-goes story lines. In one episode, Xander is seduced by a substitute teacher who turns out to be a giant praying mantis who wants to have sex with him before biting off his head. In another, Buffy's mother has an ultrasensitive boyfriend (played to campy perfection by John Ritter) who turns out to be a robot.

When I watch *Buffy* I look for cultural references, which are so plentiful that one web site has an explanation for them following each episode. There is Cordelia, the dreaded popular girl who speaks primarily in insults: "Nice dress. Good to know you've seen the softer side of Sears." And Xander, the boy who lusted after Buffy during the first season, who says to Buffy after she has just seen Death: "If he asks you to play chess, don't even do it. That guy's, like, a whiz." This reference to Ingmar Bergman's *Seventh Seal* is not what one expects to encounter on a teen TV show.

The viewer can appreciate *Buffy* on a number of levels. For some, *Buffy* is a fun show about monsters and the kids that fight them. For others, it says something much deeper about what it is to be a teenager. It all depends on the breadth of knowledge and sophistication the viewer brings with which to "negotiate the meaning" of the text.

The humour is quick, smart, often in the midst of the scariest or most serious scenes, allowing the viewer to laugh nervously. Best of all, it never takes itself seriously. When Cordelia suddenly goes blind during a driver's education course, Giles muses, "Why would anyone want to harm Cordelia?" To which Willow replies, "Maybe because they've met her." When Xander is caught having checked out every book in the library on the Salem witch trials, he protests, "It's not what you think."

"You like to look at semi-nude engravings?" Willow asks.

"Oh, it is what you think," Xander replies.

Benton Fraser: Do-Gooder

Fraser is not your typical Mountie. He's a pain in the ass. He's a man caught up in the Far North with a set of ethics and values that are old-world and they get him in trouble . . . Today, we tend to equate honesty with stupidity and forget it was once valued.

– Paul Haggis, *The Globe and Mail*

If you plan on flipping through the pages of this book looking for mentions of Canadian TV shows, I'll save you the trouble. What follows is the only extended mention you'll find.

Apart from the reasons mentioned earlier for the relative weakness of Canadian television, there are a number of commercial implications.

Consider this: *ER* costs about $20 million an episode to make, costs CTV about $75,000 an episode to buy, brings in approximate revenues of $200,000 per episode, and attracts 13 per cent of eighteen- to forty-nine-year-old Canadians watching TV at that time. On the other hand, *Traders*, Canada's own home-grown show, costs $1.2 million per episode to make, costs Global about $200,000 per episode to buy, brings in approximate revenues of $125,000 per episode, and attracts 3 per cent of eighteen- to forty-nine-year-old Canadians watching TV at that time. *ER* is cheaper to buy and attracts a much larger audience.

Canada is a successful and respected producer of children's programs around the world (*Anne of Green Gables, Groundling Marsh, Pippi Longstocking, Franklin, Dudley the Dragon,* and *Arthur*) but has never done well with drama series. The 1998–99 season's two new Canadian drama entries – *Da Vinci's Inquest* and *Power Play* – offered some hope critically but found few viewers. It is in comic satire that Canadians have excelled, from the wonderful wackiness of *SCTV* to the wit of *This Hour Has Seven Days*, to the Newfoundland humour of *This Hour Has Twenty-Two Minutes*, to the sometimes successful black humour that is *The Newsroom* and *Made in Canada*, to the best that is *The Royal Canadian Air Farce*. In an October 1998 show, the Air Farce summed up the Clinton/Lewinsky story with the following: "If Clinton apologizes one more time, he'll be eligible for Canadian citizenship."

Due South is a true Canadian success story. After making history as the first Canadian-produced series to make it into prime-time on a U.S. network, it was twice cancelled by CBS and finally shut down in the spring of 1996. However, in 1997, Canadian, German, and British support gave it another chance, with thirteen new episodes for each of the 1997–98 and 1998–99 seasons.

Due South is about the adventures of Constable Benton Fraser, played by Paul Gross, who is assigned to the Canadian Consulate in Chicago. Benton also works as a consultant to the Chicago police force where he teams up with plainclothes cop Ray Vecchio, played in the original series by David Marciano and in the new series by Callum Keith Rennie. The switch from one actor to another playing the same part is as smooth and smart as anything I've seen on television. Benton Fraser's sidekick is his pet wolf, named Diefenbaker (an in-joke for Canadians).

We look on the people with whom Fraser works as his workplace family, especially Ray. His father's ghost, however, played wonderfully by Gordon Pinsent, makes regular appearances. Gross portrays Fraser as an almost stereotypical, perhaps caricatured, Canadian – polite to a fault. Paul Haggis, the writer, says there is a serious intent to the show, which is played off the humour. "I live to lampoon things I love, which includes the way we Canadians view ourselves as inferior and yet overcompensate by being more chauvinistic than the Americans," Haggis told *The Globe and Mail* in 1993. "I love turning stereotypes on their heads. To do this, you first set up the stereotype, an archetypical Mountie who descends on Chicago, a fish out of water in big-city U.S.A. Then you take this 'typical' American, Ray Vecchio, a Chicago cop who wisecracks to Fraser after they demolish the bad guys: 'We just took out seven guys. One more and you qualify for American citizenship.'"

This playing with the notion of national stereotypes appeals to viewers and is one of the charms of the show. Clearly, the notion of national characteristics constitutes a shared interpretation of reality that we can all recognize to a greater or lesser degree. We may be Canadians who have been to Chicago or Americans who have been to Canada. The third key concept reminds us our experiences are significant.

Homicide: Life on the Street

Homicide *is addictive and I always hate when it ends. For as prickly and combative and sweat-stained as these nicotine-addicted characters are, I love having them in my living room . . . That's the true mark of success for a television show.*

– John Haslett Cuff, *The Globe and Mail*

This cop show is set in Baltimore and is based on David Simon's book *Homicide: A Year on the Killing Streets*. It is directed by Barry Levinson, who directed the films *Diner*; *Good Morning, Vietnam*; *Rainman*; *Sleepers*; and *Wag the Dog*. *Homicide: Life on the Street* is Levinson's first go at a television drama.

It is filmed mostly on location and relies heavily on handheld cameras, which gives a *cinéma vérité* feel to the show. The cast has included Ned Beatty as Detective Bolander, Richard Belzer as Detective John Munch, Yaphet Kotto as Lieutenant Al Giardello, Andrew Braugher as Detective Frank Pembleton, Clark Johnson as Detective Meldrick Lewis, Melissa Leo as Detective Kay Howard, Kyle Secor as Detective Tim Bayliss, Reed Diamond as Detective Mike Kellerman, and Harlee McBride as assistant medical examiner Alyssa Dyer.

Homicide premiered in 1993, right after *Super Bowl XXVII*. Such a launch meant that NBC had big expectations for the show. Five years later, *Homicide* continues to receive rave reviews – and low ratings. Cop shows have always done well, but in the 1997–98 season no fewer than eight new cop shows appeared on the screen. At the beginning of the 1998–99 season, not one of them returned. There are three good reasons for this: *Homicide: Life on the Street*, *NYPD Blue*, and *Law & Order*. As ABC entertainment chairman Stu Bloomberg explains: "They did it so damn well that if you're going to introduce a new cop drama, you better be up to that calibre."

Of the three top cop shows, *Homicide* finished the lowest in the 1997–98 season, rated 74th in popularity. *Law & Order*, in its ninth season, finished 24th, *NYPD Blue*, in its fifth season, placed 19th. *Homicide* stands apart from the other two shows, most significantly, perhaps, because the personal lives of the detectives are the basis for most of the episodes. All three shows begin with an "action" premise that we expect of cop shows but it is *Homicide* that more often introduces elements more typical of a drama – exploring areas of moral complexity and ambiguity. The lapsed-Catholic background of Detective Frank Pembleton became an important element in a number of episodes as did the character's struggle to recover from a debilitating stroke.

Every episode of *Law & Order* opens with the words: "In the criminal justice system, the people are represented by two equally important groups: The police who investigate crime, and the district attorneys who prosecute offenders. These are their stories." So the focus in *Law & Order* is on a criminal case, while the cops' and prosecutors' lives remain in the background. *NYPD Blue*, created by Steven Bochco (who also did the acclaimed *Hill Street Blues*), centres primarily on two cops and the harshness of their work and lives in New York City.

These three cop shows are all excellent dramas in their own way. *Law & Order* is more the thinking viewer's character-driven drama. *NYPD Blue* is more the action show, with some emphasis on the personal lives of the cops. *Homicide* takes the middle ground, paying less attention to crime-solving, more to the characters and lives of the crime-solvers.

The characters of *Homicide* sneak into our lives and stake a claim on us. In its second season, we were introduced to Lieutenant Megan Russert, played by Isabella Hoffman. "Aha!" Cuff exclaimed in *The Globe and Mail*. "They're throwing in this sexy attractive thirtyish blonde to jazz up the ratings, but I'm not buying it. Well, within a couple of episodes I was smitten. Russert is a widowed mother fighting her way up the male-chauvinist hierarchy of the Baltimore P.D. and facing all these veiled slurs, resentments and opposition common to her sex."

What attracts us to these cop shows may be the action, but what keeps us interested are the characters. In action shows there is always the promise of an easy resolution. But when we are dealing with character, there is a real complexity. Like Cuff, we are drawn into their lives and develop a relationship with them. We empathize with them and see something in them that reminds us of ourselves. Possibly the attraction is that they always care for each other, no matter what danger or dirty-dealing beset them, and we hope someone would care as much for us in our adversities.

While viewers were making such a fuss over Ellen DeGeneres's coming out in the sitcom *Ellen* in the 1997–98 season, *Homicide* quietly allows Detective Tim Bayliss to explore his bisexuality. There was mixed reaction to this character twist, but it seemed an honest development in a complex character. The detective's sensitive quandary was handled quietly, respectfully, without fanfare. In contrast to *Ellen* the show took an enlightened approach, refusing to appeal to our prurience in an attempt to gain ratings. Bayliss had been shown to have had an active heterosexual liaison, and now he would deal with the other feelings. No big deal.

Homicide also provides some excellent writing. Script writer Tom Fontana has now examined three major American institutions – a hospital (*St. Elsewhere*), a correctional facility (*Oz*) and a police department (*Homicide: Life on the Street*). Two of prime-time television's most powerful hours during the 1997–98 season happened on *Homicide: Life on the Street*.

One was the episode titled "Sins of the Father," which told of a slave's descendant who lynches a white man for crimes committed by his ancestors during the Civil War. Producer Tom Fontana used the actual sites of Harriet Tubman's runaway slave network to shoot flashbacks of nineteenth-century incidents. The other was "The Subway," which guest-starred Vincent D'Onofrio as a dying man trapped between a subway train and the platform. After the opening action, little happens as the rest of the drama is devoted to helping the doomed man come to terms with the fact that he is dying. The man is angry at having been pushed and wants the man who did this to be punished. He does not want to accept his own death. Nor do we as we watch. For this episode, *Homicide: Life on the Street* won an unprecedented third Peabody Award, television's highest honour.

Still, *Homicide: Life on the Street* remains low in viewer popularity. Perhaps it is too intense, too personal, too real. The reality which the show creates may be too close to the reality of our own world. When watching television, we have always been comforted by the knowledge that what we are seeing is not real. Perhaps we are uncomfortable with a show that causes us to wonder if maybe what we are seeing *is* real. Perhaps NBC is keeping *Homicide* alive out of a sense of noblesse oblige, because it is so damn good. And perhaps viewers in the television wasteland give it low ratings for precisely the same reason: it is too damn good.

That Quirky McBeal Woman

Ally McBeal is the male version of the new woman . . . and it's really problematic.

— Hamilton Spectator

Ally McBeal tells the story of a young lawyer, played by Calista Flockhart, who, fired from her first job, becomes an associate at another Boston law firm, run by a school friend, Richard Fish, played by Greg German. Ally's old boyfriend, Billy Alan Thomas (Gil Bellows), also works at the firm, as does his wife, Georgia Thomas (Courtney Thorne-Smith). Comedic aspects are introduced by using fantasy vignettes depicting what Ally is thinking or what she imagines happening around her. When she feels humiliated, visuals show her as small as a mouse; when her heart is broken, real arrows appear to fly into her chest. And then there is that dancing, diapered *ooga-chugga* baby.

What do you say about a program that has created its own genre and whose main character is selfish, not very likable, neurotic, and who dances with an imaginary baby? Whatever I say, I will say carefully, because *Ally McBeal* was one of the few successes of the 1997–98 television season, though it finished 59th in popularity. Of the forty-nine one-hour pilots ordered by the six U.S. networks as candidate series for fall 1997, only *Ally McBeal* actually got on the air and survived to begin a second season in fall 1998. This wonderfully quirky show reminds me of *Northern Exposure*, arguably the best hour-long drama ever to appear on television.

Ally McBeal's fantasies, the phantasmagorical and the morphed, both work and distract. When Billy invites Ally for coffee we see them in a coffee-mug-shaped tub rubbing suds on each other. When Ally discovers her Billy is married, three arrows fly into her heart. A little of this goes a long way. But when it works, it shines. A fantasy that works is the Dancing Baby, which first appeared as a hallucinatory reminder to Ally that, at the age of twenty-nine, her biological clock ticks on. The actual Dancing Baby has been on the Internet for years, from animators working at Kinetix, a software publisher in San Francisco. It spawned a generation of permutations, among them Psycho Baby, Car Crash Baby, Drunken Baby, even Madonna Baby. *Ally McBeal* is one of the first prime-time shows to integrate computer graphics into what appears to be a realistic story line. This is more than just another special effect. The use of such computer graphics has enlarged the language of television and, whether we like this show or not, its enlarged language will be part of TV's vocabulary for years to come.

Pop culture references are used to good effect. Ally is in an elevator with an attractive man she has just met. Will he ask her out to dinner before the elevator comes to a stop or not? On the sound track, as Ally waits, is the sound of the music from final *Jeopardy!*

Ally is one of the most complex characters on television. On the one hand she is a very successful lawyer who can be brilliant in court. She has no problem helping her best friend through a difficult personal crisis. But she is also insecure, jealous, demanding, and lonely. In other words she is very much like a real person. We are so used to accepting the one-dimensional characters of many TV dramas that when we are faced with Ally we need to step back and take a second look.

John Allemang summarized the pros and cons of Ally's character in his column in *The Globe and Mail* when he said, "Most of the criticism has focused on Ally's girlish dithering, which displays a weakness that women in particular don't like to see in a fellow professional. In her wish to have a child, to rekindle a romance in a hopeless situation, [in her tendency] to screw up her work because she's still lost in her private thoughts, the show implies that all working women are equally distracted and incompetent ... Ally McBeal is not a role model by any means, but her abiding conflict between what she does and what she wants to do are much more lifelike and engaging."

In an early episode of the 1998–99 season, Billy tells Ally: "Once in a while, it would be nice if life were more than just your party."

The writing varies widely, but when it is on – which is most of the time (an example: Fish's statement that "helping people is never more rewarding than when it's in your own self-interest") – and when Flockhart, a fine actor, is given the chance to use her talent, the show works very well. It's interesting to note that Flockhart, who is new to television, three years ago played Laura in Tennessee Williams's *The Glass Menagerie* on Broadway and gave an inspiring performance as the shy, crippled, vulnerable girl, which reminds us that Ally is a role, not a person.

It took time for *Ally McBeal* to grow on viewers. As James Collins observed in an article on the show in *Time*, "A viewer senses that, as with *thirtysomething* and *My So-Called Life*, two shows that could also be precious and manipulative and [which] had similar attitudes and characters, there may be stages [that the viewer has] to go through: disgust, annoyance, grudging tolerance, enjoyment accompanied by self-loathing, actual enjoyment." We are so used to letting TV wash over us that when something new comes along we are forced to sit up and take notice. The effort is worth it.

The music on *Ally McBeal* is intriguing. We pay a lot of attention to music in movies, but we tend to ignore it in television shows. This is changing, in no small part because of *Ally McBeal*. The opening theme for *Ally McBeal* – Vonda Shepard's "Searchin' My Soul" – and the one for *Dawson's*

Creek – Paula Cole's "I Don't Want to Wait" – capture perfectly what the shows are all about. Music should be an integral part of a program. Music plays an obvious role in creating emotion within a scene. It can also set a mood which can change the way we see a particular scene. Music can also evoke an association within the viewer's own mind. And because this is something the viewer brings to watching TV, the association may be something the TV producer never thought about. Overall the music we hear throughout *Ally McBeal* works well, especially at the nightclub where the lawyers relax after work. Here Shepard's songs mean something. They have been carefully selected and are as much an expression of Ally's emotions as the dialogue. A fine instance of this was in the closing episode of the first season when all the characters are dancing and Shepard sings "Alone Again, Naturally." The characters all happen to be with someone, but they don't seem happy, despite the cheery hubbub of the nightclub. They really are all quite alone.

The music becomes the voiceover.

The creator, writer, and executive producer of *Ally McBeal* is David E. Kelley, a man who has amazing creative energy. Somehow, Kelley has managed to write every episode, a prodigious output. But there's more: his other shows are *The Practice* (for which he also writes most of the scripts), *Picket Fences*, and *Chicago Hope*. He has written for *L.A. Law* and has a new feature ready to go, titled *Mystery Alaska*. A writer for *Entertainment Weekly*, who had been granted a fifteen-minute interview with Kelley, mused in print, "Time, one assumes, in which Kelley could have knocked out three scripts."

I admire the risks Kelley takes with his shows, especially *Ally McBeal*. Toward the end of the first season, Kelley blended the plots of his two shows about Boston lawyers, *Ally McBeal* and *The Practice*, a gritty real-life drama which won three Emmys in its first season, including Best Drama Series. Two very different constructed realities about lawyers came face to face. The danger was that the illusion of both would be shattered. It is to Kelley's credit that not only did this not happen but that both realities were strengthened.

The absurdity of the law office where Ally works was held up to ridicule by the city-weary, tough realists from *The Practice*. Confronted with the unisex bathroom that functions as both toilet and coffee room on *Ally McBeal*, Bobby Donnell, the head lawyer for *The Practice*, shouts at Ally and her colleagues: "You're all crazy!" It was a wonderful moment: characters from two realities confronting each other.

Ally McBeal has much of the same quirkiness that attracted people to *Northern Exposure*, and there is also a little of the surreal magic of *The Singing Detective*. Maybe Ally, Billy, Georgia, Fish, Renee, Elaine, and Whipper *are* crazy. But then so were Maggie and Joel and the rest of the gang from *Northern Exposure*.

The Out-of-the-World Experience

By the mid-1990s, television would be able to build an entire Zone-like series – The X-Files – around the notion that government agencies knew all about the supernatural and paranormal, but kept it hidden away.

– Steven Stark, *Glued to the Set: The 60 Television Shows and Events That Made Us Who We Are Today*

Two FBI agents team up to investigate unexplained phenomena, officially classified as "The X-Files." David Duchovny stars as Fox Mulder, an Oxford-educated psychologist who believes his sister was abducted by aliens when she was a child. Gillian Anderson plays Dana Scully, recruited from medical school, which enables her to take a scientific approach to the cases.

Since its inception in 1993, *The X-Files* has defied casual viewing. Yet it is very popular, finishing in 11th place overall during the 1997–98 season. It has won nine Emmys. Chris Carter, the creator and executive producer, told *Entertainment Weekly*, "This sensuous, darkly humorous, scary and gorgeous paean to free-floating evil depends on an audience willing to suspend disbelief – to buy into the paranormal, the extraterrestrial, and all manner of government deceptions, inveiglements, and obfuscations (not to mention two windmill-tilting FBI upstarts who hope to unravel it)." Carter said that he began the show "with the notion that everyone wants a religious experience."

The reasons for the success of *The X-Files* vary widely. Perhaps it is best just to summarize them.

1. The Horror Factor

Frank McConnell, a television critic for *Commonweal* magazine, says television has successfully done science fiction, the grotesque and the violent, but never horror – until now. He explains that this is because "TV wants to show you things, and real horror, as Poe knew and Clive Barker knows, is not what you see but what you're afraid you might have to see in a minute . . ." There is also the notion that whenever monsters, aliens, or the supernatural are brought into a drama, at some level they embody or represent the subconscious. *The X-Files* works on this level, playing on our fears.

2. The Characters

Mulder is not an occult vampire-hunter but an FBI agent who, as McConnell says, "feels the terror and allure of the world as Mystery, a visionary trapped in the infonet." His sidekick Scully, the career-rationalist, finds herself drawn into Mulder's universe. In his article in *The Atlantic Monthly*, James Surowiecki says, "Fox Mulder is Noam Chomsky with a Glock 9mm." Of course, having both a sceptic and a believer gives most viewers someone to identify with.

3. The Story Lines

They are open-ended, which is interesting from a structural point of view. Issues are never quite resolved, which is unusual for TV. Even when an episode finishes, it is never over. The dead don't always stay dead. James Wolcott writes in the February 1994 issue of *New Yorker*: "The success of Carter's production techniques lies in the queasy contrast between these gruesome horrors . . . and a lush, becalmed spirit of voyeurism so pure and intent that it borders on a trance state."

4. The Atmosphere

Essential to the success of *The X-Files* is the atmosphere, the result of shooting the first six seasons in Vancouver, where the damp weather and low-lying fog give the show a special feel and look. Wolcott says, "Even the sunlight looks a little ill." This pleased many American viewers because the lush, sometimes darkly gloomy texture, was comfortably foreign, but not too foreign. The opening show of the 1998–99 season began with a close-up of the sun and then a long shot of a bright desert as if to tell viewers that they weren't in Vancouver any more. Much of that special location feel was lost during the seventh season. Los Angeles has a very different feel to it than Vancouver.

5. The Writing
Duchovny says, "It's intelligent writing . . . I don't think there's anything like it on TV because all the scary shows have been kind of stupid. *The Twilight Zone* is interesting, but it's goofy, campy. *Outer Limits* is campy. I don't think we're campy. We're conceived of as an actual drama rather than some kitschy slice of Americana from this day and age."

6. The Internet
The X-Files is the first on-line hit with some hundred *X-Files* sites, official and unofficial. It was a cult hit the first season, then it became a popular show. This is an example of how media can interact with each other reinforcing the constructed reality. One of the producers explains it this way: "*The X-Files* was one of the first shows that was adopted by people on the Internet and it spread through the Internet, which is really a grassroots, word-of-mouth situation. Because of the Internet, our popularity has reached into all facets of the community."

7. Generation-X Appeal
John Haslett Cuff, when he was television critic for *The Globe and Mail*, was one of the first to notice the Generation-X appeal of *The X-Files* when he wrote: "Generation-X fans . . . think *The X-Files* is profound, that it tells truths in fictional guises that are more credible than anything they see on the evening news . . . In a world in which 'truth' is routinely manipulated at the touch of a computer key, and 'real life' role models are bought and paid for by running-shoe manufacturers, these TV constructs make perfect sense as icons for a generation bereft of heroes." Cuff also makes another interesting observation: "The natural audience for this supernatural cop drama consists primarily of the offspring of my generation, a group that is culturally and perhaps genetically disposed to distrust authority and believe in dark government conspiracies." The two familiar, cryptic catchphrases of *The X-Files* are, "The truth is out there" and "Trust no one."

8. Paranoia

James Surowiecki writes in *The Atlantic Monthly* that paranoia has been at the core of some of the most interesting products of American culture in the postwar years, including films such as *Invasion of the Body Snatchers* (1956), *The Manchurian Candidate* (1962), and *Seven Days in May* (1964). "If from one perspective America looks like a nation where anything goes," says Surowiecki, "from another it looks like a place where nothing goes at all unless a secret cabal wants it to. Paranoia, one might say, is in the American grain."

9. The Religious Factor

Writer Deepak Chopra, in a 1998 *New York Times Magazine* article, believes: "Mulder is leading Scully on a search for God – at least the kind of God one senses in these lines from Thomas Merton: 'The Lord travels in all directions at once/The Lord arrives from all directions at once.'" Chopra believes Mulder and Scully are searching for meaning in their lives – his office poster reads "I want to believe," she wears a delicate gold cross. Chopra continues: "The fact that they never conclusively prove anything is what makes them so spiritual – for them, the eternal quest is as open-ended as Parsifal's quest for the Grail."

While the conspiracy episodes are the mainstay of the series, some of the other episodes, like the monster tales, have provided some of the greatest moments on *The X-Files*. Everything is fair game, from the Frankenstein story – retold in a modern setting, in black-and-white – to televangelists. *The X-Files* also parodies itself with great success, most notably in the episode called "Jose Chung's from Outer Space." The episode involves a flashback of Scully being interviewed by a "non-fiction science-fiction" writer named Jose Chung, which becomes a hilarious character-by-character parody that recounts an alien visitation. Writer Darin Morgan lampoons not only the show, and the lunatic fringe it documents, but also the fanatical viewers of *The X-Files*.

Viewers identify with the two main characters, a reflection of the excellent writing, casting, and directing. People are intrigued by the relationship between Mulder and Scully, yet over six seasons nothing romantic has taken place between them. Chris Carter, the creator, insists that nothing ever will.

"If they ever get too romantic," he has said, "you can imagine them ignoring the aliens and genetic mutants and just staring into each other's eyes." Any romance between them is buried in dialogue like the following:

> SCULLY: I finished the autopsy, Mulder. The necrotic tissue around the clavicle is inconsistent with any known pathogen, and I'm mystified by the cutaneous puncture wound below the chin, here.
>
> MULDER: Are you kidding, Scully? This is clearly a simulated vampire attack, clumsily devised.
>
> SCULLY: But why?
>
> MULDER: To divert attention from what really happened in those woods last night.
>
> SCULLY: Which was what?
>
> MULDER: Unless I miss my guess, alien cloning.

As the summer of 1998 approached, more intrigue and interest built as *X-Files* buffs anticipated the release of the $65-million movie version: *The X-Files: Fight the Future.* Scuttlebutt was that all the mysteries would be laid bare, all puzzles solved, all questions answered. The end result? Viewers not familiar with the TV series basically liked the movie. Many fans of the series were as disappointed as I was. We learned almost nothing and marked time until the first show of the 1998–99 season, when we would find out a little more about the ongoing conspiracy theory. Film is a different medium with its own language and conventions. It's not a medium that suits an open-ended and intimate show like *The X-Files*. In fact, very few television shows have made a successful transition to the big screen. *Star Trek* has, for the most part, succeeded, because it presumes that viewers know the background and so the movie spinoffs head right into the action. *The X-Files* has such a complicated back-story that the movie can't do this.

Was producer Carter trying for some new and strange development? Perhaps the movie was just an example of brilliant marketing, conceived to lure some of the 20-million-a-week fans of the TV show into movie theatres. Duchovny says it's a clever way to make us pay for something we get free on television. He may have been joking. But he was addressing the fourth key concept of media education: all media have commercial implications, and ought to make a profit.

The compelling attraction of *The X-Files* is the overarching premise: trust no one in authority. The truth is out there – we just have to find it. It embodies a very contemporary mindset, and not just one of Generation Xers. Carter has created a show that every week remains just a little beyond the grasp of the viewer. As author Jody Duncan reminds us, "Fans of *The X-Files* may have wanted to believe, but they had to think." One last word from Deepak Chopra: "I'd rather be touched by Mulder's paranoia than by an angel."

3

All in the Family: Sitcoms as Modern Miracle Plays

⁓

Television is a hearth fire in the modern home . . . It is simply on all the time.

– Camille Paglia

Situation comedies have always been a mainstay of television, but their roots are far older. We can make a case that Aristophanes in ancient Greece and Molière in seventeenth-century France wrote the sitcoms of their time. And it is even possible to go back to the Middle Ages to consider the major form of medieval drama, the Mystery Play (known in England as the Miracle Play). These plays drew their themes from Scripture and often were filled with humorous contemporary references. They were performed on small wagons parked in churchyards or in the market square. Most often they were a not-so-subtle way of reinforcing religious beliefs.

The room where we watch television today is, as Camille Paglia suggests, the hearth fire of the modern home (the small churchyard wagon of our time). It is not much of a stretch to regard today's television sitcoms as modern mystery plays that not-so-subtly reinforce the belief system of contemporary North American culture. And, like the mystery plays, television sitcoms have recurring character types, offer broad pictures of good and evil, and concentrate on an optimistic view of human nature.

Many critics dislike the sitcom. Thirty years ago, Newt Minnow, chairman of the Federal Communications Commission in the United States, declared that sitcoms were "formula comedies about totally unbelievable families." Thirty years later, many of our cultural guardians would readily agree with Minnow's assessment. In the March 1993 edition of *Esquire*, writer Tad Friend summarized this view when he wrote: "Critics charge that even the wittiest sitcom bypasses the brain and spears the emotions, that sitcoms are really meant for children, or the child lurking in adults. They're right. We are cradled in sitcoms, rocked in their warm lap, nursed from what Harlan Ellison calls 'the glass teat.'" In the *Esquire* article, titled "Sitcoms Seriously," Friend continued: "The dismissive adult view of sitcoms is loudest espoused by highbrow cultural guardians like Neil Postman and the late Allan Bloom who want to build a fire wall around the popular art forms they claim will destroy us with their damnable intent to cause pleasure and laughter." Certainly television sitcoms are escapist art. The pleasure and relaxation which they offer is welcome.

The early television of the 1940s was filled with the sight gags and pratfalls from vaudeville. Viewers were familiar with this type of comedy but they were also used to listening to sitcoms on radio. Many of the early television sitcoms – Amos 'n' Andy, George Burns and Gracie Allen, and Jack Benny – came directly from the radio. In fact what is reported as the first successful sitcom was the 1949 show *The Goldbergs*, an adaptation of the once-popular radio show. Dealing with the conflict that rose in a Jewish family between tradition and American culture, this show ranked seventh in that year's ratings.

It did not take long for television to create its own sitcoms. Wally Cox played the mild-mannered science teacher, Robinson Peepers, on NBC's very successful *Mr. Peepers*. And then Jackie Gleason took what had been a sketch from his variety show and turned it into *The Honeymooners* – the story of that classic little-big-man Ralph Kramden, his wife, Alice, and their neighbours, Ed and Trixie Norton.

But the sitcom that will be most remembered from that time is *I Love Lucy*. Lucille Ball, one of the best comedians on stage and screen, made the transition to television as if the medium was invented for her. *I Love Lucy* is still seen today in virtually every country around the world because Lucy's humour transcends national boundaries. Images of Lucy stomping grapes, or stuffing chocolates in her mouth, her pockets, under her hat, in her dress, as they come endlessly down a conveyor belt, or of getting more and more drunk as she does take after take of a commercial for an elixir more alcoholic than medicinal, need no interpretation.

The 1950s were the Eisenhower era when America was prospering and everyone was feeling good. But they were also the era of the nuclear threat, the Cold War, and unquestioned U.S. military supremacy. It was a time of uniformity and conformity. The sitcoms of those days reflected that with the cheerful all-American family of working father, housekeeping mother, and one boy and one girl.

The 1960s belonged to the Kennedys and with them came a little more sophistication, freedom, and hope for change. While a sitcom like *The Dick Van Dyke Show*, featuring Van Dyke and Mary Tyler Moore, was still about an American family, that family now had a father who worked in show business and a mother who was a former dancer. The New Frontier was front and centre. The nuclear family became a difficult image to maintain and the networks – for whatever reason – decided that it was time for a change and we got a whole stream of "different" families – monsters (*The Munsters*, *The Addams Family*), Martians (*My Favorite Martian*), genies (*I Dream of Jeannie*), witches (*Bewitched*), talking horses (*Mr. Ed*). I think it is a toss-up as to the strangest sitcom of that time but it would be a close race between *The Flying Nun* and *My Mother the Car*.

In the 1970s there was a really radical change in sitcoms. As former CBS programming head Michael Dann said, "The genre was burned out and people were ready for something different. That something different was the truth in comedy, the satire of making fun of bigotry and hate and racial discrimination." At the same time a satiric and surreal comedy tinged with sexual humour was prominent outside of television in the work of Lenny Bruce, Cheech & Chong, and the Firesign Theater. The stage was set for the arrival of Archie Bunker.

Adapted from the extraordinary British sitcom *Till Death Do Us Part*, *All in the Family* each week brought the problems facing the U.S.A. of the 1970s – civil rights, the Vietnam War, poverty, and discrimination, to mention a few – to homes across the country, as right-winged, multiprejudiced

Archie faced off against his ultra-liberal son-in-law Michael. Possibly the most amazing thing about the show was not that it worked – it did – but that it was so popular. "America," as producer Norman Lear said, "was far more grown-up than they had thought." The show ran for twelve-and-a-half seasons and for its first five years was the number-one show of the year.

All in the Family was produced in front of a live audience, which has become the norm for television sitcoms. Some shows augment the audience response by adding laugh tracks. And some few shows, notably Canadian sitcoms, use neither a laugh track nor a live audience. While the form – the sitcom – remains the same in all cases, the end content can be totally different.

Norman Lear went on to bring to television the edgy sitcoms *Maude*, *Good Times*, *The Jeffersons*, *Sanford and Son*, and went one step further with his witty takeoff on the U.S. soap opera, *Mary Hartman, Mary Hartman*, which prepared audiences for another soap-opera satire, *Soap*.

In 1970 CBS offered Mary Tyler Moore her own sitcom, and on the strength of that offer, MTM Enterprises was formed by her husband, Grant Tinker, to produce the show. *The Mary Tyler Moore Show* (1970–77) was the story of Mary Richards, a single woman who lands a job as associate producer of the evening news at Minneapolis's lowest-rated television station. As David Bianculli writes in *Dictionary of Teleliteracy*: "Though Mary Richards was both embraced and attacked by feminists in the seventies (embraced because she was a single career woman, a small step forward for TV womankind; attacked because, for one thing, she always addressed her boss using the deferential 'Mr. Grant'), her greatest value was her consistency." The show was one of the first sitcoms to accept the breakdown of the nuclear family and to deal with the belief in the possibility of self-actualization. *The Mary Tyler Moore Show* and the other MTM shows were focused more on personal relationships than on the big issues of war and race. MTM's other shows included *The Bob Newhart Show* (1972–78), *Rhoda* (1974–78), *Lou Grant* (1977–82), *WKRP in Cincinnati* (1978–82) and *Hill Street Blues* (1981–87).

As a footnote, 1972 saw the premiere of *M*A*S*H*, possibly the ultimate war against all wars and a thinly disguised attack on the futility of the Vietnam War specifically. When the final episode aired in 1983, 77 per cent of all people watching television in the U.S.A. were watching that show.

The influence of MTM continued into the 1980s with many sitcoms coming from those who once worked for MTM – *Cheers* (1982–93), *Family Ties* (1982–89), *The Cosby Show* (1984–92), *Kate and Allie* (1984–89), *The Golden Girls* (1985–92). And they all had that MTM touch of dealing with more personal issues.

But it was also in the 1980s that sitcoms turned their focus on the darker side of family life with Fox's *Married With Children* (1987–97) and ABC's *Roseanne* (1988–97). Although both shows were sitcoms, their take on family was meant to be satirical, an approach that did not always work.

The 1990s began with the strangeness of the animated family that was *The Simpsons* (1990 to present) and went on to introduce what would become the phenomenon known as *Seinfeld* (originally known as *The Seinfeld Chronicles*; 1990–98) – the sitcom that spent thirty minutes talking about nothing. The show was the ultimate conclusion of the "me" generation's self-absorption. And it was a great success until it closed down eight years later – for no other reason than that its creator believed that eight years was a good number of years for a television show to run.

As we near the turn of the millennium, there is a variety in sitcoms that harks back to the older days of the genre. There are shows about families of all sorts – *Home Improvement* (1991–99), *Everybody Loves Raymond* (1997 to present), *Dave's World* (1993–98), *The Hughleys* (1998 to present), *Two of a Kind* (1998 to present); the return of the alien with *3rd Rock from the Sun* (1995 to present); sitcoms about the media – *Murphy Brown* (1988–98), *Frasier* (1993 to present), *Newsradio* (1995 to present), *Caroline in the City* (1995 to present), *Mad About You* (1992 to present), *Sports Night* (1998 to present); about the dysfunctional family – *Grace Under Fire, Cybill, Jesse*; and sitcoms about extended families – *Friends* (1994 to present), *Veronica's Closet* (1997 to present), *Ellen* (1994–98), *Spin City* (1996 to present), *The Drew Carey Show* (1995 to present), and *Will and Grace* (1998 to present).

When you look at the sitcoms of the 1990s one element is missing – any sort of a broad-based hit that appeals to all audiences – *Frasier* may be the closest. It has been a long time since the family sat down on any evening to watch a sitcom together. Still, a lot of people watch sitcoms. In fact, the television most people watch *is* the sitcom. Prime-time television on any given weeknight offers people a wide choice of sitcoms, all of which deal with one kind of family or another. Sitcoms, like any other television show, indeed like all media, present implicit value systems to viewers. After a time – a season or two – of watching a sitcom we come to see that the values by which those characters live could become part of our own values system. Children who grow up watching the way teenagers on television behave in school could go to high school thinking that is the way to behave.

We are usually aware of the commercial implications of the sitcoms – the spinoff products with images of Bart Simpson and the *South Park* kids, for example, available on everything from coffee mugs to school lunchboxes. But do we realize just how often social issues are presented in sitcoms? Topics such as unemployment (*Roseanne, Grace Under Fire, Maggie Winters, Frasier*), AIDS (*Designing Women*), homosexuality (*Spin City, Ellen, Will and Grace*), premarital sex (*Married With Children, Family Ties, The Nanny*), abortion (*Maude*), adolescence (*The Simpsons, Two of a Kind, That '70s Show*), racism (*All in the Family, The Hughleys*, and ageism (*The Golden Girls*). While their views on these social issues may not be to our liking, we should be aware that they can help form opinions. Usually the treatment of such issues is not done in any depth but it is present and has been since the 1970s. And perhaps the lighthearted approach has more of an effect on people than sermonizing would.

Over the years, many critics have tried to define just what a sitcom is and what it does. Surprisingly, this has not been easy. Perhaps Gerard Jones presents the best analysis in his book *Honey, I'm Home! Sitcoms: Selling the American Dream*. Jones presents his analysis thus:

1. The sitcom is a corporate product. "It is a mass consumption commodity, designed, like a sedan, to be constructed decade after decade on the same safe, reliable pattern, yet allowing enough surface variations to be resold as a new product every few years." This is one of the common complaints from television critics. If a sitcom about blue-collar workers is successful then the following season contains clones of the show – *Roseanne* begat *Grace Under Fire* begat *Everybody Loves Raymond* begat *King of Queens*. Some succeed, most fail.

2. "The ideals upheld by the sitcom are the ideals on which modern bureaucratic business and government are founded: the consensual solution is the best solution, ideology and self-interest only stand in the way of mutual

benefit . . . there is no reason we can't all end up happy." Take any sitcom –
Spin City, say – where the orderly running of the workplace – in this case
the office of the mayor of New York – is threatened by a crisis. This is
resolved only when all the workers support the plan devised by Michael J.
Fox's character.

3. Sitcoms are an expression of the family. "The sitcom is more directly
about families and workplaces than about society in the greater sense." As
we will see, the concept of family has changed considerably from the families – such as that of Jim Anderson in *Father Knows Best* – which first
graced the television screen. Families are rarely what was once the traditional family consisting of a father, mother, and two children. We are more
likely to find single-parent families (*Jesse*, for example, and any 1990s
sitcom with Tony Danza). But family has come more and more, ever since
The Mary Tyler Moore Show, to mean the workplace family on such shows
as *Murphy Brown*, *Working*, and *Caroline in the City*.

4. The sitcom is a mirror. "A foggy mirror to be sure . . . but one of its functions has always been to show the American family to itself." Sometimes
these shows hold up models of what society thinks the family should be –
the Cleavers, the Bradys, the Huxtables. Sometimes they present families
worse off than we are, allowing us to feel superior to the characters portrayed – the Kramdens, the Clampetts, the Bundys.

5. The sitcom is an escape. "In the age when the family is threatened and
coworkers are opponents and neighbors are strangers, it's pleasant to have
an imitation family to retreat to." These families can offer us what our own
– at home or at work – perhaps cannot. *Cheers* said it best with its theme
song – wouldn't it be nice if we could all go to a place "where everybody
knows your name and they're always glad you came"?

6. The sitcom is a teacher. At times, television producers treat it as such.
What we can learn from sitcoms is inconsiderable compared to what we
learn from real life. But certainly "sitcoms teach something through rein-
forcement; they make us feel good briefly by reflecting and dramatically
reconfirming that which we already wish to believe. They may not change

our behavior, but they may strengthen our confidence in continuing as we are." All media offer us values, social comment, political opinion, and some kind of ideology. In doing this they may indeed reinforce what we already believe or they may cause us to question our own beliefs. It is very difficult for us to remain totally unaffected by sitcoms.

7. The sitcom is entertainment, "... quintessential entertainment. It's small, it's intimate, it's a friendly thing to invite into the home and a comforting thing to watch with the family." And even though it may teach, there is nothing to prevent it from entertaining us as we learn. This is the best way to educate as good teachers know. Laughter is the best medicine – a cliché to be sure. When we finish a day stressed out from work of whatever kind, a sitcom that offers us a chance to laugh at someone else's difficulties can relieve our own stress.

8. The sitcom sells; "because it creates feelings of warmth and security and positive regard for modern life, it's a perfect shill for a sponsor's product." And so we have to keep in mind that at the same time a sitcom is entertaining us, and presenting values and social messages, it is also about selling products – it may be spinoff items like *The Simpsons* t-shirts or the various products advertised during the show. Television is a business and sitcoms are a wonderful vehicle for presenting us with the good we are supposed to need to lead the happy family lives of our favourite sitcom characters.

The Simpsons

> *That little hellraiser is the spawn of every shrieking commercial, every brain-rotting soda pop, every teacher who cares less about young minds than about cashing their big, fat pay cheques. You can't create a monster and then whine when he stomps on a few buildings.*
>
> – Lisa Simpson on her brother Bart

Created in 1990 by newspaper cartoonist Matt Groening, *The Simpsons* is an animated prime-time television sitcom. Animated prime-time shows for adults are not the norm. *The Flintstones*, which ran from 1960–66 on ABC, was the first successful one. ABC tried again with *The Jetsons* in 1962, but it lasted only one season. Both these shows enjoyed an extended life as Saturday-morning cartoons.

The Simpsons live in the small town of Springfield where Homer, the father, works as a safety inspector at a nuclear plant. Marge with the column of blue hair is the socially conscious mom. Bart is the underachieving brat who seems destined to remain forever in Grade 4. Lisa is his bright sister, and finally there is baby Maggie and her pacifier. Against a backdrop of cynicism and greed, *The Simpsons* examine family values in their own special way.

In June 1998, *Time* named twenty artists and entertainers who most influenced life in the twentieth century: Frank Sinatra defined American pop music, James Joyce revolutionized fiction, Pablo Picasso defined many of the art movements of the century, and Bart Simpson embodied a century of popular culture. Bart is the key to the controversial success of *The Simpsons*. He is world-weary and street-wise, with bulging eyes and post-Renaissance aggression. We know him by:

"Eat my shorts."

"Don't have a cow, man."

"I'm Bart Simpson. Who the hell are you?"

Many find this TV family, which was never intended as a show for children, downright nasty. Many love it, many hate it. There are critics who say *The Simpsons* is the show closest to the reality of the typical American family. Children often say they like *The Simpsons* because the characters fight and have money and status problems just like their own families. Consistently, since its debut in 1990, the show ends the season listed within the top twenty shows.

John Allemang of *The Globe and Mail* appeared on a television panel to discuss why *The Simpsons* should be cancelled. He went prepared to defend the program as good satire but changed his point of view when he encountered several teens in the audience who attacked *The Simpsons* as "morally and intellectually objectionable." In his column, Allemang wrote of the experience: "The father, the figure of authority in the family, is a boob who gets by on bending the rules and slacking off. He passes on these lessons in life to his son, whose motto from the earliest days of the series has been, 'Underachiever and proud of it.' The mother sacrifices herself to the whims of these ungrateful males and ends up being a bundle of neuroses. The smart daughter, the one character who might serve as a role model to young viewers, is mocked for her intelligence. The religious figures who do make regular appearances on the show – the obsessive do-gooder Ned Flanders, the opportunistic Reverend Lovejoy – are figures of mockery."

And yet, in the pages of *Alberta Report*, a right-wing, fundamentalist Christian magazine, a theology professor calls *The Simpsons* one of the most religious shows on television. "It takes religion's place in society seriously enough to do it the honour of making fun of it," says Gerry Bowler, professor at Canadian Nazarene College in Calgary and chairman of the Centre for the Study of Christianity and Contemporary Culture.

Bowler cites an early episode when Marge tells Homer she is pregnant. "Can't talk now – praying," Homer tells her, whereupon he prays: "Dear Lord, the gods have been good to me and I am thankful. For the first time in my life everything is absolutely perfect the way it is and I won't ask for anything more. If that is okay, please give me absolutely no sign. [Pause.] Okay, deal. In gratitude, I present to you this offering of cookies and milk. If you want me to eat them for you, please give me no sign. [Pause.] Thy will be done."

As for do-gooder Ned Flanders, Bowler says Ned is "television's most effective exponent of a Christian life well lived." When Homer pleads to God for tickets to the football game, Ned rings Homer's doorbell and offers him the tickets. "Prayer of all kinds abounds on *The Simpsons*," Bowler submits, citing as an example Bart's mealtime offering when he says, "Dear God, we paid for all this stuff ourselves, so thanks for nothing."

Professor Bowler really might be saying the opposite of what he meant to say, and his illustrative arguments in favour of *The Simpsons* may support the views of the teens at Allemang's panel discussion. But *Christian Century* magazine, in its summer issue of 1990, wrote: "*The Simpsons* is satire. Rather than engage in the pretentious misrepresentation of family that one finds in the 'model family' shows (from *The Donna Reed Show* to *The Cosby Show*), this program admits that most parents aren't perfect. They haven't worked out their own childhood confusion and they don't have the answers to all their children's problems. The obnoxiousness of the Simpson children and their schoolmates is their way of coping with adults who can't possibly always do right: after all, adults are only human."

It is Bart who, in his questioning of religion, best brings home the importance of religion. In one episode Bart sells his soul to his friend Millhouse. Bart figures, why not? He doesn't believe in the soul, so if Millhouse wants to pay him five bucks for it, fine. Bart may not believe in his soul, but after the deal with Millhouse he begins to notice something missing in his life. He can no longer do things other people do, such as fog up an ice-cream display case with his breath. He begins a search more desperate than comic that takes him through the streets of Springfield. Finally, he prays to God and begs for his soul. When Lisa gives him the paper on which he had written the agreement to sell his soul, she tells him that some people believe souls are given only after suffering, thought, and prayer.

The Simpsons has been attacked from the highest office in the United States. Republicans in the U.S.A. were staking out "family values" territory in part to appeal to the politically powerful religious right – a group to whom programs like *The Simpsons* are anathema. In 1990, Barbara Bush declared it "the dumbest thing I've ever seen." This prompted Marge to write to the first lady, saying, "I always believed in my heart that we had a great deal in common. Each of us living our lives to serve an exceptional man." Mrs. Bush then apologized, but two years later, at a broadcasters convention, George Bush himself said, "The nation needs to be closer to the Waltons than the Simpsons." This prompted Bart to respond, "Hey, we are just like the Waltons. Both families spend a lot of time praying for the end of the Depression."

Groening, the artist who started it all, told *TV Guide* in 1997: "Sometimes you have to watch an episode twice to catch a joke – which is a good thing. There are obvious jokes, the visual sight-gags, the subtle literary allusions, and at the most subtle – what we call the freeze-frame gags – jokes you can only get if you videotape the show and play it back in freeze-frame. What we try to do is reward people for paying attention."

Groening believes that people who think the show is subversive and anarchistic just don't get it. "My goal from the beginning has been to not get mired in this kind of sour 'ain't life horrible' kind of humor that is the hip stance these days," he told *TV Guide*. "I think we're able to get away with some fairly dark comments about our culture by leavening it with lightness. The fact is, the show is a celebration. That has been my main goal from the beginning."

The Simpsons is a celebration of the family, certainly in the sense that the family unit is always vindicated. But it is also very realistic in many ways. In one episode Marge leads a campaign to get rid of violence in children's TV programming. She succeeds, but at a price. She learns that once people in Springfield have a taste for such protest they go on to protest things that need no protest – here it is the bringing of Michelangelo's *David* to Springfield.

In the midst of all the controversy that circles round *The Simpsons*, it is important to remember that while kids do watch it, this is a show meant for adults despite the tendency to regard animation as kids' stuff. *The Simpsons* is smart, funny, and very strong in presenting family values. When we look beyond the outrageousness of some episodes, we can see that these are values which we want both for ourselves and for our families.

Two other prime-time cartoon shows that deal with the family are *King of the Hill* and *South Park. King of the Hill* is the story of Hank Hill, a common-sense, conservative Texan who sells propane, his wife Peggy, a substitute Spanish teacher and notary public, and their pudgy, unmotivated son, Bobby. There is also Hank's niece, Luanne, who is trying to graduate from beauty school. And Hank's buddies, Dale, Bill, and Boomhauer, who all seem to have a lot of time to stand around doing nothing.

King of the Hill is the 1995 creation of Mike Judge, who also brought to life another controversial animated series called *Beavis and Butt-Head*. Many non-Texans who watch the show regard the characters as stereotypes. Not Judge, who argues that his characters are real people behind what merely appear to be stereotypes. "I'm not making fun of these good ol' Texas boys, the humor comes from them just being themselves," he told *TV Guide* in 1997. "I know guys like them and in their own way they're pretty hilarious."

Just how realistic is *King of the Hill*? David Kronke, a senior writer at *TV Guide*, comes from Texas: "Nothing on the show – nothing – is exaggerated. Hank is a typical contemporary Texan: a cowboy shunted to the suburbs . . . this breed of Texan pines for the return to the mythical Texas embodied by John Wayne." Canadians tend to regard the family in *King of the Hill* as more "foreign" than the family in *The Simpsons*.

If *The Simpsons* has caused such a storm of controversy, what about

South Park? This murderous little animated sitcom is to *The Simpsons* what the film *Reservoir Dogs* is to *Lassie Come Home.*

South Park is set in a snowbound Colorado town that is home to third-graders Stan, the vile-mouthed fat kid Kyle (who's picked on because he's Jewish), and Kenny, the poor kid who gets killed in every episode. This is not a show for children. Its original intended audience was college kids – the ones who find *Animal House* and *Porky's* hilarious. It has become a "guilty pleasure" of many grown-ups.

In Canada, *South Park* starts at midnight with a stern advisory that it contains "offensive material" and is intended for a mature audience. There was an attempt in 1998 to air the show at 10:30 P.M. on Canada's Global stations. This did not last long. It seems kids are staying up beyond 9:00 P.M. In some of the gentler episodes, Kyle passes off his pet elephant as "the retarded kid," Kenny is cooked in a microwave, and their teacher plots the assassination of Kathie Lee Gifford.

There was another stern advisory, this time in an episode of *South Park* itself. When the teacher, Mr. Garrison, tells the children: "Throughout history there have always been television shows that have come and gone that have been very bad. Usually they get taken off the air. You see, you should be spending your time enlightening your minds with more intelligent entertainment." Or perhaps this was an ironic comment by the show's writers directed at their critics.

Spin magazine, March 1998, traced the origins of the show: "Take a bunch of cute li'l quaintly animated characters – redolent of early '70s instructional films and *Peanuts* holiday specials – and slam them into '90s grossness and dread. Somehow, by featuring vomiting, farting, racial slurs, and decapitation, their not particularly high-minded creative enterprise seized pole position in the culture industry. Somehow, *South Park* must speak to some hunger deep within us, must affirm some basic truths about humanity. That, or we're truly a bunch of retards."

The original show was done on video – for $750 – and shopped around till a deal was made with the Comedy Central channel. This video – *The Spirit of Christmas* – introduced us to the main characters as well as to what would become the ingredients for almost every episode – sacrilege, sadism, and non-stop profanity. Jesus appears before the kids to avenge the commercialization of Christmas. He does this via a kung fu combat with Santa Claus during which Kenny is accidentally killed.

The antecedents for *South Park* are shows like *Ren and Stimpy* and *Beavis and Butt-Head* as well as *The Simpsons*. While *South Park* holds its own against the juvenile humour of *Ren and Stimpy* and *Beavis and Butt-Head* it does not fare so well when compared to *The Simpsons*. *The Simpsons'* satire is concerned more with suburban life and popular culture. *South Park* is about puking and aliens and nothing – I can see it as being one of the favourite shows for the characters in *Seinfeld*.

An article in *The Globe and Mail* in February 1998 summarized various criticisms of *South Park*:

1. A one-note show with humour as crude as its drawing style.

2. ". . . these bad boys are so bad they make *Beavis and Butt-Head* look like Charlie Brown" (from *Newsweek*).

3. "The humour is so twisted that one can only fear for the future of civilization run by the spaced-out insomniacs who watch this show" (John Allemang).

4. "It might help if the *South Park* kids had personalities, but they're as one-dimensional as the show's cut and paste animation" (*Entertainment Weekly*).

The article says the creators of the show, Trey Parker and Matt Stone, two twentysomethings, insist that *South Park* is far more clever than at first appears evident. Parker explains, "When we sit down to write these, we don't say, 'All right, how far can we get? How can we offend people?' We just figure a story we want to tell."

Maybe today's kids know something most adults do not. In the August 1997 edition of *Variety*, the bible of showbiz, a reviewer calls *South Park* "gloriously subversive art . . . blasphemous, juvenile, preposterous, mean-spirited, defiant and politically incorrect . . . The genius is in the incongruity between the innocent look of the characters and the outlandish invective that spews from their yaps and gives *South Park* its deliciously wigged-out sensibility."

There will never be any agreement on shows like *South Park*. It will offend as many as it pleases. But it's here, it may be around for a while, and many kids who should be in bed at midnight love it. The best way to consider it is to focus on the satire it so clearly aspires to and the values which it offers.

Newsradio

I thought about something last night. What is a family? And I think I know. A family is people who make you feel less alone and really loved. Thank you for being my family.

> – Mary Richards's final words to co-workers in
> the last episode of *The Mary Tyler Moore Show*

Many sitcoms have dealt with the extended family that has grown up around the workplace. *The Mary Tyler Moore Show* was among the best and earliest examples of this sub-genre. Jilted by a long-term boyfriend, Mary Richards leaves her small town and drives to the big city of Minneapolis where her colleagues at a television station become her family. There are sitcoms that mix actual family life with workplace family life. *Mary Tyler Moore* concentrated almost exclusively on the workplace family. And there are other, newer examples. In the 1997–98 season, these included *Spin City* and *Working*, both of which were well received. *Newsradio*, which premiered in 1995, is another. Though never finishing higher than 60th, it is still on air and has a good following.

Newsradio is set in the all-news radio station in New York City. The staff is a dysfunctional collection of characters. Stephen Root plays Jimmy, the grim eccentric who owns the station, WNYX. Dave Foley, from the Canadian comedy team Kids in the Hall, is news director Dave Nelson. The late Phil Hartman (another Canadian) played the pompous anchorman Bill McNeal. Andy Dick is Matthew, an insecure, off-the-wall reporter who moonlights as a dentist. Maura Tierney is Lisa, an intelligent but neurotic newswriter. Vicki Lewis is the wacky secretary and Joe Rogan plays Joe, a technician who seems to be here for no other purpose than (as *Entertainment Weekly* suggests) to remind us of Tony Danza.

We know hardly anything about the at-home families to which these people return after work, so they represent a workplace family coping with the usual familial joys and sorrows. They support each other in hard times.

When Matthew loses his job the others try to get it back for him. They also trade jobs within the station in order to make the place work more efficiently. They care for each other in ways we would want our families to care for us. It is easy to see ourselves in them, so we care for them. Their caring is a significant but subtly stated example of the fifth key concept, which talks about all media containing value messages. Here we see Christian family values in a workplace setting. The workplace of *Newsradio* – despite all the strange antics that go on there – is a workplace that speaks of a real social concern. *Working* also attempts this but does not quite succeed. This is due to the fact that *Newsradio*'s cast, for whatever reason, works better as an ensemble. In both these sitcoms, as in the original TV sitcom families, the TV workplace families are actually more supportive, sympathetic, loving, resilient, and wise than many real-life families (at work or at home).

The writing and directing are excellent, but much of the success is due to the actors. When *Newsradio* first aired, Ken Tucker of *Entertainment Weekly* observed in March 1995: "Foley has a quality that sets him apart from other comic actors: He knows how to portray a shy, polite, introverted man who is not a total dweeb. His Dave is also smart and resourceful. Foley's shrewd, understated style here is much closer to that of the English comic Rowan Atkinson than to any American model."

As for Hartman's anchorman, Tucker writes: "Hartman is . . . doing a brilliant job in a difficult role. After all, how does anybody do a boob anchorman without aping the definitive one, Ted Knight's Ted Baxter? But Hartman has figured out how to do it. His Bill isn't a simple fool – he's a mean fool, someone who relishes making other people squirm. It's a testament to Hartman's stylized yet genuine charm – with his crinkly eyes and lizard's smile – that he makes Bill as likable as he is."

Newsradio's 1997–98 season ended with a spoof on the movie *Titanic* with the cast, in period costume, running the ship. The only survivor of the ship's sinking was, ironically, Hartman's Bill McNeal. We see him at the end of the show, floating alone in the water on a suitcase. Less than a month later, Phil Hartman was murdered. Many wondered if *Newsradio* could continue without him, but it did continue. The opening episode of the 1998–99 season began with the staff in the office following the funeral of Bill McNeal who had died at home of a heart attack.

There is no question but that this was a difficult episode to write and to act. How, in the midst of a sitcom, do you deal with death, especially with the death of one of the stars of the show? Death has been dealt with before on sitcoms – the episode of *The Mary Tyler Moore Show* which centred on the death of Chuckles the clown comes to mind. But on *Newsradio*, the star didn't just die, he was murdered.

If *Newsradio* were a "black comedy," a comedy with a dark or cynical edge, there would be no difficulty in dealing with death. Black comedy uses laughter as a defence against the tragedies and absurdities of modern life – it is essentially entertainment as survival tactic. But *Newsradio* is not a black comedy. It is a sitcom, quite a different genre. On TV, black comedy exists in the hour-long dramas. Shows like *M*A*S*H*, *Picket Fences*, and *Northern Exposure* have all dealt with real death in a black-comedy manner.

Newsradio chose to show us how each of the major characters reacted to Bill's death. They each spoke of what they did when they heard: Lisa got drunk, Joe ran home to his parents' and climbed in bed with them, Jimmy bulldozed the new house he was building, and Matthew went into denial. They made no attempt to be humorous yet there was humour in watching these characters react as they tried to express their grief. They drew a fine line between sentiment and sentimentality.

And in a way that would never have happened in real life, he remembered them as well. Bill had left letters with his lawyer in case he died – letters for each member of the staff reminding them about their relationship. And Bill left a final note, which Dave read: "Farewell, take care of each other. See you all when we get to wherever I am now." The tears in the eyes of the cast as Dave read these lines were – I suspect – real tears for the loss of Phil Hartman, a close friend and colleague, as well as for the character of Bill McNeal. This was a unique situation where real life imposed itself on a constructed reality.

Mary Richards said about her make-believe colleagues on *The Mary Tyler Moore Show*, "A family is people who make you feel less alone and really loved." Twenty-one years after she said that, we saw it happen once again as *Newsradio* mourned. The reality that was created in this sitcom once again makes us care about the characters. This is good television.

Father Knows Best Revisited?

Television doesn't try hard enough most of the time. And when it does, and succeeds in presenting something truly special, neither its creators nor its viewers take it seriously enough.

– David Bianculli, *Teleliteracy: Taking Television Seriously*

On the surface, *Home Improvement* is the very model of a mainstream sitcom: wife, three kids, a bumbling dad. It has always been a popular show, rated in the top-ten every season since it began in 1991. Standup comic Tim Allen stars as Tim Taylor, husband and father of three boys: Brad (Zachary Ty Bryan), Randy (Jonathan Taylor Thomas) and Mark (Taran Smith). The wife and mother is Jill (Patricia Richardson). Tim hosts a home improvement program on a Detroit cable TV station. The Taylors' next-door neighbour Wilson (Earl Hindman), whose full face is never seen, offers wise advice.

Interesting to note that a *TV Guide* poll among thirteen- to forty-year-old viewers determined that Tim and Jill Taylor are television parents most like their own. Have Tim and Jill Taylor become the representative parents of the 1990s? If a similar poll had been taken, say, in the 1950s, would Mr. and Mrs. Jim Anderson have been voted the television parents most like our own?

We are talking about feelings here. The title itself, *Father Knows Best*, says much about the mindset and expectations of the 1950s. The television show, which featured Robert Young as Jim Anderson and Jane Wyatt as the perfect wife and mother, grew out of an NBC radio program titled *Father Knows Best?* (The question mark is the operative punctuation.)

Home Improvement is entirely different. An article in *Time* in May 1993 summed up its appeal when it said it "covers all its bases shrewdly. It combines the ironic edge of Allen's standup comedy – a sort of macho flipside to Roseanne Arnold's beleaguered-housewife rants – with traditional family-show sentimentality. It caters to the baby-boom audience while poking gentle fun at it. It toys with the sitcom format in ways both inventive and annoying."

In the 1990s, *Home Improvement* examined – in an entertaining and enlightening way – what it meant "to be the best father and husband in an age of feminism and embattled male identity," which is how Steven Stark explains it in his 1997 book *Glued to the Set*.

Matt Williams and David McFadzean developed the concept for *Home Improvement* when they both were reading the work of noted linguist Deborah Tannen on male–female communication (*You Just Don't Understand: Women and Men in Conversation*). In *Glued to the Set*, Williams tells Stark: "Her book deals with the fact that men and women speak different languages. That right there is the piston that drives this television series. Jill and Tim will never do the same thing the same way and both sides are valid."

So *Home Improvement* focuses on gender issues. As *Time* says, "Tim is a swaggering takeoff on a macho guy who gets his kicks from rebuilding closets and working on his hotrod at 4:00 A.M. . . . For advice, he turns to his next-door neighbor, a disciple of poet Robert Bly, whose conversations usually open with an avuncular chuckle . . . and end with an anecdote about tribal customs. *Home Improvement* of course makes fun of these men's movement clichés."

The more Tim works at upholding his masculine ideals, the more it becomes obvious the show is satirizing male attitudes towards women and life in general. In one episode, Tim tries to help his son by suggesting he dab sticky glue on his hands so he won't keep fumbling footballs. When his son tells him that the label on the glue container warns against skin contact, Tim says that the warning is for "pretty little pink girl skin," not for fellows "like us" who have "man skin – calluses, warts, open wounds."

Jill is the only woman in this otherwise all-male world. As a modern everywife, she must dance a fine line as Tim tries to figure out how to be a man in a world where men and women are equals. Pat Richardson, the actor who plays Jill, told *The New York Times* in 1992 that *Home Improvement* "takes apart gender-related clichés bit by comic bit. Whether it is a question of Jill getting a job rather than staying at home with the boys or a fight over how to unclog the sink the Taylors explore a range of male–female friction points. These are dangerous issues, particularly now, with the country so polarized. Women are divided among women, men and women are divided, and racially everything is incredibly divisive. In the show, here are these two people coming from completely different points of view most of the time, who still love each other and have a sense of humor about each other's attitudes. And I think that's reassuring."

No doubt about it, Tim comes off as a chauvinist, one of those conspicuous targets of feminism. Yet one of Tim's attractive qualities is that he is a sensitive man, though often you must take a very forgiving attitude to accept this. There was the episode in which one of the boys gets into a fight at school and explains that he was embarrassed when Tim hugged him in front of the other kids. Tim gently, patiently, explains to his son how men shouldn't be ashamed to hug.

Home Improvement may be a surprise in that it succeeds in being modern while depicting a family whose members actually like one other. But how close is this representation to the suburban middle-class family in the 1990s? I suspect closer in many cases than we might otherwise have believed. Most viewers, as the *TV Guide* poll showed, like them and want to be like them. And whether the reality they have constructed is close to the reality of today's families does not matter. Their constructed reality brought them a large audience – they finished 10th overall in the 1997–98 season.

Frasier

The most important thing you look for is a writer who looks at the world from a different angle or is just a little bent . . . You have to be willing to pitch a joke that bombs and have everybody ridicule you for it and then dust yourself off and go on writing.

– Peter Casey, one of the creators of *Frasier*

At the 1998 Emmy Awards, *Frasier* won its fifth consecutive Emmy as Best Comedy Show – this is a record. Since its first show in September 1993, *Frasier* has been praised for being not only funny but also literate and intelligent. It has consistently finished the year in the top twenty. In the 1997–98 season it ended up in 13th place. At $475,000 per thirty-second commercial, it has the second-highest ad cost on TV. As it went into its sixth season, it took over the coveted spot occupied by *Seinfeld* – Thursday nights at 9:00 P.M. This is the spot also once held by *Cheers*, in which the character of Dr. Frasier Crane was originated by Kelsey Grammer.

In *Frasier*, Dr. Crane has moved to Seattle from Boston to host a radio call-in show. His widowed, ex-cop father, Martin, played by John Mahoney, has moved in with him, along with Daphne Moon (Jane Leeves), Martin's physiotherapist, and, of course, Eddie, the dog. The cast also includes Frasier's brother, Dr. Niles Crane (played by David Hyde Pierce), Frasier's producer Roz Doyle (Peri Gilpin), and the station's gruff sports reporter, Bulldog (Dan Butler).

Diane English, producer of *Murphy Brown*, was asked at a gathering of the American TV industry's more creative minds, "Whatever happened to smart comedies?" As *The Globe and Mail* reported on July 24, 1998, English responded, "Takes smart people to write them." And when her interrogator asked, "Is there nobody there to write them? What happened?" English replied: "Too many people spending too much time watching television." *Frasier*'s writers, unlike other TV writers who are deeply steeped in their medium, must not watch much television – they write so well.

The ideas in *Frasier* are not that much different from those in other sitcoms. Frasier is not the first sitcom character to work in a radio station or to have a slightly unusual family. But the writing in *Frasier* is as good as it gets on television. *Time* writer James Colins (September 28, 1998) explains it best: "On most sitcoms, all the lines but the jokes seem dispensable, and the shows seem to have been mostly put together in the editing room. In contrast, the best *Frasier* episodes seem like little 22-minute plays whose scripts have words that actually matter, and whose scenes build as they would on stage."

From the first episode, critics loved the writing and much of the credit for the show's success must go to Casey and co-producers and writers David Angell and David Lee. The three worked together on *Cheers*, also on the long-running sitcom *Wings*.

The writing team for *Frasier*, including Casey, Angell, and Lee, numbers from eight to ten at the story stage, and they have built on the success of the show's pilot. One member of the team is Christopher Lloyd, who told *Starweek*: "The pilot takes you so far and only gives you so much latitude to create characters and situations. Then you can go in any of a hundred different directions. The challenge in creating a show that started as strongly as this one did is to sample each of those possibilities and see which directions seem to give you the most potential."

Story lines – such as Roz's pregnancy, Niles's crush on Daphne, the unseen Maris, the gay manager's attraction to Frasier, the loss of the entire staff's jobs – are interesting developments of a fine pilot. The writing is at its best, however, when it delves into the relationships, especially between the psychiatrist-brothers, Frasier and Niles. They are wonderful characters, exploring every sibling rivalry that ever existed within a family. It is unusual in a sitcom to get a laugh expressing rage by shouting, "You, you . . . popinjay!" But this is how upright, uptight Niles dresses down a rival for Daphne's affection. Niles is married to (then divorced from) someone called Maris, but he is sweet on Daphne. We never see Maris, though she is a recurring offstage presence. There have been other characters in sitcoms who are either heard but never seen or, in the case of Wilson, the next-door neighbour in *Home Improvement*, only partly seen. There is a sense in which such characters act as bridges from a constructed reality to the "real" world.

The cast of *Frasier* is top-notch, with the two brothers the standouts. Most of the cast spent a great deal of time acting on stage before *Frasier*. Liam Lacey says Kelsey Grammer has "the resonant voice of Orson Welles, and a classical actor's sense of facial muscle control: with the telling twitch of a lip or flicker of an eyebrow, he can switch instantly from indignant man to leering wit." As for David Hyde Pierce's Niles: ". . . blond, tight-lipped and prissy, but his comic style is defined in smaller, subtler strokes. Unlike Frasier, Niles has not met real disappointment, just missed opportunities. So, Hyde Pierce's performance suggests what Frasier would be like in his budding form, waiting to burst out."

Frasier and Niles try to work together. In one episode an attempt to collaborate on a book results in the brothers coming to blows. And when Frasier falls ill with the flu, Niles replaces him in the call-in studio, where he succeeds masterfully. An outraged Frasier staggers back to the studio, glassy-eyed and numbed by medication, and takes back his show, terrifying his staff and insulting his callers. And it works, as Liam Lacey writes in *The Globe and Mail*, because "the viewer can say: yes, I know someone just like that (or I am just like that) and I can understand that behaviour not as distressing but laughable."

Liam Lacey again: "Frasier has a sense of a man who has seen failure, who has a lived-in rakishness. Niles is still fresh-faced, pristine, tight and trembling with repression. Beyond that they have a neat naturalness of a younger/older relationship that is often ignored on TV."

David Bianculli says in his *Dictionary of Teleliteracy* that *Frasier* is "the best sitcom to be spun off from another sitcom in the entire history of television. In terms of quality humor, no one-two punchline in TV history packs as great a punch as *Cheers* and *Frasier*. Line for line, performance for performance, laugh for laugh, nothing comes close."

At one of our sessions, O'Malley and I got to talking about *Frasier*.

O'MALLEY: What I like about *Frasier* is the way they mix highbrow and lowbrow without being patronizing. You have Frasier and Niles, the snobs. And Martin, their ex-cop father. And Roz, the vamp, and Bulldog the jock. Think of the episode in which Frasier and Niles are competing to buy the perfect gift for their father. It keeps escalating, until Niles sees a monster television set in the living room, with humongous speakers. Niles strokes his chin and says, 'Ah, just what we need . . . Stonehenge.'

PUNGENTE: Because they don't explain it. Niles doesn't go on to say Stonehenge is a famous English monument of stones, erected by an ancient race.

O'MALLEY: The subtle way they did it would fly right by fans of *Married With Children* or *Jerry Springer*.

PUNGENTE: It's like peeling layers off an onion, or understanding a poem. You may understand a poem at a level of "Roses are red, violets are blue," but if you go into the mythological symbolism of roses and violets, perhaps you'll understand it better and enjoy it more. The writing in *Frasier* allows the viewer to bring his or her own knowledge of the world to the interpretation of each show. And the more knowledge you bring, the greater the enjoyment.

Strangers in a Strange Land

I want to be offensive to at least somebody in every episode. Comedy should outrage as much as it entertains.

– John Lithgow

3rd Rock from the Sun is about four aliens from a distant planet who have come to earth as an advance scouting party led by the High Commander (John Lithgow) who masquerades as Dick Solomon. He becomes a brash physics professor in the small college town of Rutherford, Ohio. The male security officer finds himself in the body of Dick's sister Sally (Kristen Johnston); the team's information officer and oldest member has taken the form of Dick's earthly son, the adolescent Tommy (Joseph Gordon-Levitt); and an alien who came along for the ride becomes Dick's brother Harry (French Stewart). Dick's love interest, a fellow professor, is the very human and prim Dr. Mary Albright (Jane Curtin of *Saturday Night Live*).

3rd Rock from the Sun started in the 1995–96 season, was a surprise hit, and has remained successful, ending the 1997–98 season in 43rd spot. It is a family sitcom featuring a special family unit whose job is to examine the larger family – the human race. It does this with broad satire and slapstick. Bonnie and Terry Turner, the executive producers and the writing team for *3rd Rock*, spent seven seasons working on *Saturday Night Live*, so they are no strangers to this genre.

The tradition of slapstick can be traced back to the Middle Ages in drama, though we probably are most familiar with it from the films of Charlie Chaplin, Buster Keaton, and Laurel and Hardy. Slapstick is tricky. Two actors can slip on a banana peel and fall; one will be funny, the other won't. John Lithgow was perhaps an odd choice to play Dick Solomon, a character the writers describe as a cross between Errol Flynn and Bugs Bunny. Lithgow was best known for film roles that were either serious (*Distant Thunder, Terms of Endearment*) or sinister (*Cliffhanger, Raising Cain*). He was nominated for his role as a transsexual football star in *The World According to Garp*.

But Lithgow was the writers' first choice. They had worked with him when he hosted *Saturday Night Live* and were impressed by his comic talent. He brings his comic genius to every episode of *3rd Rock*. In one, Dick wears leather pants to impress Dr. Albright only to discover he is incapable of sitting in them, incapable of moving at all, without making egregious noises. Of course, it helps to have on hand another *Saturday Night Live* veteran, Jane Curtin, playing opposite him as his love interest. The comic timing of these two provides many of the highlights of the show.

Although the constructed universe of *3rd Rock from the Sun* is absurd, the script delivers recognizable truths about our lives here on earth. The alien Solomons show us a lot about ourselves, whether it be our attitude to Christmas (Buy! Buy! Buy!), the elaborate ritual that goes into the making of an American Thanksgiving, or the long lineups and paperwork required to get a driver's licence (which results in the wickedly telling remark: "Imagine what it must take to get a gun"). The Solomons also tell us much about earthly social issues like racism and ethnicity from the perspective of curious aliens, which they do without preaching. When Dick learns that on earth no matter what you do, you can still count on the forgiveness of your family, he says, "Why, that's so beautiful!"

At the start of the 1998–99 season, Dick and Sally became Henry Fonda and Katharine Hepburn in *On Golden Pond*. They did it by a slight change in the tone of their voices, by putting on a hat, by sitting in a certain way, and by small gestures – the way Sally reaches out to touch Dick. It is not only satire – it is also both touching and humorous – and it is very difficult to pull off. That they can do this within the reality they have created of aliens in a human world – that they can create another reality that draws us instantly into the movie world of *On Golden Pond* – is a tribute to both the writers and the actors.

Above all, consider what Bonnie Turner, one of the writers, says about why she thinks *3rd Rock* works. "It's about being human," she told *Entertainment Weekly* in 1996. "But because they're alien, we can distance ourselves from being human rather than doing a microanalysis like *Seinfeld*."

There is nothing new about alien sitcoms. A new one seems to come along every decade. There was *My Favorite Martian* in the 1960s, *Mork and Mindy* (with Robin Williams) in the 1970s, and *ALF* in the 1980s (ALF meaning "alien life form"). As *Entertainment Weekly* suggested in 1996: "The stranger in a strange land is a wonderful, classic notion that works. And *3rd Rock from the Sun* remains true to the satirical bent of outsider-looking-in, while managing to be sexier than *Martian*, raunchier than *Mork*, and hipper than *ALF* and more sophisticated (by a hair) than Coneheads."

Sitcoms present us with a wide variety of family types – from earnest Marge Simpson to the quirky news anchor in *Newsradio*, to madcap Dick Solomon in *3rd Rock*. There is something of us in all of them. We can learn from the way these characters act and react within their television families something of the world and our beliefs and biases, something about ourselves. And as we learn we laugh. Laughter that educates, something Ignatius of Loyola would have liked.

4

Bishop Sheen Touches an Angel: Values on Television

~

Tens of millions of Americans now see the entertainment industry as an all-powerful enemy, an alien force that assaults our most cherished values and corrupts our children.
— Michael Medved, *Hollywood Vs. America*

The values we hold have great influence on the way we live our lives. But where do we get them from? The three traditional agents of education, through which values are passed on to children, have been the home, the school, and the church. For some time now it has been accepted that these have been joined by a fourth: the media.

The Ontario Ministry of Education once defined values "as those qualities that the individual, the society, or both consider important as principles for conduct and as major aims of existence. Personal values are held by the individual. Societal values are the values generally accepted by society as demonstrated by its cultural traditions, structures, practices, and laws."

The family has changed substantially from the comfortable old shoe of mom, dad, and two kids (ideally one male, one female). Schools are being turned into businesses by provincial governments. The church has lost its clout, the pews are sparsely occupied. More and more young people get their values from television.

All media contain values in everything they present, sometimes explicitly, sometimes implicitly. Values are neither passive nor neutral. They are, on the contrary, dynamic – they either repel or attract. When a viewer comes to identify with a character, even though that character exists only in an imaginary, media-constructed universe, it is possible that the viewer will be influenced by that character's value system.

William Fore in *Television and Religion* points out that "for the first time in history, children and adults live in two worlds." One is the reality system of face-to-face encounters with other people: at the office, taking care of children, visiting neighbours, reading books, telling stories, remembering the past, planning the future. We call this "the real world."

The other, as Fore describes it, "is the far more vivid and appealing pseudoreality" world. This world provides instantaneous and transient sensation, immediate gratification and a torrent of words and pictures in a never-ending flood of moving images. There are no face-to-face encounters. The processing of data is not the same. There is little connection to our past or our cultural traditions. We call this "the world of media." This is the world of the second key concept – all media construct reality.

It is impossible here to detail all the images, symbols, and myths that go into making the complex "world of media." People have their own ideas about this. In 1987 when Fore wrote *Television and Religion* he discussed the way media affect our values, sense of reality, and lifestyles. He analyzed the implicit values and cultural significance of television from which emerge the central myths of the world of media.

To Fore the mass media worldview is that we are basically good, that happiness is the chief end of life, and that happiness consists in obtaining material goods. To be rich is good; the ultimate good is to be able to buy anything. How this wealth is obtained may or may not be material. For example, cops in shows like *NYPD Blue* who obtain their money from bribes or threats will never really be happy. But at the same time television advertising shows the glamorous lifestyle of the rich and famous without considering how they obtained their money.

Fore believes that media transform the value of sexuality into sex appeal, the value of self-respect into pride, the value of will to live into will to power. Acquisitiveness becomes greed. Media change the value of recreation into competition, the value of rest into escape. Media construct our experience and substitute the world of media for the real world so that we could become less able to make fine value-judgments.

Fore is negative about the values presented by the media. I believe there are more positive values than negative presented to us on mainstream commercial television. There is the real and obvious love of Jill and Tim Taylor on *Home Improvement*, the self-respect of Benton Fraser on *Due South*, the selflessness of the doctors and nurses on *ER* and *Chicago Hope*, and the generosity and caring of the characters in *Touched by an Angel*.

Some of us, it is true, do have problems distinguishing between the "real world" and the "media world." An extreme (but entertaining) exploration of this theme within the media itself is Peter Weir's 1998 movie *The Truman Show*, which tells the story of Truman Burbank (played by Canadian Jim Carey) who was born, raised, and grows to adulthood on a gigantic television soundstage disguised as an island village. With the lone exception of Truman Burbank, who is totally unaware of the artifice, everyone on the set is an actor. The "show" is a "documentary soap opera" and Truman's every move is broadcast twenty-four hours a day to a global audience. As *Entertainment Weekly* points out, "the film takes off from a culture – ours – that erases privacy by turning reality into television and television into reality."

This is not a new concept. Years ago, Northrop Frye, Canada's great literary critic, talked about "the protective wall of play," the wall that used to divide fact from fiction. The contemporary erosion of this wall has, at the extreme, resulted in two views of the world. When *The Truman Show* was released in June 1998 it prompted Rick Groen of *The Globe and Mail* to remark of these two worlds: "The naive view, with its literal-minded insistence that everything is real, these are the people who can no longer distinguish the actor from the role . . . and the cynical view, with its ironic contention that everything is fake, these are the folks who believe that even the moon landings were a hoax."

Two Kinds of Values
While I am aware that the argument can be made that all values are both moral and spiritual, for discussion purposes I would like to keep them separate.

For my purposes, social values are values we hold about issues around which our society is built, such as the family, ways of raising our children, matters of life and of death, the treatment of people.

Spiritual values may or may not be religious in nature but deal with issues in our lives such as morality, honesty, selflessness, integrity, care for others, and using our abilities.

Social Values

The personal values that are endemic to American culture are deeply embedded in the programming material of its most favoured entertainment medium. These values are played out in endless scenarios and in countless dialogues, and range in magnitude from subplot foundations to passing observations. They appear in many forms and are expressed by many types of characters at various levels of involvement.

— Gary Selnow, *Journal of Communication,* 1990

It was May 1992, an election year for Dan Quayle and George Bush. Riots had devastated parts of Los Angeles, and the conservative politicians were at it again. Quayle attacked *Murphy Brown* because the fictional character chose to have a baby and raise it by herself. Quayle said Murphy's decision was symptomatic of Hollywood's scorn for traditional family values.

Robert Lichter, Linda Lichter, and Stanley Rothman noted in the book *Prime Time* that Quayle's attack "smacked of the surreal, as the vice-president . . . criticized the child-rearing techniques of a fictitious anchorwoman. Yet it inaugurated a serious debate over family values that would not have taken place without the participation of a fantasy character whose recognition factor probably approached Mr. Quayle's." It later was revealed by a Quayle spokesperson that the Vice-President had never seen *Murphy Brown.* The last show he had followed regularly was *Perry Mason.*

As the show's response to Quayle, *Murphy Brown*'s 1992–93 season opener was an hour-long special, which began with Murphy hearing Quayle's remarks on television while she tends to her new baby.

"I'm glamorizing single motherhood?" Murphy remarks with incredulity. "What planet is he on? I agonized over that decision. . . . I didn't just wake up and say, 'Oh jeez, I can't get in for a facial, I might as well have a baby.'" Later, at work in the fictional newsroom, Murphy goes on air and says: "Perhaps it's time for the vice-president to expand his definition and recognize that whether by choice or circumstances families come in all shapes and sizes. And, ultimately, what really defines a family is commitment, caring, and love."

The controversy didn't end there. The same season a senator in the sitcom *Hearts Afire*, on hearing that Quayle is upset at Murphy Brown having a baby out of wedlock, asks: "But she's not real, is she?" During the 1992–93 season some other programs ventured into contentious issues. A popular medical show, *Doogie Howser, MD*, opened with a show depicting the panic and confusion in the Los Angeles hospital at the time of the riot. No political stand was taken, but young Dr. Doogie ended the show by typing into his computer-diary, paraphrasing Martin Luther King: "A riot is at the bottom of the unheard."

One last word on the Quayle/Murphy Brown episode goes to Richard Zoglin, who wrote in *Time* in September 1992: "The irony is that one area where TV espouses unmistakably conservative values is the very one that Quayle chose to focus on: the family. Though single-parent households are common on TV (as they are in real life), the family bond is nearly always portrayed as strong and indispensable. If TV has any prevailing sin, it is its sunny romanticizing of that bond: no matter what the conflict or crisis, family love makes everything come out all right. If Dan Quayle were to look at TV a little more clearly, he might find the stuff of Republican dreams."

The loving and supportive family, in this view, is a significant component of television's prevailing ideology. The medium offers us other values as well, though not always obviously.

Once every decade, the World Values Survey examines values in the Western world. The survey found that between 1981 and 1990 values such as loyalty, honesty, prudence, chastity, deference, patriotism, and fidelity had changed in Canada. An article on this survey in *The Globe and Mail* in May 1998 observed: "Canadians became more willing to approve such behaviour as cheating on taxes, avoiding paying fares on public transit, keeping money they have found, lying in their own interest, or claiming government benefits they were not entitled to. Those approving of at least one of these dishonest actions jumped from 40 per cent to 44.2 per cent."

Yet, over that same decade, Canadians were found to be more patriotic, diligent, charitable, and compassionate. When parents were asked to choose values they would like to pass on to their children, they listed hard work, perseverance, responsibility, thrift, unselfishness, and good manners. Contrast this with a report in 1998 by the Institute for American Values and the University of Chicago Divinity School, which found that moral values are on the decline in the United States. The report, titled "A Call to Civil Society: Why Democracy Needs Moral Truths," advocates such measures as tougher divorce laws and tax incentives for couples who marry. It also calls on television networks to police themselves and urges religious institutions to reassert their influence on society.

Because a show contains what one group considers "good" values, does this make it television worth watching? Or should we ask who it is who decides what constitutes "good" values on television? Obviously, there are some who feel that our morals are made by the media.

Every year the U.S.-based Media Research Center, a conservative watchdog group, publishes *The Family Guide*, in which it tells parents what shows are and are not suitable for children. While I doubt many would quibble with the fact that a lot of television is needlessly vulgar, we might have trouble with *The Family Guide's* approach. In December 1996, Ken Tucker of *Entertainment Weekly* took aim at *The Family Guide*. He pointed out that the *Guide* believes that *The Drew Carey Show* should be avoided because ". . . 'it celebrates debauchery, irresponsible drunkenness and a lascivious lifestyle.' Cripes, if it actually did that, the show would probably be even funnier than it already is." The *Guide* does not approve of *Friends* because it has "given the nod to homosexual marriage and parenting." After telling us how the *Guide* disapproves of the language used in *Spin City*, *3rd Rock from the Sun*, and *Homeboys from Outer Space*, Tucker concludes by referring to some of his favourite shows under attack by the *Guide*. These are ". . . shows I enjoy immensely that I don't want my children to watch, such as *The X-Files* and *NYPD Blue*, because they are clearly intended for adult sensibilities. But the knee-jerk standards applied by this book would lead you to think that . . . *Nick Fresno: Licensed Teacher*, a drecky sitcom full of insufferable wiseacres, is healthy fare because it doesn't 'introduce offensive subject matter.'"

All television shows are value-laden. A few, however, appear to sell values actively – it's like the difference between hard-sell and "lifestyle" advertising. But surely it's simple-minded to believe that only the hard-sell is effective. Television devotes considerable time to examining social values explicitly in current affairs shows, sitcoms, dramas, public service announcements – even commercials. Television has examined issues such as AIDS, gender equality, health, ideology, violence, war, business ethics, and education. Sometimes it has done this brilliantly, as it did in Home Box Office's *And the Band Played On*, which traced the history, beginning in 1981, of the struggle to identify and find a cure for AIDS. It also sometimes does it lamentably, with pop-medicine disease-of-the-week teleplays. What must be understood is that television has no obligation to present only a sanitized "happy" side of life. As Tucker says in *Entertainment Weekly*: "TV isn't an arm of social policy or government propaganda; it has no more responsibility to be upbeat and positive than does, say, poetry or the theatre."

Even when television shows consciously set out to be virtuous, the message they convey may be less than constructive. They may suggest that the good life can be achieved without effort and that evil can be vanquished right after the next commercial break. When *60 Minutes* goes after the bad guys, confronts and exposes their corruption, couch potatoes across the nation go to bed relieved, perhaps uplifted. Simply by watching *60 Minutes* somehow they have made their world better, without even letting go of their remotes. Want to feel racially tolerant? Watch *Cosby*. Want to feel spiritual? Watch *Touched by an Angel*. Want friends? Watch *Friends*.

Yet television also offers shows that have presented positive values in a way that is neither simplistic nor neatly packaged. *Julia* and *All in the Family* used comedy to confront issues of race. *M*A*S*H* examined the horror of war. *Growing Pains*, *Who's the Boss*, *Family Ties*, *The Cosby Show*, and *Parenting* examined family life in a positive way. *Designing Women* did an especially good job on AIDS. And *The Golden Girls* took a serious look at what it means to be old in today's youth-oriented society.

In 1990, PBS brought us Ken Burns's *The Civil War*, an enthralling eleven-hour series that attracted an audience of 14 million viewers. This was no boring history lesson. Yet we learned about the battles without once actually viewing a single frame of battle footage – no reenactments, no docudrama. Instead, Burns used 16,000 still photographs, and he used real letters written by real people who fought in the war. We learned of the role of blacks and women, how the Union ranks had more than 100,000 soldiers who were not yet fifteen years old, how a fifth of Mississippi's entire budget was spent on artificial limbs. This program succeeded in conveying a powerful anti-war message through the way in which it presented original material.

Who can forget the letter Union Major Sullivan Ballou wrote to his wife the week before he was killed at Bull Run:

> If the dead can come back to this earth and flit unseen around those they love, I shall always be near you; in the gladdest days and darkest nights . . . always, always, and if there be a soft breeze upon your cheek, it shall be my breath, as the cool air fans your throbbing temple, it shall be my spirit passing by.

Northern Exposure (1990–95) consistently presented viewers with an interesting and positive take on values. A New York doctor goes to work in Cicely, Alaska, a town where people live according to their own individual rhythms, not the stereotyped rhythms of television. A sixty-two-year-old man, one of Cicely's most respected citizens, marries a nineteen-year-old woman. The local disc jockey stops the music to read *War and Peace*. The bush pilot is a young woman who loves losers and loses lovers. A young native dreams of making films like those of his idols, Bergman and Fellini. A moose wanders benignly down the main street.

In an episode titled "Seoul Mates," Maurice, the mayor of Cicely and an ex-astronaut is confronted by his grown son, the result of a long-ago affair with a Korean girl. Maurice is uneasy about accepting the son because he is Korean (Maurice is a racist). Chris, the local disc jockey, however, convinces Maurice that racism is learned behaviour, not natural, and what can be learned can be unlearned. Chris taught Maurice all about the value of tolerance.

The role of women in prime time has evolved considerably from *That Girl* and *The Mary Tyler Moore Show* to *Murphy Brown* and *Ally McBeal*. Professor Robert Thompson, director of the Center for the Study of Popular Television at Syracuse University, told *The Globe and Mail* (June 2, 1998): "Since 1970, television's portrayal of women has vastly and self-consciously altered. There are more professional women. They're in positions of more power. The change, however, isn't as big as it first may seem. A lot of television still presents professional women as a premise. Their status as fish out of water is what drives the series."

There are many examples of these "career women": Brooke Shields as a San Francisco magazine writer in *Suddenly Susan*; Captain Kathryn Janeway in *Star Trek: Voyager*; Calista Flockhart's *Ally McBeal*; Lea Thompson's cartoonist in *Caroline in the City*; Ally Walker as forensic psychiatrist Dr. Sam Waters in *The Profiler*; and the women professionals in ensemble shows such as *ER*, *Chicago Hope*, *Law & Order*, *NYPD Blue*, and *Homicide: Life on the Street*.

But the argument can be made that in the majority of shows on primetime television the man is the accepted "professional" and the woman remains "the fish out of water." Do the career-women shows reflect the real world? According to the American Bar Association, female attorneys now make up 24 per cent of lawyers, compared with 2 per cent in 1971. And according to the American Medical Association, the percentage of women doctors rose from 7 per cent in 1970 to 21 per cent in 1996, and the ratio of men and women entering medical school now is about 50:50.

And the image of men on television is also changing. Yes, we still have the image of man as swaggering macho buffoon (most supporting male characters in sitcoms), man as protector of the weak (*Walker, Texas Ranger*), man as ignorant and perhaps racist (*Living in Captivity*, *The Hughleys*), and man as womanizer (the character of Fish on *Ally McBeal* or Joey on *Friends*). But in recent years we have television presenting a whole new set of values for men, a set of values that might be best described at aiming to make men "sensitive." As John Allemang writes in *The Globe and Mail* on September 30, 1998, "The new season is full of men who have the time and the patience to listen to the problems of others, who are kind and caring and in touch with their feelings."

Allemang was referring to the 1998–99 television season and gives examples. There is Will from *Will and Grace*, a gay lawyer who seems to spend much of his time involved in solving the problems of Grace, his best friend. And Evan on *L.A. Doctors* who skimps on what he spends for himself so that his ex-wife can raise his son in the style to which they have become accustomed. Or poor Conrad from *Conrad Bloom*, who seems destined to have nothing else to do but listen and deal with the various anxieties of almost everyone with whom he comes in contact. And both *Sports Night* and *The Secret Lives of Men* are about men whose marriages are falling, or have fallen, apart, and who have to figure out ways to rebuild their lives.

Television advertising also sells values, usually implicitly, values which we may or may not share or like. The best ads now often convey a message we approve of while still, of course, selling a product. In effect, the strategy is to sell the product by associating it with something "good." In 1998, Kellogg's launched an advertising campaign that showed women discussing what to wear, while struggling to fit into clothes too small for their bodies. The ads are explicit, yet clever and intelligently understated. The message is: "Look good on your own terms." But it's the same old sell: eat Kellogg's Special K.

British Airways for years has been running advertising on television that punches up the "togetherness" button. The ads show people from all over the world coming together, usually as a family being reunited in some way: happy, smiling, embracing. They pluck heavily on our heartstrings as a God-like voiceover informs us that British Airways brings people together. Watching these ads makes us feel good about life and people and the world – and British Airways. We may not run out and buy a ticket to Capri or London, but next time we are planning a trip overseas that ad will spring to mind and we may choose British Airways to take us there.

Speaking of ads, there is a startling contrast between two "ads" – I think we can call them that – once used as sign-offs at the end of the day's programming. An American sign-off shows an F-16 fighter plane patrolling a deserted American landscape of fields, valleys, rivers, and mountains. The pilot is invisible inside the cockpit of the killer jet. The only indication that people once lived here are the stern visages on Mount Rushmore, hard as stone. It could be the pre-credit roll for a post-Doomsday movie, the irony being the anthem itself, "the rocket's red glare, the bombs bursting in air . . ." The second "ad," the broadcaster's Canadian sign-off, shows children playing, laughing, all across the country while hearts are uplifted as we hear "glorious and free." Values are on display in both these sequences as they are wherever we choose to look on television.

Very young children were once seen on many popular sitcoms: little Ricky on *I Love Lucy*, Opie on *The Andy Griffith Show*, and Joey on *All in the Family*. But, as *Entertainment Weekly* pointed out in November 13, 1998, things changed. *Dharma and Greg, Frasier, Spin City,* and *Friends* all had story lines in the 1998–99 season involving small children. The networks found that such story lines were not holding viewers. While the numbers for *Murphy Brown* and *Mad About You* rose during pregnancies of the main characters, they dropped off after the babies were born. The demographic that the networks want to hold on to was not interested in stories with small children. The children soon disappeared.

There have been many studies focused on children and television – one of the best being Kathleen McDonnell's book *Kid Culture* – and I have no intention of trying to do justice to this topic in a chapter. But I do want to discuss the values that television offers our children.

For young children there is *Sesame Street, Rolie Polie Olie,* and *Jack the Pirate.* There is *Bill Nye the Science Guy, Arthur, The Magic Schoolbus, Reading Rainbow, The Puzzle Place, Theodore Tugboat.* CBC gave us *Anne of Green Gables* and *Road to Avonlea, Wind at Our Back,* and *Emily of New Moon,* which have much to say about family life. And *Ready or Not* explored many value-laden issues for young teens.

While it is doubtful that *Beverly Hills 90210* (set in an upscale California high school) or *Dawson's Creek* (twentysomethings playing fifteen-year-olds) offer much in the way of worthwhile values for teenagers, there was a long-running Canadian show that did: *Degrassi High.* It began as *The Kids of Degrassi Street* in 1979 and evolved through *Degrassi Junior High* until it finally ended in 1991.

It was innovative, courageous television. The regulars in the cast started as eight- and nine-year-olds, growing to eighteen- and nineteen-year-olds by the time the series ended. None of them were actors when the series began, merely children who wanted to tell their stories on television. They kept adding to the story line and characterizations, encompassing topics such as teenage pregnancy, abortion, homosexuality, drugs, leaving home, sexual abuse, and AIDS. At the same time the shows presented ways to deal with these issues.

A six-part documentary series called *Degrassi Talks* followed, showing teens across Canada talking about the issues raised in the ninety-six earlier episodes, which have been shown as reruns in fifty countries around the world, including the United States, China, France, Australia, Germany,

England, and Israel. The *Degrassi* shows won four Gemini Awards in Canada and two Emmys.

The Beat Goes On

Popular music is an important part of a teenager's life. Many grown-ups, especially parents, believe, sometimes with justification, that the new music is totally opposed to their beliefs and fundamental values. But I wonder how many listen to their children, or dare ask what some of these tumultuous, raucous lyrics mean? After you've waxed on about Benny Goodman (or the Beatles, Janis Joplin, jazz) have you ever asked them to tell you about *their* music?

Popular music brought home the plight of the Ethiopian famine when, in 1984, Bob Geldof assembled a group of British singers and musicians to record "Do They Know It's Christmas?" The record and video raised more than $5-million for the Ethiopian relief fund. This led to similar efforts in Canada ("Tears Are Not Enough") and the United States ("We Are The World"). It culminated in Live Aid, a sixteen-hour television special that involved 180 pop musicians in London and Philadelphia. The live musical marathon on July 13, 1985, was seen by some 1.5-*billion* viewers in 169 countries. It raised more than $110-million in donations for famine relief in Africa. It also raised the awareness of millions of young people to the problem of world hunger. Worthwhile values?

Sell-a-Tubbies

In March 1998, I flew to London for the second World Summit on Television for Children. There was an interesting dust-up over the then-new BBC children's show *Teletubbies*, the $20-million production that has taken England and much of North America by storm. It features four adorable thingamajigs with antennas on their heads and TV screens on their tummies. Their names are Tinky Winky, Dipsy, Laa-Laa, and Po. They hug and romp on grass that looks as if it overdosed on chlorophyll. We're not even talking children's television here, we're talking "baby" television; the demographic for *Teletubbies* is said to be eighteen months.

Teletubbies raises interesting questions, perhaps some worries, about television. Most of the delegates at the conference were engaged in the production and marketing of television, so one assumed that not all of them were overly concerned at the commercial grab of *Teletubbies* – Teletubby dolls, Teletubby books, Teletubby games – "Roll the bassinet to the tube, get 'em hooked in the crib, there's money to be made." There was no discussion of "television addiction," or television-as-babysitter (television-as-pacifier?). No, it's a business opportunity, an entire generation of giggling burpers on the demographic horizon, not one of whom has yet mastered the channel-changer.

At first it seemed the delegates at the second World Summit on Television for Children would have some fun at the BBC's expense. Some stood up to condemn *Teletubbies* as empty-headed entertainment. Another suggested it was "vaguely evil" because it lacked moral structure. A delegate complained there was too much "babytalk." There were snide suggestions that eight months may be a good time to hit 'em with nuclear physics or comparative religion.

Then Ada Haug, head of preschool TV programs for NRK in Norway, stood up to denounce *Teletubbies* as "the most market-oriented children's program I've ever seen in my life." She criticized the show's repetition, poor plots, and the fact that the show has no sense of place. "No wonder the series is proving popular on the world's commercial channels," she said.

This was too much for Alice Cahn, director of children's programs for PBS, the American public broadcasting service that had purchased *Teletubbies* for showing in the United States. She called Haug "an ignorant slut."

There was a collective gasp from the six hundred global delegates. It certainly got my attention.

What Cahn actually said was, "As they say on *Saturday Night Live*, Ada, you ignorant slut." Cahn assumed that everyone would recognize the old *Saturday Night Live* exchange between Dan Aykroyd and Jane Curtin, when Aykroyd always got a laugh saying, "Jane, you ignorant slut!" Many Americans really do believe that anything that has ever been popular on American television is globally recognizable, like some sort of television Esperanto.

I watched *Saturday Night Live*, but Cahn's reference wasn't immediately recognizable to me, nor to many of the delegates from England, Australia, New Zealand, Bosnia, Scandinavia, Japan, China, the Philippines, Germany, France, South Africa, Spain, Italy, Guatemala, and Mongolia.

After the smoke cleared, there were screenings of other new television shows for children, including one introduced by Ada Haug. The Norwegian show, called *Trobbel*, is a cartoon that warns children of pedophilia and incest. None of this Tinky Winky, Dipsy, Laa-Laa, and Po stuff. The *Trobbel* script asks: "Do you know what trouble is? A fierce dog . . . someone smoking . . . you feel sick. When you sit by your uncle, he's nasty as well . . . wants us to take our clothes off . . . I had to touch his thing . . . I was frightened." (An earlier version used "father" instead of "uncle," but it was changed so as not to "demonize" fathers.)

Germany's presentation was *Dr. Mag Love*, which targets an audience of twelve- to-sixteen-year-olds and it too eschews subtlety. The episode screened was titled "No screwing without rubbers" and featured a model of an erect penis (17 centimetres) with comments on 1) how to put on condoms, 2) how to avoid tearing them, and 3) why two are better than one.

Needless to say, the United States declined to purchase these shows for American viewers.

Soon, *Teletubbies* sparked a debate in North America among those who quarrelled with its empty-headedness, those who thought it was "too damned cheerful," and those who considered that even the diapered demographic has a right to have fun. In *The Globe and Mail*, columnist Rick Salutin wrote: "Do one- to-two-year-olds really need to learn the world can be a troubled place? They recently passed through *the birth canal* and possibly, eight days later, circumcision, not to mention earaches, the inability to roll over or scratch, or make your needs known to the giants hovering above you?"

To some, it is neither the cheerful empty-headedness of *Teletubbies* that is disturbing, nor the pretend-violence of *Mighty Morphin Power Rangers*: it is the selling game. If *Teletubbies* is simply an innocent, harmless delight for toddlers, as the producers say, why not develop a similarly mindless delight expressly for semi-comatose, bed-ridden adults? It will never happen because they can't sell them anything.

Is it possible to form values in the minds of babies? Those in favour of the show, such as Anne Wood, its creator, say "children have a right to enjoy themselves." She argued that programs like *Teletubbies* were not designed to cure the world's ills. Rather, she suggests, they should be a mirror of their own lives, a window to the experiences of other children. She told *The*

Independent in March 1998 that *Teletubbies* has a positive effect on young children by helping them to develop speech.

Critics of *Teletubbies* wonder why children at such a young age – diapered, sucking pacifiers – need to watch educational programs at all. In *The Globe and Mail*, John Allemang expressed serious concerns about how child-rearing is portrayed on *Teletubbies*. He found that the producers of the show want to make children feel confident enough to face the world beyond *Teletubbies*. But as Allemang writes: "How do they increase self-confidence and build self-esteem and celebrate individuality? A periscope rises out of the ground and starts blurting out a song, and all the Teletubbies feel compelled to pay attention. This could as easily be teaching authoritarianism and group-think. And it doesn't stop there. Whenever the Tubbies like something, they shout out 'Again!' And obedient to their commands the item is repeated . . . Yes, this teaches thinking skills of a kind. But what thoughts, and at what costs?"

I'll tell you at what cost: $34.99. That's what Toys 'R' Us charged when the first *Teletubbies* dolls appeared on the counters of its outlets. And sales were brisk, demonstrating once again that there are fewer more powerful marketing tools than television. Sales of *Teletubbies* dolls and paraphernalia were compared to those of the phenomenally successful Cabbage Patch Dolls, Tickle Me Elmo dolls, and the Furby. What is *Teletubbies* really out to teach – skills, values . . . or the joy of shopping?

Eleven years ago, in a column in *Newsweek*, the writer Nicols Fox examined the nature of American values: "real American values are expressed not by what we say we wish for, but what we really do. We love our families, but we can't count many friends with intact ones any more. We love our old people but not for more than an hour or two at a time . . . We are a people full of compassion but it extends more freely to three trapped whales than to the homeless huddled over heat grates on the streets of our richest cities."

Fox says that what we really value can be seen in what we read, what we watch on television, what we do with our free time. "We complain about the invasion of drugs but our culture tells us that no discomfort can be tolerated and that every desire needs to be satisfied. We complain about crime but our system demonstrates that good guys finish last – that crime pays.

We complain about the moral decadence of our young and high incidence of teen pregnancies but our young have been carefully taught, by example, that responsibility is old-fashioned."

If we are to change, Fox suggests we begin by looking at ourselves as we really are. When we've done that, by whatever means, when we come to see ourselves and our values as we want them, then we should make certain those are the values we pass on through our families, and through our media.

Spiritual Values

The sitcom has taken the place of the church, of religious training. In his novel Generation X *Douglas Coupland defines tele-parabolizing as "morals used in everyday life that derive from TV sitcom plots" . . . In many families, watching sitcoms together is an almost sacred obligation: When the set goes on, the couch becomes a pew.*

– Tad Friend, *Esquire*

Part of St. Augustine's definition of God – a Being whose centre is everywhere and whose borders are nowhere – may, with good reason, remind us of television. The Church was one of the traditional mechanisms for passing on spiritual and religious values from generation to generation. It seems television has taken over some of this role.

Murphy Brown often was a trailblazer in television's approach to value-laden topics. The show had a long run, from November 1988 to May 1998, with Candice Bergen as Murphy Brown, a recovering alcoholic and high-strung reporter. It won eighteen Emmys, a Golden Globe, and a Peabody Award.

During the final 1997–98 season, Murphy faced a personal battle with breast cancer. Somehow the writers managed to explore this terrifying and emotional issue through comedy. In the final episode, Murphy dreams during her operation that she has snagged the ultimate scoop: God has agreed to an interview (God being played by a well-tailored Alan King).

Murphy looks across at God and asks: "Do our actions in life make a difference or is our future already planned for us?"

GOD: Your life is a series of choices. How you choose determines where you end up.

MURPHY: I don't remember choosing to have cancer. With all due respect, why did you give it to me?

GOD: Your illness was a gift.

MURPHY: No offence, but a nice pair of driving gloves would have been more than enough. . . .

GOD: You know what celebrity is, Murphy? It's an invitation to service. It's everything you do attracts attention. If you get cancer people sit up and take notice. Maybe they'll work harder to find a cure.

MURPHY: Why don't you cure it?

GOD: There we go again. Then you wouldn't have a purpose. . . . You still have work to do, Murphy. Work. You use your work to make a difference. That's what you're all about.

I ran Murphy Brown's interview with God at a workshop for teachers and parents in Niagara Falls, Ontario. They watched it silently, in rapt attention. I also showed a CBC-TV clip of the Princess of Wales's funeral to demonstrate how effectively television, by arranging and compressing reality, can pack an emotional punch. During a break, some people wandered outside. A high-school vice-principal standing by herself on the grass looked shaken, near to tears.

"Was it the Diana funeral?" someone asked her.

The woman looked away, almost trembling. "No, Murphy interviewing God."

During the broadcast of the 1998 Emmy Awards people across the U.S.A. were asked to express their thoughts about television. One woman with breast cancer indicated that the continuing story on the final season of *Murphy Brown* presented her with a model for her own life. Murphy's courage and determination gave this woman strength to continue her own battle. And a man spoke of the profound impact television had had on forming his own values. He referred specifically to the character of Andy Sipowicz in *NYPD Blue* who has to deal both with alcoholism and racism. Through all of this, Andy has a strong values system to which he clings and which is of considerable help.

There is much "religion" on television, even on animated sitcoms like

The Simpsons. There was the popular Bishop Fulton Sheen on television in the 1950s. There are the Billy Graham crusades, televised as expertly as any World Series or Super Bowl, and Graham's interesting (and accurate) remark that because of television he can "preach to millions more than Christ did in His entire lifetime." There are the evangelical, send-us-your-money programs that appear regularly throughout the schedule. There are the religious talk shows, usually with a pronounced evangelical, fundamentalist attitude hosted by men with easy smiles and blow-dried pompadours. My colleague O'Malley calls this strand of religion "They'll know we are Christians by our hair." The message conveyed by such programs is mixed at best. Many of them, as the scandals in recent years have made all too clear, are more concerned with raising money than in presenting the values of the Gospel.

According to the Parents' Television Council study in 1997, there has been a fourfold increase in "religious depiction" on American prime-time television since 1993. A *TV Guide* poll in March 1997 found that 61 per cent of Americans who responded want more references to God on prime-time television. Why?

Perhaps with the approaching millennium and talk of "millennial anxiety" people are being drawn to religion, seeking answers, reassurance. Perhaps the Big Questions are back in favour and the networks, sensing this, are giving viewers what they want. Of course, the explanation may be more prosaic, as a television producer suggested to *Time* in September 1997 when he said: "People are sniffing a dollar, I guess."

Is Nothing Sacred?

After a few dismal attempts – such as *Going My Way* (1962–63), based on the 1944 Bing Crosby film, and *The Flying Nun* (1967–70), a sitcom about a novice nun who discovers she can fly – religion finally hit prime-time in the 1990s. Dramas and sitcoms are tackling religious issues. Their goal is as much to entertain as it is to preach or present explicit values. Sensitive, delicate, troubling issues are explored: abortion, homosexuality, premarital and extra-marital sex, murder, suicide.

When we think of religion and religious values on television we think of shows such as *Touched by an Angel* (1994 to present), about angels who come to earth to help mortals deal with problems; *Promised Land* (1996 to present), which deals with a Christian family living in a trailer, going from town to town doing good; *Nothing Sacred* (1997–98), about a liberal priest in a beleaguered inner-city parish; *Teen Angel* (1997–98), a sitcom about a dead teenager who returns as his best friend's guardian angel; and *Soul Man* (1997–98), about a reformed widowed gang-member-turned-minister who is raising four kids.

At another of our morning sessions, O'Malley turned on his tape recorder, anxious to discuss *Nothing Sacred*, which he had watched for the first time the week before. He seemed momentarily disappointed when I told him I found it rather boring.

> O'MALLEY: Why boring? Because you're a priest and it's all old-hat to you?
>
> PUNGENTE: I find it boring because it's all been-there, done-that on television. The Father Ray character doesn't have to be a priest to deal with a drug-addicted brother who's separated from the family. He doesn't have to be a priest to fall in love with someone else's wife.
>
> O'MALLEY: But he *is* a priest. That's what I find interesting. I don't think it's a 1990s gimmick. To me it's fresh. And I think there's a yearning for some explicit spirituality outside of Jimmy Swaggert and Jerry Falwell.
>
> PUNGENTE: Being a priest adds a little dollop in hopes of getting people to watch –
>
> O'MALLEY: It got me to go to mass last Sunday.
>
> PUNGENTE: It's not always good television. It's become predictable.
>
> O'MALLEY: Last night the big deal was *glossolalia*, speaking in tongues.
>
> PUNGENTE: Turns out there was a dove up in the ceiling.
>
> O'MALLEY: A hospital patient starts speaking Aramaic.
>
> PUNGENTE: But he turns out to be a schizophrenic.
>
> O'MALLEY: There have been fascinating movies with religious themes, but not much on television. *Nothing Sacred*'s finally trying to convey something intelligent about religion. And in prime-time, on Thursday evening.
>
> PUNGENTE: It's in a terrible spot. You can't go up against *Friends*. Nothing can. And *Nothing Sacred* is not an eight o'clock show, it's a ten o'clock show. But ABC doesn't want to put it on at ten o'clock because *Chicago Hope* is on at ten o'clock.

O'MALLEY: Thursday night is *Frasier* and *Seinfeld*.

PUNGENTE: And *Friends* and *ER*. Why are they putting *Nothing Sacred* against that stuff? They should put it up against *Touched by an Angel*, see what happens.

O'MALLEY: Would you put *Nothing Sacred* in your list of the 90-per cent-schlock TV?

PUNGENTE: No, it's worthwhile.

O'MALLEY: You have to like the writing. The episode when the young woman in the rectory is pregnant and is considering an abortion. Father Ray, after some soul-rendering, ultimately tells her it's up to her conscience. Father Leo, the old curmudgeonly priest, over-hears this and is mad as hell. Then a subplot involves Father Ray dealing with one of his parishioners who is a rapacious slumlord. He's on the telephone to this guy and tells him if he doesn't stop his evil ways he'll go after him from the pulpit. He'll – *excommunicate* him! Father Leo overhears this, too, and quietly admonishes young Father Ray: "Notice you didn't tell him it's up to his conscience."

PUNGENTE: The writing is good. The principal writer is someone called Paul Leland. It's actually Bill Cain, a Jesuit in New York who used a pseudonym because he didn't want *Nothing Sacred* marketed as written by a priest.

O'MALLEY: Next thing I'll hear a Jesuit is managing the Yankees.

Nothing Sacred didn't survive its first season of 1997–98, though in its brief life it generated more controversy than shows that have lasted much longer. *TV Guide* called it, "one of the most compelling dramas to grace a TV schedule since *thirtysomething*. It's gritty, gutsy, and extremely potent . . . pulls no punches and packs a wallop. The next time someone bemoans the poor quality of network programming, tell them to watch this show."

Writing in *The Catholic Register*, September 1997, freelance writer Kevin Burns said: "Just as *ER* uses the emergency room as a metaphor and anchor set for a compelling drama about the fragility and value of human life, so does *Nothing Sacred* use the confessional box as a location and as a metaphor for the possibility of forgiveness, reconciliation, and grace . . . In a world of dumb, tabloid, put-down and exploitation, it glows with the glimmer of the momentary presence of the divine."

On the other side of the ring, powerful Catholic lobby groups in the United States loathed *Nothing Sacred*. The New York-based Catholic League for Religious and Civil Rights organized an advertising boycott, accusing *Nothing Sacred* of anti-Catholic, offensive propaganda that seeks to "convince viewers that those Catholics who challenge the Church's teachings on women and sexuality are more compassionate than those who uphold church teachings."

Nothing I saw in the show convinced me that the priests acted against church teaching. Both sides of controversial issues such as abortion and the ordination of women were presented, though for reasons of drama the show often skated on thin ice. Cardinal Roger M. Mahony and Bishop Gerald Wilkerson were among the defenders of the show. "I don't see anything terribly wrong with the show," Wilkerson told a freelance writer for the *Toronto Star* in December 1997. "I guess nobody really wants to believe that a priest is human, that he never has any doubts or questions." Cain, the Jesuit writer for *Nothing Sacred*, explained what he attempted when he said: "What I'm trying to do is depict genuine people struggling to be faithful to the church, something that is no more easy to do than to raise a family."

Kevin Burns finds a parallel between the struggle to keep the fictional downtown church alive and the struggle to keep *Nothing Sacred* alive. In the final, unseen episode, the church accidentally is destroyed by fire when a rehearsal for the Easter vigil goes wrong. The line of dramatic action seems to mirror *Nothing Sacred's* experience with the network. Cain himself agrees: "We always felt that what we were writing reflected what was going on around us. There were constant parallels between what we were going through with the network and what we were going through on the show. The first show begins with Ray, saggy-baggy, hauling his tired butt out of bed, and the series ends with Ray having celebrated Easter in a show that has to do with nightmares and his having a dream of dolphins. So there is a journey from chaos to peace, encompassed in it. There's a journey of destruction in a way, too, where the actual building of the church is destroyed but the people remain whole."

Viewers were not to enjoy the promising youth, mature middle age, and gentle decline of a show that has had a full span. In the end, it was not the critics who killed *Nothing Sacred*. When it premiered in October 1997, it was 54th in the ratings. By mid-October it had slipped to 92nd, making it the lowest-rated show on the four major networks in the United States. ABC renewed *Nothing Sacred* for the entire season, moving it to another night, then abruptly cancelled it, leaving a number of episodes unshown. In April 1998, *Nothing Sacred* won a Peabody Award for "honest portrayal of the complexity of faith in the modern era." ABC replaced *Nothing Sacred* with *America's Funniest Home Videos*.

Nothing Sacred was a quality show which didn't make it. *Northern Exposure* was a quality show which did. One of the surprises about this earlier show was the important role religion played. Robert Thompson, writing in *Television's Second Golden Age*, calls it religion in which God "showed Her/His benevolent self in the form of Native American spirits or a New Age non-denominational presence whose gospel was preached by the morning deejay." Every episode of *Northern Exposure* dealt with an issue which one might confront respecting spiritual beliefs or the search for identity and meaning in life.

Another successful quirky show, *Picket Fences* (1992–95), treated the values of organized religion on a regular basis. Catholic, Protestant, and Jewish points of view were presented in a way that was neither dogmatic nor melodramatic. When nine-year-old Zach brings charges against the school board for including creationism in the curriculum, his family has to look carefully at what their Protestant faith means to them. And for all of its off-the-wall black comedy, the episode in which cows were used as surrogate mothers for human embryos brought forth serious discussion about surrogate motherhood.

You Are Now Leaving Media World

T. S. Eliot observed that "television is a medium whereby millions of people can listen to the same joke and still remain lonesome." This is true for those who watch television unaware that what they are watching contains values that could mean much to them when they leave "media world" to re-enter "real world." Whether the issues are religious or secular, an intelligent treatment of them on television can have repercussions in "real" life. This may be most obvious when people discuss last night's episode of *ER* at work the next day. But "media world" and "real world" impinge upon one another constantly in small and big ways.

As I was walking out of the movie theatre after seeing *The Truman Show*, I overheard a teenager say to his friend, "Kind of makes you think about the world around you, doesn't it?" Too often we accept the "reality" of the media world without thinking how it impacts on our "real world." Often, too, we accept the values of "media world" without thinking about them. They may or may not be the values we share or admire. But becoming literate about the medium of television can help us to decide.

5

He Shoots, He Kills! Violence on Television

~

Research has found that the more children watch television, the more it influences them. Researchers also tell us that developing media literacy skills reduces TV's impact on kids. The more kids think and talk about TV, the less influence it has on them.
— *Live TV: Activity Guide* (1996) to accompany
the National Film Board of Canada video *Live TV*

There is a wonderful Latin saying, *scinduntur doctores*, which means *the experts are divided*. On the issue of whether or not television causes children to be more violent, the experts certainly are divided. Since the 1950s, there have been more then 3,500 studies on television violence. Two recent studies examine network programming over the same period of time and emerged with opposite conclusions.

The U.S. National Cable Television Association determined that the incidence of violence in television programs increased from 53 per cent in 1994 to 67 per cent in 1997. The U.S. National Association of Broadcasters determined that over the same three years violence on television declined steadily. Same data, opposite results. The only thing the two groups agreed on as reported in *The Globe and Mail*, April 28, 1998: "It is not uncommon for social scientists to look at the same phenomenon and get differing results."

Social scientists may be more or less confused but that doesn't stop some politicians and others in authority from pointing an accusing finger at television.

In October 1997, a sixteen-year-old killed his mother and two class-mates in Mississippi. In December 1997, a fourteen-year-old killed three girls with a semiautomatic Rutger. In March 1998, an eleven-year-old and a thirteen-year-old ambushed their school in Arkansas, killing five people. In April 1998, a fourteen-year-old in Pennsylvania attacked classmates and teachers at a school dance, killing a science teacher. In Oregon, May 1998, fifteen-year-old Kim Kinkel murdered his parents, then killed two school classmates, and wounded eighteen others.

President Bill Clinton blamed the carnage on "a changing culture," meaning, in particular, violent movies and video games. Vice-President Al Gore cited the oft-quoted statistic that the average child watches 20,000 "simulated murders" on television by the time he or she graduates from high school. "Exposure to this amount of media violence is not healthy for children," Gore said. And *The New York Times* summed up: "It was guns. It was the violent culture of the South. It was the violent culture of the American media. It was bad parenting. It was the breakdown of the family caused by liberal politics or economic stress. It was violence against women. It was lax juvenile laws."

For some others, placing blame is more complicated.

Health and Welfare Canada's statement on "The Effects of Media Violence on Children," 1993: "For some children, under some circumstances, some television is harmful. For some children under the same conditions, or for the same children under other conditions, it may be beneficial. For most children, under most conditions, most television is probably neither particularly harmful nor particularly beneficial."

Gary Dunford, *Toronto Sun*, January 25, 1996: "If only we could turn off TV's violence faucet our problems would vanish! Bring on that Silicon Valley snake oil. Step right up, gimme a dollar. There are no bad kids. There is only bad TV. It makes them do zombie deeds."

Geoff Pevere, *Toronto Star*, March 28, 1998: "For if there seems to be violence everywhere – on and off our screens, in fiction and fact, in lurid dreams and dull reality – it's because violence, like soap and sex and cigarettes, is an incalculably lucrative product to produce, package, and sell."

Lieutenant-Colonel Dave Grossman, an expert on the psychology of killing and a member of Arkansas Governor's Working Group on Juvenile Justice, *The Globe and Mail*, May 23, 1998: "The data linking TV violence and violent crime is more scientifically sound than that linking tobacco and cancer. More than 200 studies have identified a clear cause-and-effect relationship. Thus, we are probably very close to a time when TV networks will be treated like the tobacco industry and brought to their knees by lawsuits."

In 1996, The National Film Board of Canada released a short video titled *Live TV*. The purpose of the video and accompanying study guide was to help children think about how television and movies influence them. The language is clear and concise: "Thirty years of scientific research have shown that television violence makes children . . ."

- ". . . think that the world is a scary and dangerous place." This is based on what media analyst George Gerbner calls the "mean world syndrome." In this theory the television audience believes the world to be more violent than it is in reality. The audience believed that crime rates increase year after year in North American cities when as a matter of fact they have tended to decrease.
- ". . . think that violence is a normal part of life." This can lead to them becoming violent themselves or at least desensitized to violence. However, as Kathleen McDonnell points out in her book *Kid Culture*, not everyone agrees on this point. "Some media experts, like the University of Toronto's Jonathan Freedman, have serious reservations about the desensitization theory. Freedman claims that children do indeed become desensitized, but only to TV violence itself, which they know to be fake. Their abhorrence of real-life violence, he admits, remains undiminished."
- ". . . think that violence is a good solution to many kinds of problems." Children will come to condone the violence in real life because of what they see on television where at times violence appears to be the only solution in a difficult situation.
- ". . . less sympathetic to victims of violence." This is the supposed result of desensitization.

- "... more interested in violence, both as a form of entertainment and a real-life experience." This presumes that children are entertained and influenced strongly by the violence they see on television.

What to do? Close our eyes and pick a cause? Or are they all correct? Perhaps what passes for analysis is nothing more than advocacy. Mark Crispin Miller, who teaches media at New York University, says: "Instead of just going there and yanking on the heart strings, we've now got armies of pundits ready to hold forth on a moment's notice with various simplistic notions of what just went down. We don't use the word 'propaganda' much any more, but the constant heavy drone of knowing voices out there is largely a chorus of propagandists talking at us."

The truth probably resides somewhere in the middle. Yes, some children can be affected in an adverse way by some of what they see on television. However, many researchers have concluded that television violence alone does not make kids violent. Other factors may be far more significant, such as real-life violence, abuse, poverty, drugs, family problems, and neglect. Researchers, as the National Film Board of Canada's notes for *Live TV* point out, have also found that the more children watch television, the more it influences them. They also tell us that developing media literacy skills reduces TV's impact. The objective of media education is not to get kids to turn off TV, but to ask themselves: "Who is smarter – the TV or me?"

Blood and Al Gore

We should not be surprised to hear that television is to blame for society's ills. It is not only Al Gore who quotes statistics about the number of bloody murders children watch on television. After all, TV is the new kid on the block in terms of media (yes, the Internet is here to stay but that's another battle, just heating up). The new kid always gets blamed. In *Preposterous Violence: Fables of Aggression in Modern Culture*, James B. Twitchell traces the history of cultural explanation of social ills. He notes that Plato complained that the written word was spoiling the spoken one. Monks in the Middle Ages were not all that thrilled by the invention of the printing press which made their handwritten manuscripts obsolete. Twitchell points out that many Victorians thought that the novel ruined literature. And in the 1870s, with the invention of the telephone, there was widespread concern that people would do nothing but talk on the phone. Twitchell writes: "Radio was excoriated because it carried the mass-marketed fantasies of soap operas and detective and Western violence to a popular audience. And if cheap novels and radio dramas were not enough to debase western culture with sensationalism, just look at how Hollywood was ruining what was left. Lucky for the studies that the television networks came along to shoulder the blame."

Joey Slinger of the *Toronto Star* took up this theme in a column he wrote in May 1997. "The *Iliad* – now that goes back. Bronze spearpoints lodging in foreheads, smashing through skulls. Some poor fellow, lanced through the navel, 'his bowels uncoiled, spilling loose on the grounds.' This goes on page after page . . . Follow the flight of Diomede's spear as it 'split the archer's nose between the eyes, cracked his glistening teeth, the tough bronze cut off his tongue at the roots, smashed his jaw and the point came ripping out between his chin' . . ."

How any of us survived Homer when the *Iliad* became a best-seller is a sociological mystery. The politically correct forces of ancient Greece doubtless lacked the requisite clout to banish this new poetry from polite society. Slinger, moving on through the pages of history, examines Mark Twain's Connecticut Yankee, who thought the Knights of the Round Table lacked good old American know-how, so he introduced them to the Gatling gun. "Within ten short minutes after we had opened fire," Slinger quotes Twain, "armed resistance was totally annihilated, the campaign was ended, we 54 were masters of England! Twenty-five thousand men lay dead around us."

And then there were the penny dreadfuls of the 1800s such as *Joanna Polenipper, Female Horse-Stealer, Footpad, Smuggler, Prison-Beater and Murderer* (what an amazing title). It is referred to in a spirited attack on the dreadfuls in the *Edinburgh Review* of 1887.

Al Gore may think that TV violence is destroying civility, but it seems there have always been people appalled by media excess. The media, however, are hardly the only determinants of social behaviour.

Dr. Edward Blackstock, chief psychologist for the Peel Board of Education in Ontario, suggests that at least nine "personal" and seven "situational" factors contribute to children's behaviours and attitudes. It is not necessary to go into all of them. What is significant is Dr. Blackstock's belief that media violence is only one of many factors that contribute to real-life violence. But, for some reason, few people campaign against the other factors.

In an article titled "Imagebusters" in the publication *American Prospect*, author Todd Gitlin is reminded of the fool on his hands and knees under a streetlight.

> "What are you looking for?" asks a passerby.
> "My watch."
> "Where did you lose it?"
> "Over there," says the fool, pointing to the other side of the street.
> "Then why are you looking over here?"
> "Because it's dark over there."

It is dark in the world of real violence. There is little will for an all-out war on poverty, guns, or family breakdown. Instead, we are offered a crusade against media violence. This is largely a feel-good exercise – moral panic substituting for practical action.

A Made-in-Canada Solution
> *TV violence is one of those abstractions that's easy to pontificate about, but it's much harder to figure out what it actually does or what to do about it.*
> — Kathleen McDonnell, interviewed in
> *The Globe and Mail*, October 12, 1998

In March 1996, after two years of hearings and discussions across Canada, the Canadian Radio-Television Telecommunications Commission (CRTC), the regulatory body for radio and television in Canada, issued an important document dealing with violence on television titled *Respecting Children: A Canadian Approach to Helping Families Deal With Television Violence*. In it the CRTC said, "The Commission believes that industry codes, program classification, and parent-empowering technology are extremely valuable in dealing with television violence. But it considers, as the indispensable underpinning to such measures, that a national and international commitment to public awareness and media literacy will be the decisive factors in changing attitudes."

When the report appeared, the media latched onto the notions of program classification and parent-empowering technology and ignored what the CRTC had to say about media literacy. We should not be surprised. The media often prefer a simplistic or high-tech solution to one that is merely practical.

The CRTC also advocated "the cooperation of the broadcasting industry to develop strong, credible, self-regulatory codes." The Canadian Broadcast Standards Council (CBSC) is the self-regulatory agency that ensures adherence to the Canadian Association of Broadcasters' (CAB) code – known as the "Voluntary Code Regarding Violence in Television Programming." This recommends that broadcasters not air programs that contain gratuitous violence or programs that sanction, promote, or glamorize violence. The code also includes guidelines for the depiction of violence in children's programs that take into account the vulnerability of young viewers. The guidelines stipulate:

1. Animated programs targeted to children shall not invite "dangerous imitation."
2. Violence will not be shown "as a preferred way of resolving conflict."
3. The consequences of realistic scenes of violence will be portrayed.
4. Violence will not be the central theme in animated programs.
5. Programs containing scenes of violence that are intended for an adult audience shall not be broadcast before the 9:00 P.M. "watershed hour."
6. Programs broadcast prior to 9:00 P.M. that contain scenes of violence not suitable for children must contain appropriate viewer advisories.

In addition, the CRTC requested the development of an acceptable classification system for television programs. Thus, starting in September 1997, Canadian TV began using distinctly homegrown screen icons to inform viewers of program content. The icons were designed by the Action Group on Violence on Television, an alliance of Canadian broadcast, cable, and production companies. The icons identifying the level of violence or mature themes all include a stylized maple leaf to distinguish them from icons intended for audiences in the United States. The icons must appear on the screen for fifteen seconds at the beginning of entertainment shows. They do not have to be used for news and sports programs. The six rating-levels, which are meant to supplement, not replace, existing viewer advisories are:

C: Children. No offensive language, sex, nudity, but might contain occasional comedic violence.

C8: Suitable for all aged eight or older. No sex, nudity, or profanity, though it may have language considered socially offensive employed within the context of the story, and violence that is infrequent, discreet, and of low intensity.

G: Family viewing. Minimal violence and no gratuitous frightening special effects. No profanity, sex, or nudity, though it may contain inoffensive slang.

PG: Parental advisory. Conflict and aggression are limited or moderate. May contain mild profanity, suggestive language, and brief scenes of nudity.

14+: Not suitable for viewers under age fourteen. Violence could be a dominant element of the story line. Could contain strong or frequent use of profanity and nudity or sexual activity.

18+: Adult. Might contain depictions of violence intended for adult viewing, graphic language, and explicit portrayals of sex and/or nudity.

The television industry in the United States launched its own rating system in February 1997. The ratings estimate suitability by age, the key factors being violence, language, and sexual material. The ratings flash at the start of all programs, with the exception of news and sports. The six ratings-levels are:

TV-Y: Suitable for all children, especially those under age seven.

TV-Y7: Children seven or older.

TV-G: General audience, suitable for all ages.

TV-PG: Parental guidance. Programs may contain material some parents might find unsuitable for children.

TV-14: Parents "strongly cautioned." Many parents would find the material unsuitable for children under fourteen.

TV-M: Mature audiences only. May be unsuitable for viewers seventeen and under.

There has been strong opposition to a ratings system based solely on age, the thrust of the opposition being that children tend to be attracted precisely to those shows identified as inappropriate for their age. Many of those opposed prefer to rate programs on the basis of material instead, the criteria being the nature and amount of violence, sex, and coarse language in the program. The logic fails me. Is it not possible that children would be as keen to watch inappropriately violent and inappropriately sexual programs as they would inappropriate-age programs?

The Kaiser Family Foundation surveyed reactions in the United States to the new rating system. At the end of the 1997–98 television season, the poll of 1,358 parents and 446 children found:

- 90 per cent of parents regard rating-advisories as a good idea.
- 93 per cent of parents who use the ratings say they are "very" or "somewhat" useful.
- 36 per cent of children have decided not to watch a program because of the rating.
- 31 per cent of boys are more interested in a program with a violent rating.
- 79 per cent of youths aged ten to seventeen had watched an R-rated movie with their parents on video or at a theatre.

An Associated Press poll in April 1998 found that "seven in ten adults pay little or no attention to the television show ratings already applied to shows. Even in homes with children, 51 per cent of parents pay little or no attention."

To V-Chip or Not to V-Chip
In 1993, Tim Collings, an engineering professor at Simon Fraser University in Vancouver, invented what has come to be known as the V-chip. The V-chip allows parents, by using a handheld remote, to set the ratings-levels of violence, language, and sexual explicitness they will permit their children to watch. Too much and, *zap*, the V-chip blocks out programs and the

screen goes blank. News, documentaries, and sports programs are exempt. The V-chip will be introduced in North America in 1999.

It gets murky here, things are not as simple as they might first appear. The broadcasters have to do the ratings themselves. About six million hours of programming are aired every year in a seventy-channel universe. As a point of comparison, each year there are some 1,000 hours of Hollywood films to be classified. Television rates programs on the basis of sexual content, profanity, and violence, using a scale of 0 to 5 ("5" being the most objectionable). Parents are expected to use an on-screen guide to program their V-chips so as to block out programs they might consider objectionable. For example, violence in a Saturday-morning cartoon may be acceptable, but violence in an R-rated movie may not. The V-chip monitors the frequency band that carries the rating-designation of each program and blacks out any deemed objectionable.

There are kinks to be worked out. The networks must agree on how much violence warrants a "5" on the 0 to 5 scale. And how much sexual content is too much? What about *The Young and the Restless*, the steamy soap opera some office workers watch on their lunch breaks? Or *Xena the Warrior Princess*, the leather-bustiered, leggy beauty clanging her sword against the forces of doom? Perhaps the most stubborn kink to be worked out is, how do you use the damned thing? Many, if not most, grown-ups are flummoxed by the clock on their VCR. (For most kids, it's a cinch.) What are the chances they'll get the hang of programming the V-chip?

Collings, the V-chip inventor, says the purpose of the V-chip is to "deal with television violence while still protecting creative expression. It remains the viewers' responsibility to make a final selection."

Champions of the V-chip argue it is useful for working parents who can't always monitor what their children watch on television. More and more children are home alone after school, parked in front of the TV set, so the V-chip works as an automatic absentee censor.

Those not keen on the V-chip say that it merely fosters the illusion of control, giving parents an excuse not to watch television with their children. They maintain that parents who go to the trouble of acquiring and programming a V-chip probably already take an active interest in their children's viewing habits. They also worry that the V-chip may provide television producers with an excuse to increase the amount of violence, figuring the V-chip protects children from the worst of it. Opponents argue, as well, that the V-chip ignores "psychological violence" – name-calling, put-downs, cruel manipulation – because it concentrates solely on "sticks-and-stones" violence. Keith Spicer, former head of the CRTC, likes the V-chip, but he said it cannot replace parents, nor can it replace a responsible television industry.

"The V-chip," Spicer said, "is just 10 per cent of the solution."

I discussed the V-chip with Pat Kipping, past president of the Association for Media Literacy in Nova Scotia, who also is a mother of two. "Instead of empowering parents," she told me, "the V-chip technology could very well disempower parents and further endanger kids. Relying on the V-chip will let parents avoid their obligation to teach their children to be wise users of media. It will allow them to abdicate their important role of mediating their child's relationship to the world. Parents need to use words, not gadgets, to communicate their own thoughts, values, and ideas to their children. They need information to develop those words."

Lance Henriksen, the cerebral, sometimes acerbic star of *Millennium*, says it's not the violence on television that does the damage, it's indiscriminate viewing, which he believes will be heightened, not lessened, by the V-chip. "The V-chip is absurd," he says. "It isn't about what's on television. It's about the fact that you're letting kids watch television unsupervised. If you want a V-chip, what you're really saying is you want *more* lack of supervision. You want a V-chip to take the responsibility for your life rather than you."

In 1996, President Clinton signed a bill to legislate the mandatory inclusion of the V-chip in all television sets manufactured in the United States after 1997. This was later changed to July 1999 to give manufacturers time to retool. Starting in July 1999, the Federal Communications Commission, the broadcast regulator in the United States, will require that all television sets larger than thirteen inches include the V-chip. By January 2000, all sets must have the V-chip. The legislation also requires that current television sets be retrofitted with set-top equipment for the V-chip.

No such legislation exists in Canada. There was an initial burst of enthusiasm for the V-chip in Canada, but this has waned considerably. Still, the CRTC stated in June 1997 that it "expects the implementation of encoding and deployment of V-chip devices to occur as soon as is feasible."

The Brits don't think much of the V-chip at all, which might reflect their longer tradition of media education. Virginia Bottomley, The National Heritage Secretary, told *The Financial Times* in March 1996 that the impracticalities of the V-chip outweigh any benefits. Andrew Brown, director-general of the Advertising Association, which represents the advertising industry in Britain, told *The Financial Times* that his concern is that the V-chip "is seen as a panacea and becomes adopted through a knee-jerk, if well-intentioned, reaction to real problems in society."

And what about media education – the "media literacy" which the CRTC called the foundation of any attempt to deal with television violence? While the press was concentrating on V-chip and ratings, media education continued to develop across Canada. Appendix One is a summary of those developments both in the field of education and within the media itself.

It has been said that the cumulative impact of indiscriminate viewing of violence is damaging to children because it "desensitizes" them to violence. Perhaps, but if this is true it is the result of watching television passively, uncritically, accepting its values as your own, having no criteria to discern the shoddy from the excellent, the intelligent from the stupid. In other words, lacking the critical thinking skills that come with media education.

Desperately Seeking Violence
The critics all take it for granted that there really is a lot of violence on prime-time television. Yet knowledgeable observers dispute that assumption. In her column on television in the *Toronto Star*, Antonia Zerbesias writes: "Yes, people are brutalized on cop classic *NYPD Blue* and the cerebral *Homicide: Life on the Street*, but viewers see only the bloody aftermath – the shock, the sadness, the revulsion – not the dastardly deed. This is not to say there is no violence on TV. Wile E. Coyote is still trying to blow up the Roadrunner and Batman is still doing his BIFF! BAM! thing. But, the way the critics carry on, you'd think murder and mayhem were all over the tube – which they aren't except when big-screen movies make it to TV."

Let's see what violence we can find on NBC's "must-see-TV" on Thursday evenings, Thursday evenings being the primest of prime-time television during the week and NBC's lineup having the most viewers on that evening. At the start of the 1998–99 season it began at 8:00 P.M. with *Friends*, all about six Generation Xers whose only quarrel seems to be what channel to watch on their television and who's got the best seats in the coffee shop. *Friends* was followed by *Jesse*, considered to be a "family sitcom" about a working-class single mother. So far, so good. Then comes *Frasier*, which replaced *Seinfeld* in the coveted nine o'clock slot. The closest *Frasier* ever came to violence was the time Niles challenged his wife's trainer to a sword fight. As for the departed *Seinfeld*, well, George's fiancee died after licking bad glue on the envelopes containing wedding invitations. And there was the time Kramer signed up for karate lessons, where he had some fun winning skirmishes against the ten-year-olds in his class.

Frasier is followed by *Veronica's Closet*, all about the "exciting" times had by the staff of a lingerie design house. Finally, Thursday evening ends with *ER*, with Steadi-Cams following the doctors and nurses trying to save lives in a big-city emergency room. There are injured people, some of them victims of violence, but for the most part the images of injury and trauma are restrained.

Okay, so these are all successful shows on prime-time. But even the not so successful shows in the 1998–99 network prime-time are violence-free. There were family sitcoms such as *Maggie Winters*, the story of a young woman who, when her marriage fails in the big city, moves back home to small-town mid-America where the drag races on the main street are as close to violence as it gets. There's *Maggie*, whose title character works in a veterinary clinic, which brings her into contact with such violence as barking dogs and wandering porcupines. Or *That '70s Show* where teens risk a violent fall down the stairs should they trip over their bell-bottoms. And *King of Queens*, about a blue-collar worker in Queens whose daily trip on the subway is as close as he comes to violence. And then there was *Meego*, which tried to capture the "other-worldly" audience by introducing a 9,000-year-old alien into a middle-class American family, which it did without any violence. (Or humour, for that matter, which may explain why it didn't survive.)

The ten o'clock fare consists mostly of cop shows, hospital shows, and lawyer shows. When there is violence, or a violence-related theme – unavoidable considering the work of cops and doctors and lawyers – it is in context with the drama, not gratuitous, prurient, or excessive.

But what about *Oz*, the award-winning series about a maximum security prison? It is probably television's most unrelentingly violent show. It is shown on a cable specialty channel, but that does not excuse the violence. In August 1998, the *Vancouver Sun* newspaper's television critic Alex Strachan called *Oz* "the most brutal television series ever made, and watching it is a brutalizing experience." And I agree. The grim, graphic violence within the walls of that prison is shown in detail. Strachan explains: "It's not meant to be entertainment – at least I hope not – and it doesn't pretend to be a documentary. It clearly wants to be an indictment of the U.S. prison system, but in its rush to judgment, it has the opposite effect." Despite the superb acting, writing, directing, and photography, I find it almost impossible to watch *Oz* because of the violence. Yet, perhaps because it is on a specialty channel, there have been few complaints about the show.

So where is the network violence? Saturday-morning cartoons? World Wrestling Federation brawls? Yes and yes. Kids have watched this form of whomp-'em, stomp-'em violence for decades, with no discernible harm done. Kids know the difference between animated, make-believe violence and real violence. Critics have called the cartoons and the make-believe mayhem of professional wrestling "the central fables of our time."

Once you've seen these or similar shows, then consider what James B. Twitchell says in his insightful book *Preposterous Violence*:

"The stories are interchangeable variations of ancient fables of aggression that usher in audience after audience. The dramatization of danger, the laying down of the rules and boundaries of hostilities, the simulations of crisis, the rehearsal of conflict, the alternate scenes of dominance and submission, the playing out of roles, the centrality of masquerade, the half-hearted resurgence of authority at their conclusion – all give the genres their incantory and ritualistic power."

And yet, these are the television shows the V-chip is designed to protect us from. It is difficult to find objectionable violence in the prime-time network shows – *Friends*, *Frasier*, *ER* – unless you really work at it, which some people have done. A university group in the midwestern United States actually counted individual "acts of violence" during one week of television, after which the "survey" concluded that *Briscoe County Jr.*, a science-fiction western, was the most violent show in the study. This was because there were more than one hundred (count 'em) "acts of violence" in the one-hour show. The producer of the show, understandably upset by this dubious honour, decided to watch the episode his accusers had watched. He was astonished at what he found, and what the study group deemed acts of violence. The show in question happened to contain two boxing matches and the researchers had counted every punch thrown in the ring as "an act of violence." In this sense, every time Dr. Frasier Crane stubs his toe or an *ER* doctor makes an incision we would have what this group would call an act of violence. The study group would have been better advised to watch the pushing, punching, kicking, biting, hair-pulling, bleeped-out profanity, and smudged-over nudity we see every night on *The Jerry Springer Show*.

Kids know violence. They appreciate the difference between cartoon violence and real violence. A dead bad guy struck down by a superhero is not as disturbing as a real person shot dead at a McDonald's and shown on the six o'clock news. This is why the V-chip won't work, because it exempts the worst of television violence: news and sports.

If It Bleeds, It Leads
We will examine news in a later chapter, but for now, let's consider the advice some television reporters were given to help them assess the newsworthiness of any item under consideration on a given day: *If it bleeds, it leads*. Why? The competition for news is intense and one sure way to capture an audience is with a particularly grisly bit of video footage. You can only watch one channel at a time, the remote is always at hand, so let's not have any boring talking-head discussing the sublime and theoretical. Let's show fires, floods, car crashes, earthquakes, tears, anguish, blood! Get the highest ratings, charge the most for commercials. Television must make money. News is television. News must make money. And news is exempt from the V-chip.

What about children and the news? I watched a special report on media violence on Citytv in Toronto in which a ten-year-old boy said he was not frightened by violence on television because he knew it wasn't real. What did scare him, he said, was seeing a dead body on the news because that was real. Similarly, an episode of *20/20* dealt with TV violence. It showed a group of five-year-olds watching *The Mighty Morphin Power Rangers*, a live-action show about teens with superhuman powers that once was considered among the most violent programs on television. *The Mighty Morphin Power Rangers* is still on television – only with a new look as *Power Rangers in Space* and *Power Playback*.

The pretend-violence of *The Mighty Morphin Power Rangers* never bothered me. I was more troubled that the show was one long advertisement for Power Rangers paraphernalia. On *20/20*, one of the five-year-olds was asked if he thought the Power Rangers were real.

"No," he replied.

"Why not?"

"Because they're on television," the boy said. "If they were real they wouldn't be on television, they'd be on the news."

Slapshot

Another large segment of television is also exempt from the V-chip: sports. Watched any hockey lately? It bears little resemblance to the game I remember as a teenager, despite the errant elbows of Gordie Howe and the Kitty-bar-the-door brawls that occasionally erupted (and didn't seem as if they had been scripted into the game). There is no question that fighting now is an integral part of the National Hockey League, more so as league officials try to entice American viewers to the sport. An NHL player probably has a better chance of seeing himself on television in a game highlight by socking an opponent than by scoring a goal. And if he's bleeding profusely he'll likely see himself on the front page of the newspaper. They now count stitches as fastidiously as shots-on-goal.

An interesting insight into the wonderful world of hockey was brought to us by Chris Zelkovitch of the *Toronto Star* when he monitored TSN's *Sports Desk* and Global's *Sportsline* for six days in April 1998. In his report, Zelkovitch wrote: "Over those six days, there were 168 goals scored in the NHL and 23 fights. *Sports Desk* showed 99 goals, or 59 per cent of the total. It showed 16 fights, a whopping 69 per cent. *Sportsline* wasn't much better, airing 86 goals (51 per cent) and 13 fights (57 per cent). You can argue with the scientific validity of my statistics . . . but there's no denying, fighting is overplayed on TV."

The producers justify showing hockey fights, along the lines of what's good for business is good for everyone. Keith Pelly, vice-president of TSN, responded to the criticism by declaring that fighting is part of hockey and attracts viewers. Case closed.

In Martin O'Malley's book *Gross Misconduct: The Life of Spinner*

Spencer, much attention is paid to the violence of hockey and the validity of fighting as an integral part of the game. The book examines the life of hockey player Brian (Spinner) Spencer, a tough winger who came out of the wilds of the British Columbia interior to play in the NHL. Spencer discusses with O'Malley the existential experience of The Hockey Fight:

"You're wearing maybe twenty-five pounds of equipment, so first you have to throw your gloves down. And you can only hit the guy in the face. You can't hit him anywhere else. I mean, what's the use? You might break your hand. You've got no footing so you try to anticipate what the other guy's going to do. Try to brace yourself and keep upright, because if he puts you on the ice he has an advantage. Try to block him, stay on your feet, maybe throw him on his back and get a few in. You use discretion, of course, but I can take all kinds of punches and I know I'm not going to get hurt. If he hits you with a stick, fine. You bleed a little, you get sewn up."

Brian's father, Roy Spencer, drilled into his son the importance of being tough, being willing to dish it out and take it in order to make it in the NHL. Even when Brian was a boy his father would routinely level him on a backyard rink with full body checks, once knocking his son unconscious during one of these practices. His father had been a soldier, and he described the intricacies of hockey in military terms. Spencer passed on this wisdom when he said, "Hockey is a reckless-abandon game. You've got to be aware of 360 degrees at all times. If you're not, you're going to get hurt. Only a fighter-pilot in the sky has more dimensions to worry about."

In *Gross Misconduct*, O'Malley points out that hockey fights sell. "Hockey is the only sport outside of professional wrestling that encourages rule violations and regards penalties as valid statistics. Brian began his NHL career when the league expanded from six teams to twelve teams in two divisions . . . Because Americans were not intimately acquainted with the essence of hockey, the violence and the fighting became part of an unofficial marketing strategy best captured in the remark, 'I went to the fights and a hockey game broke out.' There are videos produced consisting entirely of hockey fights, one flailing battle after another, often set to music. It is primitive, atavistic, a modern version of the spectacle of the gladiators."

The gladiatorial contests in Rome, the medieval tournaments, and many of the contact sports of today have at least two things in common.

Physical violence is an inherent part of them. They are all commercial ventures. And, usually, the more physical contact there is in the sport, the more violence, and the larger the number of spectators.

Sports are big business today. In 1998, 800 million people around the world watched *Super Bowl XXXII* and two billion watched the World Cup final. The size of the audience is the main reason why advertisers did not even blink at the $1.2 million charged to air a thirty-second ad during the Super Bowl. And The Olympics, held up as a time for goodwill, sportsmanship, and patriotism, can cost a country millions of dollars, guarantee a winning athlete a healthy sponsorship contract, and give a company like Roots exposure which they could otherwise only dream of having.

Neither the Olympics nor soccer games are intrinsically violent. Still, sports and sports culture encourage both participants and viewers to believe that problems and issues can be resolved decisively inside of four quarters or three periods or whatever. From every conflict there emerges a winner and a loser. It's an aggressive view of life and it is the background to all sports.

So?

Kathleen McDonnell makes a critical point when she says in *Kid Culture*: "Stating the common-sense fact that there is a relationship between media violence and real-life violence, between male consumption of pornography and violence against women, is not the same as saying media violence and pornography cause violent behaviour. Unless this relationship is understood in all its complexity, censorship-type solutions, for all they appear quick and easy, will fail to yield the resulting behavioral and societal changes."

What to do?

The Center for Media Literacy in Los Angeles has published *Beyond Blame: Challenging Violence in the Media*, a five-part video-based curriculum for children, youth, and adults. It suggests five ways in which media education can lessen the impact of media violence:

1. Reduce exposure to media violence, especially of the young, by educating parents and caregivers about media violence and helping them

to develop and enforce age-appropriate viewing limits. Media violence today is much different than when parents were growing up.

2. Change the impact of violent images by deconstructing the techniques used to stage violent scenes (what is used to make "blood," the use of special effects to create bomb blasts), by decoding the various depictions of violence in different genres – news, cartoons, music, sports, drama.

3. Locate and explore alternatives to storytelling that use violence as the preferred solution to conflict. Change undesirable images from popular culture into opportunities for positive models. One father let his child watch *Teenage Mutant Ninja Turtles*, but only if the child would "imagine" a fifth turtle named "Gandhi." Afterwards, they had discussions on how "Ninja Gandhi" would get the Turtles out of trouble without resorting to violence.

4. Expose and challenge cultural, economic, and political support for media violence – militarism, greed, competition, dominance, poverty – as well as the personal ways each of us may be contributing to media violence. The kit encourages participants to ask hard questions of themselves, of others and of society, by applying the principles of critical thinking to experiences that look like "mindless entertainment."

5. Break the cycle of blame by promoting intelligent discussion of media violence at school and home, and with community and religious groups and representatives of media.

An informed public is less vulnerable to extremist views of actions.

In *Beyond Blame: Challenging Violence in the Media*, the authors suggest three criteria to distinguish between violence that is acceptable and appropriate and that which is unnecessary, perhaps even dangerous. These criteria relate to (a) the significance of violence to the story, (b) the depiction of the consequences of violence, and (c) the character and motives of the individuals engaged in violence.

With respect to the story, the point of the exercise is to gauge whether the violence is essential or gratuitous. In *Giant Mine*, for example, a CBC drama based on a real-life labour dispute in Yellowknife that resulted in the murder of nine miners, the violent incident is clearly central: without it, there would be no story. In this case, violence provides the occasion for an exploration of people's lives at a time of stress – a labour dispute – and delves also into larger social issues relating to class warfare and the quest for justice.

Quite different would be an episode of *Martial Law* where outbreaks of violence serve as little more than visual punctuation to break up an otherwise turgid story. Such violence is much harder to justify.

Another way to assess the acceptability of violence is by examining the shown consequences. Most dangerous, perhaps, are programs that gloss over the consequences: pain is signified by a grunt or exhalation; repeated blows to the face or body leave no mark; dead bodies simply disappear from the screen. This is violence in a cartoon world. The approach advocated in *Beyond Blame: Challenging Violence in the Media* emphasizes that the consequences not be shirked. Shows like *Law & Order* and *Homicide: Life on the Street* make certain that the consequences of violence are shown.

Finally, the least justified depiction of violence is one that makes a simplistic distinction between good guys and bad guys. In the everyday world of our daily experience, motives are always mixed, and character is always complicated. Even the most virtuous among us is flawed. Even our worst enemy has his good points. But in prime-time television, too often the good guy's halo is never dimmed and his arch-enemy's character is painted solid black. Good guys wear smart clothes, are gallant in the company of women, and drive desirable cars. Bad guys are unshaven and lecherous and are denied possession of designer labels. This is often the case in *Nash Bridges*.

From the beginning of time violence has often been an important part of drama on stage, in movies, on television. But such violence should always have a reason and a context. When there is violence it should be inherent to the story, and the consequences must be appreciated. In *Oedipus Rex*, Oedipus puts out his eyes when he learns that he has, unwittingly, murdered his father and married his mother. His most violent act is done offstage. The Greeks realized that necessary violence did not have to be shown. Shakespeare's plays are filled with violence. At the end of *Hamlet* there are many dead bodies on the stage and not one of them died of a heart attack. I wonder what the V-chip would make of that scene?

6

Buy Me That! Television and Consumerism

~

Oh Georgio, my soul, Calvin, my sinew, Eternity, my every breath. You are the quintessence of my being. I don't know what it means, but I read it in an ad once. Abandon me and I am spent. Naked. A shell. I buy, therefore I am.

— *UTNE Reader*, January/February 1992

On a bright, warm morning in April 1998, Michael Cameron pulled on his Pepsi-Cola shirt and headed off to Greenbrier High School in Evans, Georgia. The high-spirited nineteen-year-old had no idea how grievously he would transgress the bounds of good taste that day.

It was "Coke Day" at Greenbrier High. This is serious business in Evans, a two-hour drive from the Atlanta headquarters of the Coca-Cola Bottling Company. Coke Day was part of a campaign by the school to win a $500 award from Coca-Cola for the school that comes up with the best method of distributing promotional discount cards to students. There would be Coca-Cola executives at Greenbrier High visiting classrooms as "resource speakers." The big event would be in the afternoon when the entire student body would assemble outside for a group photograph, arranging themselves so as to spell "Coke" on the school field. And there was Mike Cameron in his Pepsi shirt.

Later in the day he relented and pulled on a Coke shirt, but the deed had been done. The assistant principal took Cameron out of his class and demanded to know if he had indeed worn a Pepsi shirt on Coke Day. Cameron 'fessed up, so the assistant principal administered a one-day suspension. When Cameron was asked why he did it, he said, "I don't like to follow the trend of everyone else."

Responding to Ads

McLuhan wrote: "Ads are really doing their work when you don't notice them."

That probably was true when McLuhan said it in the 1960s. Those were the days when you would go to the movies for a night out, perhaps to escape the commercialism of television. Remember the first time you saw commercials before the movie? Remember the reaction? Moviegoers actually hissed and booed. I remember one angry patron shouting, "I've already paid my five dollars!"

No more outrage. Now, the movie you've paid to see often is preceded by two or three commercials, the volume at full blast, and the price of the movie itself has gone up. Moviegoers take their seats and passively let the commercials wash over them, as they do with television commercials, except that in movie theatres they can't change the channel or turn down the sound. No hisses or boos. And don't think advertisers didn't anticipate this from the beginning.

Some people deliberately arrive late, knowing the feature they want to see will start ten, fifteen minutes after the listed starting time, what with the usual parade of trailers and now the commercials. The product-placers are working on this, too. If the audience will grudgingly accept commercials *before* the movie, why not go the next step and insert them *during* the movie? This is exactly what happens in the movie *Major League* when the baseball players assemble and perform a commercial for American Express. It's in the script, and it looks like part of the story, but you could run it during any television show and no one would know the difference. At the end, a player dashes home from third base, flashes a loopy smile at the camera, and says: "American Express, don't steal home without it."

Advertisers want you to try on new lifestyles, shape new cultures, alter your beliefs and values. The people who make sitcoms and dramas can say they are only trying to entertain you, the people who bring you news and documentaries can say they are only trying to inform you, but the people who make commercials grind a much more conspicuous axe: they want you to buy something, usually something you don't need, probably something you don't even know you want.

We know ads are there to sell us products. By understanding and keeping this in mind, we can focus on the creative techniques advertisers employ to get and keep our attention. This might mean shorter ads, more images, better music, genuine humour – Canadians are good at humour – or a more concerted attempt to win our attention with intelligence and savvy.

The Advertisers

Len Masterman, in his book *Teaching the Media*, suggests that any serious examination of advertising should be "an attempt to develop an understanding of how advertising works, of the role of advertising agencies, or of the function of advertising within contemporary society."

This leads to a discussion of a number of issues including the protection of personal privacy as corporations and credit bureaus collaborate to compile information about our lives and buying habits. Without a doubt we have become a shopping culture, the economy depends on it. Media, in a variety of ways, support and are a part of this culture – though sometimes, too, media act as a cultural critic. Some people are reacting against escalating commercialism with measures such as "counteradvertising," demanding taxes on advertising, and restrictions on telemarketing and direct-mail advertising. And then there are media terrorist groups that espouse defacing ads they consider offensive.

The people who make television advertisements are among the least likely people to be critical of consumerism, but they are often astute and self-aware in describing what they do. This makes for fascinating reading, especially if they are explaining advertising techniques. Gene Del Vecchio, in his 1997 book *Creating Ever-Cool: A Marketer's Guide to a Kid's Heart*, mentions that the Children's Television Workshop, the originator of *Sesame Street*, has helped educate more than 120 million children worldwide. Eight per cent of the American population visit a McDonald's on an average day. Two Barbie dolls are sold every second in the world. "By all measures, this is success!" Del Vecchio exclaims. "People who helped create and develop brands such as these understand what most others do not. They understand the timeless, emotional needs that all children share."

When he wrote the book, Del Vecchio was a senior partner and director of planning and research in the Los Angeles office of Ogilvy & Mather Worldwide, the world's sixth-largest ad agency, with billings in 1996 of $8.3 billion. He had been working for twenty years in children's advertising when he wrote *Creating Ever-Cool* to explain how to sell products to kids.

He provides an overview of the magnitude of the children's market, and a marketing strategy for achieving "Ever-cool." He then probes the essence of the child's timeless psyche, filled with needs and desires demanding satisfaction. Next he examines a child's world and culture, comprised of trends and fads that will help the marketer keep a brand eternally fresh while expanding its role in a child's life. Then Del Vecchio reviews the tools marketers can use to develop the best possible children's brands, marketing programs and issues related to ethics. "In a marketer's rush to fulfill a child's emotional needs and desires, care must be taken to ensure that the child is not harmed in the process," Del Vecchio says.

I found the book a revelation of the methods of media advertising and how they pertain to a child's desires and needs. After reading Del Vecchio's summary alone I knew I would never be able to look at children's advertising the same way again.

In one instance, Del Vecchio develops a simple matrix. One column lists categories a marketer may target (e.g., sports, toys, snacks). The second column contains the key elements of a kid's emotional psyche (e.g., win, control, affection). The third column is a reminder to gratify the child's senses. The fourth column lists the child's world and culture: from fads to family. The final column offers marketing options to keep the product "ever-cool" year after year. Using this matrix, Del Vecchio tells us that in less than thirty minutes he developed nine new products for kids from a cookie that changes from dull brown to a rainbow of colour when dipped in milk to a yo-yo that makes gross sounds.

In my own writings on advertising I point out that we often make important decisions based not on what is logical but on what we feel is right. We do this with people we meet with whom we want to be friends.

And we do it with decisions about things we buy. Like many important decisions, we make them not because they are the logical choice but because they "feel right." For example, you do not count up points for and against people when you consider making them your friends. It is not surprising then that when you buy something you often do so because it feels like a good idea. Advertising appeals to emotion. The most powerful way advertisers have to make you buy has been proven to be to appeal directly to your emotions.

Connecting the Dots

We respond differently to movies than we do to television. Ever wonder why you feel "buzzed" after watching too much television, yet can emerge from a showing of *Titanic* relaxed and refreshed, despite watching for more than three hours without a commercial break? It is because with movies you are watching pictures and with television you are watching dots.

The response I usually get at my workshops is, "Get outta here! That's a picture!"

No it isn't.

The television image consists of a busy configuration of tiny dots that your brain must assemble. It is hard work, so hard that if there were no commercial breaks we probably would have to invent them. Also, some people see more of a television image than others because their brains work differently, perhaps more efficiently.

With movies, the image washes over you. It is more relaxing than television because you are watching pictures, not dots. This is why movies don't look as good on television as they do in theatres. When a movie appears on television it has been downloaded into dots, then uploaded by your brain into what looks like a visual picture. With the new digital TV screens it's the same process, but your brain will have to work even harder because the dots are smaller and there are more of them. The process works at a certain level as a metaphor for the interactive nature of media education, especially as it relates to television: the more you work at it, the more you get out of it. But I'm not sure I like this metaphor: clever, yes, but not entirely apt as it implies that the process of watching television is hard at all levels when in fact when you have connected the dots and are watching quality television the process is pleasing. (Sorry, an English teacher can't resist qualifying metaphors.)

In many ways, we welcome the respite from television that is provided by ads. A movie takes up a specific block of time, about two hours, during which we have decided to do nothing else. A movie audience, therefore, is usually very attentive. A TV audience is much less attentive – willing to get up and leave at any time, start a discussion with someone, even talk on the phone or read a book – and the commitment may be open-ended.

Ad breaks offer a change of pace. They may offer relief from the tension of the drama and many TV dramas are written so as to reach a high point just before the commercial. And ads are often small dramas in themselves. Taster's Choice coffee ran a series of ads about a developing romance between two apartment dwellers who borrowed coffee from each other. Characters from your favourite TV show may appear in an ad and so, in a sense, the ad becomes an extension of the show. One of the best known examples of this was the appearance by the cast of *Friends* in a series of Coke ads during the Super Bowl and prior to their show after the game. All of these are aspects of television which affect viewers as well as the advertisers who are out to sell something.

*

Target Markets

We know that different programs have different demographics. Some programs appeal to men, some to women. Teenagers watch their own shows and often have scathing comments about what their parents watch. Advertisers obviously have an interest in locating their advertisements in programs that appeal to their particular markets. You won't find many ads for feminine products on a football game or ads for beer during an afternoon soap opera. Advertisers pick their spots. And they have a particular interest in those segments of the population that either have money to spend or, as in the case of children, have money spent on them.

Preschool children are not exempt as marketing targets. The *Teletubbies* show, launched in Britain in 1997, was watched by two million people every day by the end of 1998. It had been sold to twenty-two countries, rapidly joining *Barney* and *Sesame Street* as one of the top-five kids' shows in the United States. It has been estimated that spinoff products inspired by *Teletubbies* could be worth some $2-billion in retail sales. Along with the Teletubby dolls there are Teletubby slippers, backpacks, puzzles, videos, pyjamas, books, board games, baby bottles, cups, key chains, stacking toys, records, and a monthly magazine – much of it aimed at mere toddlers. Anne Howe, one of the creators of *Teletubbies*, says that this merchandising is "now part of life for children" and that "parents expect it."

In the summer of 1998, more than 700,000 people gathered on the streets of midtown Toronto to watch the annual Gay and Lesbian Pride Parade. These people were a marketer's dream: in the week before the parade and on parade-day itself they would spend $43-million on restaurants, hotels, entertainment, and shopping. Some 40 per cent of the 700,000 watching the parade were tourists visiting Toronto expressly for Pride Week. Two breweries, Molson and Labatt, were key sponsors of events during Pride Week. Their research had indicated that gays and lesbians exhibit uncommon brand loyalty and have above-average disposable incomes. This has not gone unnoticed by television advertisers. Ikea runs an ad featuring a gay couple.

Advertising That Works
Advertisers know exactly whom they want to reach. Their task and challenge is to slip their message past whatever defences the viewers may put up and win them over. The boy who wore the Pepsi sweater in order to buck a trend is not entirely untypical. Most of us want to rebel sometimes against conformity or the too-slick sales pitch. But the urge to rebel sits side-by-side with a desire to belong, to be part of the group, a regular guy. Advertisers play on both urges.

Product placement, properly executed, may lead us to believe, if only subliminally, that a particular product is everywhere – like Coke. After all, the Coca-Cola logo is the most recognized symbol in the world after the Cross and the Star of David.

In the movie *The Gods Must Be Crazy* one of the star characters is an empty Coca-Cola bottle. Coca-Cola took another starring role in the 1994 film *The Paper*, prompting a *Globe and Mail* reviewer to hail Coca-Cola as "the world's first carbonated movie star . . . There's Coke in the foreground and background, Coke sharply in focus and teasingly blurred. Coke at

[Michael] Keaton's lips, in his hand, at his elbow. And he's gotta have it. Arriving in the newsroom, he heads straight for the Coke Machine. . . . But eventually his luck runs out and tragedy strikes: the machine is empty! He pounds on it in frustration and rushes off to the other one – the newsroom has two, so no matter which way the camera turns there is always a big red glowing Coke-box nearby, as warm and inviting as a ski-lodge fireplace on a cold January night." A Coca-Cola spokesperson confirmed there had been a "product placement" deal between Coca-Cola and the producers of *The Paper* but said the producers initiated the deal.

Product placement has become as much a part of movies as casting; in fact, it is a form of casting. The lovable alien in the 1982 film *E.T.* munched on Reese's Pieces. In *Sleepless in Seattle*, when Meg Ryan and Rosie O'Donnell watch *An Affair to Remember* on video, they sip from bottles of Snapple. There were the Junior Mints the Seinfeld gang were always popping. In the movie *Free Willy*, the parents give their foster child new clothes, making sure that the labels of the Nike shoes are facing the camera. All the principal characters in the film *The Firm* consumed and discussed the merit of Red Stripe beer. In *Coneheads*, ample screen time was devoted to Subway Sandwich Shops. And in both *The Firm* and *Another Stakeout*, important members of the supporting cast were sleek Mercedes-Benz convertibles. One of the most blatant examples of product-placement is in the 1993 movie *Jurassic Park*, which features a gift shop in a theme park stocked with Jurassic Park merchandise, all with the JP logo.

In *Walker, Texas Ranger*, Chuck Norris slambams around in a Dodge Ram pickup, which becomes as much a character in the TV show as Norris himself. Bob Hadler, vice-president of Hadler Public Relations, a product-placement firm hired by Chrysler, explains: "You couldn't get anybody better than Chuck Norris. Across the Midwest he is like a god, and that's the demographics you're looking for. It is an opportunity to drive home the message: the pickup is as tough and macho as the man driving it. That kind of identification is like gold."

Product placement is a highly efficient way to advertise a product. Norris takes the vehicle on wild chases that go on and on, far longer than any television commercial. This is valuable exposure in an industry where the average thirty-second commercial costs $175,000. Every automaker uses one of fifteen product-placement firms in Hollywood that specialize in cars and trucks, paying fees for their services that range from $200,000 a year to more than $2-million.

From product placement in a single movie or TV program to product placement as but one element of a carefully orchestrated, mutually reinforcing, multi-media extravaganza – the game becomes ever more sophisticated. In October 1998, *Daily Variety* noted that fashion designer Tommy Hilfiger's clothing will make up 90 per cent of the clothes worn by the stars of the teen sci-fi movie *The Faculty*. So product placement goes one step further. Instead of just a few seconds of exposure, the product will be on display for almost the entire movie. Hilfiger is funding $15 million of the $30-million ad campaign for the film. There will also be a series of print ads in magazines and on television featuring the film's cast members wearing Hilfiger's clothes. This is part of a growing trend. In the past, celebrity actors, as themselves, have promoted products, but now Hilfiger and others are using fictional movie characters who step out of their fictional settings to promote real-life product. Once again "media world" meets "real world."

Product placement is as widespread on television as it is in the movies. In the summer of 1998, Jeff Giles, president of the Canadian Football League, warned players and coaches that they could be forcibly removed from games if they continued to wear Nike products. The reason is that the CFL has signed a three-year deal with Adidas, a deal that would provide the league with some $1.8-million in cash and products. The 1998 season also was the final year of a deal between the CFL and Starter, which provides equipment and clothes to CFL coaches and players. The problem is that many high-profile players – Tracy Ham of Montreal, Danny McManus of Hamilton, Damon Allen of British Columbia, David Archer of Edmonton, Jeff Garcia of Calgary – had personal deals with Nike. The players refused to end these deals to satisfy the CFL's deal with Adidas.

Most viewers probably are aware of the commercial implications of televised sports. Certainly, Michael Jordan's relationship with Nike has been widely publicized. Indeed, he is often referred to as "Air Jordan," a direct reference to a brand of shoes Nike manufactures. Interestingly, if the connection is well known, it appears not to be much resented. Nike products have achieved a ubiquity in North America that its rivals must envy.

Using sports celebrities to sell products is one thing. Using historical figures is another. In the United States, advertisers have had great success using figures such as George Washington to inspire trust and brand loyalty. We tried this in Canada in the 1920s, using Sir. John A. Macdonald holding a bottle of Coca-Cola, but the ads didn't work. Canadians do not like to be hit over the head with patriotic allusions, and as *The Globe and Mail* (June 27, 1998) pointed out, Canadians knew Sir John preferred the hard stuff.

This may be changing. Canadians may respond to patriotism if it's done, as the same article suggested, "gently and from the side," using ads with references that only Canadians are meant to get. Thus, Canadian Airlines shows a Canada Goose strutting by The Seine. American movie stars wear Roots clothing with the Maple Leaf. The voyageurs in Labatt Blue ads paddle through the Canadian wilderness in search of beer. Maple Leafs Meats lists national achievements – folksinging, wilderness travel, excessive courtesy, auto racing, Canadian bacon – without bothering even to mention the accompanying high-profile Canadian names of Joni Mitchell and Jacques Villeneuve. The Maple Leaf Meats people take the high road by simply presuming that Canadians recognize their own.

One of the cleverest campaigns using this technique is the Molson ad showing a young man in a beer store ordering "24 Canadians." Out of the storeroom, through the curtain on the conveyer belt come 24 people, all ages and genders, hugging their knees and smiling. The young man shrugs, smiles back, and takes them home. This is one of Molson's TV ads about what it means to be Canadian. These ads include the four monkeys typing in what appears to be a Gothic cathedral. We never see the beer so the question has to arise – do these ads really sell beer? Do they even define what it means to be Canadian? There is no reason why viewers should not enjoy well-made advertisements even as other advertisements, by their inanity, drive them mad. There are those who believe, incidentally, that dumb ads are meant to irritate. By being maddening they achieve memorability. The point is, as Neil Postman and Steve Powers write in *How to Watch TV News*, "Television not only delivers programs to your home, but, more important to the advertising community, it also delivers you to a sponsor. Be aware."

We should watch commercials carefully and think critically about them. One way to do this is to keep an eye out for programs such as Citytv's *Media Television* and CBC's *Undercurrents* which regularly examine advertising and show you how it is made and how it is meant to work on you. These programs demystify what we see.

There is a wonderful three-part TV series from Home Box Office, *Buy Me That*, which shows how TV ads are constructed. One excerpt demonstrates how a fast food burger is prepared for its "star turn" in a TV commercial. A woman demonstrates the off-camera work that goes on before the burger, shake, and fries are ready for lights, camera, and action. First, the meat is seared to make grill burns, even though it is essentially raw. No matter, it *looks* juicy. It is then painted with a red-brown dye so it *looks* cooked. Sesame seeds are glued onto the bun so they will *appear* conspicuously seedlike. A strip of thin cardboard is placed under the raw meat so the bun won't get soggy. Lettuce is held in place with pins. Some white vegetable lard that won't melt under hot television lights is poured into a milkshake container, with a curlicue on top. Carefully selected brown fries are wedged into a red container, like a flower arrangement, behind which chemically produced steam rises.

Another excerpt is for a toy called "Flipball." First, it presents in full the TV commercial, which shows exuberant young people on a beach having a swell time flinging the "Flipball" to one another, catching it on the run, catching it while they leap in the air, catching it behind their backs. "Flipball" resembles lacrosse, except the ball and catcher are plastic. Looks easy, until we show the next clip, an unedited version of the raw footage. Now we see kids *not* catching the "Flipball." They look clumsy and frustrated as the plastic ball flies off in every direction, never landing in the catcher, rolling away on the sand.

Buy me that? I think not.

Television advertisers are constantly looking for new ways to keep our fingers off the remote control during ad breaks. In July 1998, Master Lock became the first national advertiser to run a one-second ad on television. As *Time* (August 3, 1998) reports: "The commercial – call it a blink ad, for obvious reasons – depicts the company's signature image, a bullet shredding but not opening a lock, together with the logo." The question, of course, is what kind of an impact will blink ads have on sales. While it is too early to tell, it is probably safe to say that blink ads will not work to introduce new products but could help reinforce already familiar icons – the Golden Arches or Coke, for example.

The Monster Under the Table

So we have an idea of the advertisers' pitch. What about the media they work with, mainly the print and electronic media (and now, as we have shown, movies)? The media themselves keep us informed on things like newspaper ownership and concentration, how, for example, Conrad Black's Southam Inc. publishes thirty-three newspapers in Canada, including *The Ottawa Citizen, The Montreal Gazette, The Vancouver Sun,* and *National Post.* The other major newspaper player is Thomson Corp., which owns sixty-eight daily papers in Canada and the United States. These two groups own and control nearly every newspaper in Canada.

Television's a different story, right? After all, the viewing public in Canada has access to eighty cable channels – Canada is the most wired cable country in the world – and access to hundreds of other channels because of satellite technology. This must mean television affords us a huge and diverse picture of the world, with a breathtaking sweep of different views, opinions, ideologies, and values. Right?

Wrong.

Most of the television we watch in Canada comes from the United States and most of it is owned and produced by seven companies, which also own many other media-related concerns. Mark Crispin Miller, who teaches media studies at New York University, explained in an article in *The Nation* in June 1998 that these seven companies produce about 90 per cent of what we see during prime-time on all six networks. The article, which used research funded by the Investigative Fund of The Nation Institute, is an excellent piece of journalism, invaluable for anyone interested in what makes media tick.

The seven companies *The Nation* lists are Tele-Communications Inc. (T.C.I.), Time Warner, Disney, Rupert Murdoch's News Corporation, General Electric, Viacom, and CBS. These giants run TV and their stranglehold may be growing. In 1998, the Federal Communications Commission in the United States reviewed the rules of ownership, which means if corporate lobbyists prevail the big-business stranglehold on TV may get tighter. It could allow a single corporate entity to own several TV stations in a single market, or the cable system *and* TV stations, or the cable systems, TV, *and* the daily newspaper.

As Miller looks ahead to the age of digital television he sees the horror of "All Garbage, All the Time." He warns that national news will concentrate on sex scandals and disasters with very little world news. And local news will continue to concentrate on crime and grief, "keeping everyone as frightened of the city as they are bone-ignorant of what is really going on there.

"And our 'entertainment' will become at once more violent and more boring, with all the hits of yesteryear, or yesterday, recycled, only now with desperate crudity: lots of skin and rape and torture, anything to keep the audience from moving on or passing out. While there will still, as ever, be a few good shows, tomorrow's *Law & Order* and *The Simpsons* will be even more extraordinary than they are today, quite overwhelmed by the great sea of crap that is the beast's own element. . . ."

The Nation's chart listed seven companies and what they owned. Since then there have been, and continue to be, many changes. I have tried to update the list from various sources. It is not complete and no doubt will have undergone further changes by the time you read this.

1. General Electric. 1997 revenue: $91 billion. Owns NBC Television Network, American Movie Classics (67 million subscribers), CNBC (68 million subscribers), MSNBC (38 million subscribers), Bravo! Cable Network (30 million subscribers), MuchMusic U.S.A. (8.5 million subscribers). Also owns TV stations that reach 27 per cent of homes in the United States. Produces aircraft engines, household appliances, nuclear and electrical power-plant parts, light bulbs and fixtures, diesel and electric trains, industrial motors, medical equipment, and plastics.

2. Disney. 1997 revenue: $22.5 billion. Owns ABC Television Network, Disney Channel (35 million subscribers), ESPN (73 million subscribers in 150 countries), ESPN-2 (52 million subscribers), Lifetime Channel (69-million subscribers), A&E (67 million subscribers), The History Channel (48 million subscribers). Also TV stations that reach 24 per cent of homes in the United States. Also television production operations such as Walt Disney Television and Touchstone Television. Also motion-picture studios Walt Disney Pictures, Touchstone Pictures, Hollywood Pictures, Miramax Film Corp., Buena Vista Home Video.

144 ~ MORE THAN MEETS THE EYE

MORE THAN MEETS THE EYE

Also hockey's Anaheim Mighty Ducks and baseball's Anaheim Angels. Also theme parks and resorts such as Disneyland, Disney World Animal Kingdom, Disneyland Paris, Tokyo Disney World, Disney Vacation Club, and Disney Cruiseline.

3. Time Warner. 1997 revenue: $13.3 billion. Owns Cartoon Network (45.8 million subscribers), TNT (72.4 million subscribers), Comedy Central (44 million subscribers), Court TV (33 million subscribers), CNN (71 million subscribers and a 24-hour penetration in 20 countries), CNN Headline News (66.9 million subscribers), TBS Superstation (73 million subscribers), HBO (32 million subscribers). Also television operations such as Warner Bros. Television, Telepicture Production, Warner Bros. Television Animation. Also motion-picture studios Warner Bros., Castle Rock Entertainment, New Line Cinema. Also operates 625 movie screens in seven countries. Owns baseball's Atlanta Braves, basketball's Atlanta Hawks, and the new Atlanta NHL franchise. Owns 30 magazines, among them *Time, Life, People,* and *Sports Illustrated.* Owns book-publishing operations such as Warner Books, Little Brown, Time-Life Books, and Book-of-the-Month Club.

4. Viacom. 1997 revenues: $13.2 billion. Owns The Movie Channel (17 million subscribers), Showtime (17 million subscribers), Nickelodeon (66 million subscribers, 100 million homes worldwide), UPN Television Network (reaches 93 per cent of homes in United States), MTV (67 million subscribers, 300 million homes worldwide). Also book publishers such as Simon & Schuster, The Free Press, Pocket Books. Also movie theatres such as Famous Players in Canada. Also motion-picture studios such as Paramount Pictures. Also theme parks such as Canada's Wonderland north of Toronto. And retail outlets such as Blockbuster Video.

5. News Corporation. 1997 revenue: $11.2 billion. Owns Fox Television Network, Fox Family Channel (66.9 million subscribers), Fox News Channel (23 million subscribers), Fox Sports Net (5.4 million subscribers). Also TV stations reaching 40 per cent of homes in the United States. Overseas: British Sky Broadcasting (40 per cent), Star TV (Asia),

and Fox/Liberty Media (50 per cent). Also Twentieth Century Fox Television. Also motion-picture studios Twentieth Century Fox, Searchlight Pictures, Fox 2000, Fox Family Films, and Fox Australia. Owns *The New York Post, The Sun; The Times* and *News of the World* in Britain, and newspapers in Australia. Owns basketball's New York Knicks and Los Angeles Lakers (option for minority stake), hockey's New York Rangers and Los Angeles Kings (option for minority stake), baseball's Los Angeles Dodgers, and Madison Square Gardens (20 per cent through Fox/Liberty) in New York. Also Manchester United soccer team (pending).

6. Tele-Communications Inc. 1997 revenue: $7.6 million. Owns The Learning Channel (73.4 million subscribers), USA Network (69.7 million subscribers), BET (53.5 million subscribers), Sci-Fi Channel (47 million subscribers). The Travel Channel (20.5 million subscribers), Telemundo (17 million subscribers). Also owns Cable Franchise, the largest cable company in the United States with 14 million subscribers. Also has an interest in cellphones and pagers through joint ventures with Sprint, Comcast, and Cox.

7. CBS. 1997 revenues: $5.4 billion. Owns: CBS Television Network, The Nashville Network (reaches 70 million homes in United States), Country Music Television (42 million homes), TV stations that reach 31 per cent of homes in United States, 175 radio stations.

Miller ends with a plea for vigilance and cooperation between those who watch TV and those who work in it. He insists that such measures as anti-trust laws, a public service code, and sufficient public funding are a necessity. Why? Simply because television "has become our hearth, our home, our country and the very air we breathe. So what's at stake today is, simply, everything."

Miller's survey reminds us that the expression "free press" has become an oxymoron, unless, as the writer A. J. Liebling said, you happen to own your own. It also should remind Canadians of the merits of a publicly funded broadcast system, the original underpinning of the CBC, threatened year by year by forces similar to those identified by Miller in the United States.

The obstacles of corporate control are formidable in all media, but especially in television and movies. In his marvellous book *Monster: Living Off the Big Screen*, John Gregory Dunne tells of the long and arduous process of trying to do a screenplay for Hollywood. He and his wife, Joan Didion, worked for a number of years and countless drafts on a movie that originally was based on a book by Alanna Nash called *Golden Girl*, the true story of network correspondent and anchorwoman Jessica Savitch. What it eventually became, when it was released in 1996, was the frothy, mediocre *Up Close & Personal*.

Dunne tells of an encounter over dinner at a Sunset Strip restaurant between a screenwriter and a producer for Walt Disney Pictures. The writer was having difficulty accepting certain changes foisted on his script by the studio. When the writer's protest escalated, a Disney executive told him he was forced to take the monster out of the cage, whereupon he reached under the table and pretended to pull up an invisible monster from an invisible cage. The executive then tells the writer he is putting the monster back in its cage and the writer must never force him to take it out again. The executive asks the writer if he knows what the monster is. The writer shakes his head.

The executive says, "It's *our money*."

And money is important. While it is difficult to arrive at a set formula for how much various TV shows charge for ads – it is a question of how popular the show is, when it is on, who the advertiser is – it is amazing to find out just how much advertisers will pay to be part of a top-rated show. *Advertising Age* magazine gave these examples for the 1998–99 season: Thirty-second commercials for *ER* cost about $565,000; for *Frasier* about $475,000 (up from last season's $200,000 before *Frasier* took its time slot over from *Seinfeld*, which got $600,000 in its final season); for *Friends* about $425,000; for *Monday Night Football* $375,000; for *Home Improvement* and *NYPD Blue* some $200,000 each; *Ally McBeal* could bring in $250,000 per spot, while sitcom *Everybody Loves Raymond* comes in at $120,000. Just multiply by the number of thirty-second spots during any of these shows to see how much money a successful show can bring in.

Today's Lesson Brought to You by Coke, Pepsi, Reebok

Coca-Cola Day in Evans, Georgia was small potatoes compared to some of the newer inroads being made into the education system by commercial interests. I was a high-school principal in the 1970s and am familiar with the overtures schools get from people who want access to the captive audience of a high school. So how about a shiny new Coke (or Pepsi) machine for the school cafeteria? Maybe two, three? And if you use only Pepsi (or Coke) machines, we'll donate a new scoreboard for your football field. There will be a Coca-Cola (or Pepsi-Cola) logo on the scoreboard, but it won't cost you a dime.

School districts are clueing in to this apparent largess, striking better deals for themselves, or so they think. If the school can get two Coke (Pepsi) machines and a new scoreboard, why not go for more – cash advances, scholarships? This is what has been happening, according to a fascinating report by writer Mark Walsh. It was published on the Internet in April 1998, titled "Schools Are Latest Front in Cola Wars."

Walsh cites the example of Berkeley High in California, a school that was prepared to accept a seven-year $100,000 contract with the local Pepsi-Cola bottler. Members of the local school district agonized over the "deal," but eventually rejected it, convinced it would be "too much of an intrusion by corporate interests." Walsh quotes a student at Berkeley High, fifteen-year-old Sarah Church, as saying: "We have to be very careful going into any sort of a deal with a corporate power. When a corporation bring advertisements onto our school campus and has an influence on what is taught, that is a severe issue."

Ah, but this is Berkeley territory, radical centre of the hippie movement I remember from my own student days in northern California. Other educational jurisdictions in the United States have no radical tradition to draw on. The school district in Colorado Springs, Colorado, signed an exclusive deal with a Coca-Cola bottler in November 1997 by which it will receive $8-million over ten years, on the understanding that the 33,000 students in the district's fifty-three schools sell 70,000 cases of Coca-Cola products a year over the life of the contract.

Canadian schools have been drawn into the cola wars too. In 1994, a $1.2-million deal gave Pepsi exclusive rights to sell pop in Toronto schools.

This decision is still cited across Canada as a symbol of the way in which a corporate sponsor inveigled its way into the schools. Critics of the deal were worried for a number of reasons. Not only was Pepsi to have sole rights to install its machines in the schools but also – as *The Globe and Mail* reported on March 27, 1997 – "Pepsi offered to sponsor motivational school rallies and give away corporate paraphernalia." The Toronto board has since developed guidelines for dealing with corporations. Among the requirements laid down in the thirteen-point checklist is this one cited by *The Globe and Mail*, that: "any projects enhance the quality and relevance of education for learners and benefit their education. Such projects should not replace public funding of education and there should be opportunities to involve teachers and other unions."

And on May 21, 1996, CBC radio reported that an Ottawa high school had negotiated with American Express to run a travel and tourism course as part of the curriculum. This meant a group of Grade 11 students spent their time planning virtual trips to Venice seeking out lowest airfares and the best deal in hotels. So what did the school get in return for giving up one-third of an academic program? According to CBC radio, the school received "volunteer teacher time and reassigned school resources" – whatever that means.

Not all schools are opposed to linking commerce to education. Assumption Catholic Secondary School in Burlington, Ontario, entered into a deal with Coke in 1995. In return for allowing Coke to provide all the pop in the school, Coke provided the school with prizes for draws, promotional t-shirts, guest speakers, videos, sponsored the school's charity walk, and donated a school sign. Neither the school board nor the students saw anything wrong with this arrangement. Without such sponsorship such items would not have been available. And, also in 1995, Rocky View School Division No. 41 near Calgary allowed advertising to be placed on its 160 school buses. Again, they needed the money that the advertising would bring in.

The reason for this interest in schools by advertisers is obvious. Erica Shaker writing in the Fall 1995 issue of *Education Forum* quotes a Statistics Canada study as showing that Canadian children "aged 2–12 spend $1.5 billion each year, and influence another $15 billion. Total spending for 13–24-year-olds is $7.8 billion . . ." Obviously advertisers see these as markets they cannot afford to ignore.

This is not the first controversy over commercials at schools and it will not be the last. The commercializing of the educational system is escalating, especially in the United States, but there have been similar commercial assaults in Canada. And these commercial intrusions into educational jurisdictions involve much more than a free Coke and a Pepsi scoreboard.

The debate began in 1989, with the start of Channel One, originally owned by Whittle Communications, which was sold in 1994 to K-III Communications Corp. for $250-million. Channel One is shown daily in 40 per cent of secondary schools in the United States. The deal is this: in return for broadcasting a twelve-minute news program – consisting of ten minutes of "news" and two minutes of flashy, MTV-style commercials for companies such as Pepsi-Cola and Reebok – the schools receive free TV monitors for every classroom as well as VCRs and satellite receiving dishes.

It seems innocuous enough. All this "free" equipment looks on the surface like an irresistible package for cash-strapped schools. The schools can use the equipment any way they want; the only catch is that in return the schools must play, every day, for the entire student body, their twelve-minute "news" program. The equipment comes with a device that monitors the volume, which means teachers can't turn it off, can't even turn it down.

If one ignores the obvious propaganda dangers involved, it looks like a sweet deal for both sides: Channel One grosses more than $1 billion a year from the four commercials that run every day on the classroom monitors in schools in the United States, based on $157,000 for each thirty-second commercial. Several states have banned Channel One operations in their schools, and Channel One has met vigorous opposition from the 2.1 million members of The National Education Association, the largest teachers' union in the United States.

We have successfully fought this off in Canada, so far, but it is accepted, entrenched, and growing in the United States. In a worst-case scenario, this means that powerful commercial interests have total access to high-school students for twelve uninterrupted minutes every school day to push a specific and particular view of the world. Kids are used to advertising, but like most television viewers, they tend to believe that the news is an unbiased, accurate portrayal of reality. By making the TV show part of the daily routine in school, the program acquires far greater authority than the same program would have at home.

What if this entity is a racist lobby? Or the right-to-bear-arms people? Or any group with a narrow vested interest? It frightens me to think programs like this might be sponsored by some politicians or provincial governments I know, or by influential people who happen to have a lot of money. Television is powerful, for good or evil. We have examined the enormous influence television can have on values, on one's perception of the world. If kids passively watch such "news" twelve minutes a day, five days a week, don't be surprised to find a graduation class of young citizens supporting whatever philosophy was given them from that program during their high-school years.

An attempt to get into the schools of Canada with a similar approach began in the early 1990s, but it has met with considerable resistance, and not only from teachers. It was not the Channel One folks, however; in Canada it was the Youth News Network (YNN), led by Roderick MacDonald, a former Montreal-based independent TV producer and radio talk-show host. In the 1992–93 school year, YNN offered Canadian schools a deal that would involve a daily news and information program broadcast via satellite to high schools. As with the Channel One deal in the United States, the YNN proposal was for a twelve-minute program that would include two-and-a-half minutes of commercials and public service announcements.

YNN told school boards that schools in their jurisdiction that subscribed to the service would receive television sets for every classroom, VCRs, a satellite dish, basic television production facilities, and computers for all classrooms. In return, the schools had to agree to show the twelve-minute news and information program, with commercials, to all students every school day for five years. The YNN package was backed by corporate funding from companies such as Unitel and Granada Television.

The initial targets were schools in Alberta, Nova Scotia, Ontario, and Quebec. YNN concentrated its sales pitch on school trustees, not teachers. YNN had some early success, signing up about a dozen school boards, but it ran into solid opposition from teachers and other members of local communities. From August 1992 to April 1993 there were newspaper articles and editorials, letters to the editor, articles in teachers' magazines, and eventually major television network coverage of the controversy on CBC and CTV. Nearly all the coverage was negative toward the YNN proposal.

In the end, the major school boards in Nova Scotia rejected the YNN offer, which led in turn to the provincial government withdrawing its loan. Similar opposition in British Columbia, Alberta, Ontario, and Quebec, most of it led by teachers, so far has managed to keep YNN out of the classrooms of Canada.

The objections to operations such as Channel One and YNN seem obvious. It is not ethical to force students to watch commercials on TV in their classrooms when this may be against their wishes and the wishes of their parents. We have no knowledge of the beliefs, values, politics, and commercial interests of the people at YNN. No commercial interest should have the right to present its exclusive spin on the news, with money-making commercials, to a captive audience of students.

The issue is not free equipment, no matter how cash-strapped schools may be in this time of austerity and cutbacks. Nor is it an issue of selling out to big business. It is an issue of choice. Never before have Canadian schools allowed commercial interests to decide what is to be done with lesson time, or what the content of a class will be, or the slant, or the text.

Finally, at a time when every corner of our world is considered "advertising space" — church bulletins, the ice surface for hockey games, t-shirts, Boy Scout merit badges, even the bottoms of the cups on golf greens — should our classrooms also be for sale?

There are alternatives to programs such as Channel One and Youth News Network for teachers who wish to show news and other TV programs to their students. One is from YTV, and produced in cooperation with Canada's CTV network, which offers a thirty-minute, commercial-free, weekly news program for students. Teachers are allowed to tape the YTV program for classroom use. YTV also produces print and Internet material. Another alternative is CNN *Newsroom*, a fifteen-minute daily news program produced by Turner Multi Media and provided to schools with no commercials. In Canada, CNN *Newsroom* is distributed by Calgary Television. A third alternative is CBC *Newsworld*, a daily fifteen-minute news broadcast aimed at high-school students.

A valuable Canadian innovation is "Cable in the Classroom," launched in September 1995 by Canada's cable companies and specialty channels. It allows students to watch a variety of commercial-free, copyright-cleared programs, taped by teachers for use in their classrooms. The programs offered by "Cable in the Classroom" include some twenty-five specialty channels, among them CBC *Newsworld*, TVOntario, TFO, YTV, Much Music, Bravo!, Discovery Channel, A&E, CNN, and TLV. The "Cable in the Classroom" program includes resource material for teachers in print and on the Internet. The cable companies pay for the cost of cable hook-up and provide free monthly service to the students. Perhaps it is a noblesse oblige response by the cable companies, but it has proved to be a useful tool for media educators in Canada.

Just when you thought it was safe to go in the water, along comes Visual Impact Systems, a company in British Columbia that wants to install a TV system in the schools of Kelowna. According to a *Globe and Mail* report in June 1998, the purpose of the Visual Impact Systems is to "improve communications between staff and students. But it would also carry commercials to the captive audience congregating in school halls and cafeterias."

Oops, here they come again, knock-knock-knocking on the classroom door.

7

Television's Funhouse Mirror: Soap, Talk, and Trash

~

Marshall McLuhan said we'd be a tribal unit, eventually. He didn't realize that we'd really be one big talk show. Children and their parents can't even interact without being on a talk show. It's the only forum left.
– George Hamilton, *Rolling Stone*, November 2, 1995

We've got television talk shows, e-mail, computer list serves, chat lines, call-in radio, call-in television, hot lines and support groups for everything from bed-wetters to chocoholics. We've all got something to say about something. As a result we spend more time talking than listening.

Writing in *The Wall Street Journal* in August 1997, Cynthia Crossen offers one reason. "In late 20th Century America, talking is seen as active and dominant, listening as passive and deferential. There's the old joke, the opposite of talking isn't listening, it's waiting to talk." And, of course, television is made out to be the culprit since, as Crossen writes, "television also encourages passive, rather than active, listening. When you watch television, you're listening in a way that doesn't require that you retain anything and doesn't object if you leave the room." Yet becoming literate about television can change a passive viewer into an active one.

Caesar, so many centuries ago, was talking of France when he reminded us that *Omnia Gallia in tres partes divisa est* (All Gaul is divided into three parts). But he might have been talking of TV talk shows which, like Gaul, can be divided into three parts – morning, daytime, and late-night talk shows. North Americans love talk.

Prime-time television is expensive to produce and usually consists of sitcoms and dramas. Game shows, syndicated reruns, and soap operas are other genres the networks use to fill the morning, afternoon, and late-evening slots. But, short of showing a test pattern, talk shows are among the least expensive programs for those hours. All you need is a congenial or controversial host, guests, and a few chairs. And while talk shows began as late-night programming, they now more or less fill the networks' days outside of prime-time. While we are concentrating on daytime talk shows, there are also some points to be made about morning and late-night talk shows.

Talk shows are not just Made in the U.S.A. There are talk shows on Canadian television as well: *Pamela Wallin, Dini, Gabereau Live!, Jane Hawtin Live,* and *Studio Two,* not to mention *Canada A.M., Sunday Morning Live, Midday, Linehan, Imprint, Dialogue, On the Arts,* and on and on. Nighttime talk shows have not always worked well in Canada – think of Peter Gzowski's *90 Minutes Live* – or the disaster that was *Friday Night! With Ralph Benmurgui.* Ed the Sock did well with his local cable show, and the recent late-night talk show *Open Mike with Mike Bullard* has proved to be another exception, successful because of the personality of Mike Bullard but also because the producers keep the shows "small and funky" (*Maclean's,* September 28, 1998).

Perking Up the Morning

Well, here we are, and good morning to you. NBC begins a new program called Today. *And if it doesn't sound too revolutionary, I really believe this begins a new type of television.*

– Dave Garroway, host of the first *Today* show, January 14, 1952

Today (running 1952 to the present) was the first morning talk show. It was never designed to be watched from beginning to end. Rather, viewers could get the news, weather, and sports, as well as interviews with the famous and not so famous, as they got up, ate breakfast, and got ready for school or work.

Today gives viewers both information and entertainment, though sometimes the entertainment seems to take over, resulting in "infotainment."

Many people begin their day with "perky" Kathie Lee Gifford and "acerbic" Regis Philbin on *Live with Regis and Kathie Lee*. The show, which began in 1988, consists of bantering between the two hosts, silly "contests," some make-overs, and interviews with celebrities. *TV Guide*, in June 1998, says: "Critics are quick to dismiss their daily chatfest as little more than an empty hour of gushing enthusiasm and self-promotional grandstanding. Cynics skewer Kathie Lee's Norman Rockwell lifestyle and gripe about the constant on-air references to her tow-headed tykes Cody and Cassidy."

But the show is popular, has good ratings, and devoted fans. The hosts know what their audience wants and they provide it. They were the fore-runners of kinder, gentler talk shows. They have always treated their guests with courtesy, making them feel welcome. Kathie Lee has said she could not imagine doing otherwise. Both hosts have had personal problems – Regis's heart problems, Kathie Lee's marital difficulties and the accusations about the use of child labour to produce her clothing line – yet they faced these on the air winning sympathy and support from viewers. As *TV Guide* says: "It's their ability to play his jaded gruffness against her wide-eyed enthusiasm [that accounts for their popularity]; but, it's also their skills at balancing a see-and-be-seen worldliness with a common touch that speaks directly to the heartland." They appear to care for their viewers and their viewers certainly believe this is the case. It is as if the viewers are invited to join a TV family.

Daytime Distractions

Soaps are appallingly goofy. That is one cause of their disrepute. Admit to enjoying them and you admit to extracting pleasure from a dramatic world where the prevalent ailment is amnesia, where the most common human activity next to sex is blackmail, and where the question most likely to be posed about murder is how to break the news to the murderer's child.

– Walter Karp, *Channels*, July 1985

All media have commercial implications. Daytime on the networks belonged for years to the soap operas. They were relatively inexpensive to produce, had an almost fanatical following, and brought in good revenue from advertising. Their audience demographics were fairly constant. In 1992, the average daytime serial had a total of some 6.5 million viewers. Of those, 11 per cent were under eighteen years of age; 29 per cent were men over eighteen; 38 per cent were women aged eighteen to forty-nine; and the remaining 31 per cent were women over fifty. Statistics vary, but it would seem that on any given day some 25 million Americans watch soap operas.

Daytime soap spawned prime-time soap. There were huge audiences for *Dallas*, *Dynasty*, and *Falcon Crest*. The appeal of these night soaps was purely voyeuristic. They were about the rich and the famous, about what many of us would love to be. The "Who Shot J. R." episode of *Dallas*, broadcast November 21, 1980, was the most widely watched TV show of all time. This was a record not topped until the final episode of *M*A*S*H* in 1983, which was seen by 77 per cent of all Americans who were watching television that night. At the time of writing, that record still stands.

By 1996, you could catch cybersoaps such as *East Village* and *The Spot* on the Internet. These soaps are much like the soaps on television in portraying the lives and loves of larger-than-life characters. Only here you can not only see and read about them, you can also communicate with the stars, create your own characters, and even play a role in the soaps yourselves. Now that advertisers have become aware of the large audience for cybersoaps, the producers are making money.

It all began on radio in the 1930s in the U.S.A. *Ma Perkins* and *The Romance of Helen Trent* were two of many continuing radio dramas which told about star-crossed lovers and their affairs. These shows were sponsored by the big soap companies, such as Proctor and Gamble, who realized that housewives were prime targets for their products. Soaps moved to television in the 1950s and it was at that time that the "opera" element was added to the phrase. *Search for Tomorrow* was one of the first TV soaps, premiering in 1951 on CBS and lasting until 1986. The show followed the lives and loves of Joann Gardner Barron Tate Vicente Tourneur, a compassionate and much married (and widowed) woman. *The Guiding Light* has lasted even longer. Debuting in 1952, it was originally a radio soap and mainly centred on the Bauer family of Springfield. It is the only radio soap that survives on television.

Although the soap opera has usually centred on two families and their lives and loves, the 1970s and 1980s added more stories about younger people, tackling issues such as child abuse, abortion, alcoholism, and drugs. *The Young and the Restless*, which began in 1973, went a step further with shows about frigidity, rape, impotence, and all manner of sexuality. To this mix was added the attainment of love and success by young women whose fantasies became reality. Other soaps which have remained popular include *Days of Our Lives, General Hospital, All My Children*, and *As the World Turns*.

The fifth key concept tells us that all media present us with values and ideologies. Ruth Warrick, one of the actresses from *All My Children*, says in *Soap Opera History*: "We in soaps have a certain responsibility because we are role models . . . But we do show that people will pay for irresponsible actions, that you won't win or get off scot-free. It's good that soaps are more honest and real, but for a time we went overboard, just like society did in terms of permissiveness. We've definitely pulled back from that . . . Putting that in a story element makes it so much more immediate to people because many viewers relate to us as a family and mimic our actions." I doubt that soaps are either "real" or "honest." And while, the characters may pay for their "irresponsible actions," they certainly take the time to enjoy them first.

Soap opera is popular because viewers almost believe in the characters. These characters become friends they care about and who, were the truth to be told, the viewers would not mind trading places with. Karp explains that soaps ". . . seize upon disreputable cravings and indulge them shamelessly." Soaps are filled with beautiful people – male and female. Soaps have a never-ending appetite for erotic romance; and a craving for revenge driven by hatred and resentment. For Karp, what makes the soap opera appealing is "its unabashed indulgence of an insatiable craving for emotional scenes." Every day on every soap we can watch such scenes. They may well be a cry for what Karp calls "the dignity of foolish hearts and feckless lives." For years, nothing else on television could do what soaps did. But then there came upon the scene the natural extension of the soap opera, the daytime TV talk show which some refer to as "Trash Talk" because of the nature of the topics under discussion.

Caught in the Act

*Try to remember one thing and that is we are professionals. We are in busi-
ness to make money. To make money, we have to get ratings. A lot of time to
get ratings we have to make you look stupid, not ourselves. We will always opt
to make you look stupid. So if you want to be famous for being stupid, get on
a talk show.*

– Morton Downey, Jr., talk show host

There are a lot of people who want "to be famous for being stupid." The
most recent Trash Talk success, *The Jerry Springer Show*, receives two thousand requests a day from people who want to be a guest on the show and
display their stupidity for everyone to see and hear. They are willing to be
humiliated, demeaned, pushed, hit, bitten, kicked, to have their hair pulled
and be screamed at. They do not get paid for this (though they are flown to
Chicago and put up in a nice hotel for a few days). All they want is a few
minutes of national television exposure. And they get it – do they ever.

By January 1998, *The Jerry Springer Show* was attracting 6.7 million
viewers a day, making it the top-rated talk show on television, surpassing
even *The Oprah Winfrey Show*, which had dominated the genre for ten
years. However, Oprah retained the talk-show crown for the period from
September 1997 to September 1998 when she averaged 6.9 million viewers
per day compared to Springer's 6.5 million.

Gina Bailey, writing in *The Democratic Communiqué*, February 1996:
"American talk shows falsely infuse the notion of democracy into the
format itself. Audience participation has become synonymous with citizen
participation. This displacement serves to obscure the *raison d'être* of both
the home and studio audiences; that being, of course, profit. Audiences are
bought and sold according to ratings. They are commodities. Topics are
chosen based on their potential exchange value and not on the social needs
of the people."

This issue of the economics of talk shows must be considered. They
may be the natural successor to game shows and soap operas, both of
which are far more expensive to produce. Soap operas require writers,
actors, and directors, all of whom need to be paid, some quite handsomely.
Talk show guests usually are free. Even the experts, especially authors on a

book-promotion tour, are happy to accept exposure in place of remuneration. The talk shows, certainly the Trash Talk shows, provide more of the requisite jolts-per-minute that keep viewers from channel surfing. In 1985, there were fourteen hours of soap opera and four hours of talk show on daytime television. By 1998, by my count, there were eleven hours of soap and sixteen hours of talk.

Why do people want to be famous for being stupid? It could be the final confirmation of Andy Warhol's prescient observation that everyone would be famous for fifteen minutes. Or perhaps it is a super-charged television equivalent of the old press-agent take on gossip-journalism, that there is no such thing as bad publicity, that it doesn't matter what is said about you so long as they spell your name right. If you look like an idiot, fine, as long as you're a *famous* idiot.

Norman Chad, in his 1995 book *Talk Stupid to Me*, offers another reason: "On these shows, America seems to be searching for the lowest common denominator, and *we haven't found it yet*. But ask yourself this: Are we more dysfunctional than ever before? I say no, it's just that, before Marconi, we didn't broadcast all this activity across the land. And, curiously, we have not only a limitless supply of folks watching this stuff, but also a limitless supply of folks wanting to tell us they're doing this stuff . . . Everyone wants to be on TV. To be on TV gives you an identity. . . . It doesn't matter that you beat your wife or cheat on your husband or ate your children – YOU'RE ON TV!"

Trash Talk TV bumps into all of the key concepts, whether they be values, ideology, structured reality, commercialism, negotiated meaning – you name it. Some of this becomes clear when you look at a sample list of some of the topics from Trash Talk TV:

- A woman eight months pregnant boasts of having eight sexual partners during her first two trimesters (*Montel*).
- The maid of honour at her best friend's wedding tells the bride she slept with the groom a week before the wedding (*Rolanda*).
- A woman boasts that she pulled a gun on her boyfriend's wife (*Ricki Lake*).
- Two sisters who hate each other mud-wrestle in a pit against a background of pig noises (*Richard Bey*).

The hosts seem oblivious to the sensationalism and transparent inauthenticity of these shows, or they have come to believe their publicity releases, or they have raised suspension of disbelief to an absurdist art form. On *Sally Jessy Raphael*, a thirteen-year-old guest is urged to share her sexual experiences, which began when she was ten. Other titles: "Nude-Dancing Daughters," "I'm Marrying a 14-year-old Boy," "Sex Caught on Tape," "Wives of Rapists." Without blinking, Sally Jessy Raphael explains to *Variety*: "I'd like to think that honesty of purpose is winning over gratuitous sensationalism." On *Maury Povich*, Jason, an eighteen-year-old from a small town in Ohio, says he is in love with Calvin . . . Calvin is having an affair with Jamie, Calvin's twin sister . . . Jamie is attracted to Scott, who had sex with Calvin and someone named Tiffanie . . . Tiffanie had sex with everyone except Jamie. Povich explains to *Variety*: "It's not the topics that are tackled in the shows, it's how you treat them . . . the important thing is treating the topics with sensitivity." On *Jenny Jones*, a woman says she got pregnant while making pornographic movies, a husband who has been seeing a prostitute for two years is confronted by his wife, a mother runs off with her daughter's fiancee. Without a trace of irony, Jenny Jones tells the *New York Daily News*: "We try to use a little restraint."

Taking Trash Seriously

During the 1997–98 television season the five shows most watched by teenagers in the United States were, in descending order: *The Simpsons*, *South Park*, *Dawson's Creek*, *Jerry Springer*, and *WWF Wrestling*. And there are young people who take their television-watching very seriously, like the four Grade 6 girls in New York who beat their teacher for refusing to turn on the classroom television set so they could watch a *Springer* episode on the topic "Bisexual Relationships Hurt Marriage."

Jane M. Shattuc, in her 1997 book *The Talking Cure: TV Talk*, lists a number of characteristics of popular daytime talk shows. Jeanne Heaton and Nona Wilson, authors of *Tuning In Trouble*, published in 1995, provide a perspective on talk shows from a psychologist's (Heaton's) and social behaviourist's (Wilson's) point of view. By combing through both works, we learn the following about Trash Talk shows.

First, they are issue-oriented and their content centres on social and personal problems generally involving substance abuse or sex. The people with these problems – the guests – are the source of all the drama that follows.

A social worker who works with teenaged street kids in downtown Toronto says many of these young people regard *The Jerry Springer Show* as the most realistic depiction of the abusive, dysfunctional families from which many of them have fled. They know well those parents who, when they don't know what to say, when they can't articulate their emotions, start hitting. It is an illustration of how basic illiteracy, the frustration of not being able to express yourself, can result in violence.

Second, audience participation is encouraged. A great deal of attention has been focused on the people who appear on these shows. Almost as interesting are the people watching them. In many ways, they are as much participants as the people on stage and – like a Greek chorus – they indicate to the viewers at home what their own response should be. And while many of them may be there for the fun of it, some are there to try to work out their own problems and to get a few seconds of fame if called on to ask a question.

As Joe Chidley pointed out in *Maclean's* magazine in February 1996, "[W]hat makes talk shows so popular in the ethically fixated '90s is that they allow the viewer to be exactly the opposite – to be politically incorrect, to take guilty pleasure in someone else's problems. As one viewer put it: 'You know, you turn it on and somebody's crying and you laugh at them.'"

Third, these shows are structured around the moral authority of experts. The host is what Heaton and Wilson call "a beacon of familiarity." The host is assisted by a counsellor, a doctor, a lawyer, or a self-help expert. They also play an important role, providing the illusion of The Answer, or The Resolution, however specious they may be. (As Ward Cleaver, Beaver's patient dad on *Leave It to Beaver*, once explained – a line that could be carved in stone in any media-literacy archive – "Well, Beaver, this may be hard to believe, but life isn't exactly like television.")

Fourth, the target audience is primarily female.

Finally, while shown on network-affiliated stations, these shows are produced by non-network companies.

A Brief History of Trash

Not so long ago, the television-viewer had to get up and walk to the set to change channels, and there were many fewer channels to choose from. Phil Donahue addressed this issue in an interview he did on a documentary on talk shows called "Talked to Death," which appeared on *Newsworld* in January 1998. "What once titillated us in drama is now titillating us with real characters who are on the stage and are often encouraged to be animated . . ." Donahue said. "The noise will stop channel-surfing."

On the same documentary, Geraldo Rivera opined that "talk shows replaced game shows that were totally mindless soap operas that distorted reality." One might respond to Geraldo's observations by asking, "How mindful and real are daytime talk shows?" They are carefully constructed to "look" real. Are the fights staged? The guests are prepped to a point where a fight could be a natural consequence. Notice how, on *The Jerry Springer Show*, just before they go to commercial, previews of upcoming fistfights and chair-throwings are shown, a visceral jolt to get the viewer to click back when the commercials are over. What about the entertainment value of daytime talk shows? Jerry Springer says that's all there is to them. Oprah Winfrey says "entertainment is the last thing I'm looking for . . . my goal is to uplift, encourage, and enlighten you."

It is true, historically, that daytime talk shows are a mixture of other shows. In his 1997 book *Glued to the Set*, Steven Stark says the new talk shows borrow heavily from the appeal of television soap operas and game shows. He says the talk shows "borrowed a feminine style of disclosure and a focus on issues considered to be of particular relevance to women, like family and relationships." Stark shows how game shows like *The Price is Right*, *Strike It Rich*, and *Queen for a Day* taught the new talk shows about the entertainment value of having "contestants" who will talk about their personal tragedies with copious tears for money or fame. And Stark informs us that from "*Family Feud* they learned that conflict sells in the daytime. Throw in a smattering of TV religion . . . melodrama . . . and the pieces were in place for a profitable genre – especially because daytime talk shows are so inexpensive to stage."

In *Dictionary of Teleliteracy*, David Bianculli takes us back down the road to the beginning of the genre that eventually resulted in *The Jerry Springer Show*, *Geraldo*, and *Ricki Lake*. According to Bianculli, the "grandaddy of them all" was Mike Wallace's *Night Beat*, which started in 1956 on DuMont's WABD-TV in New York City. It was tough and confrontational, but hardly brainless, not with guests such as Salvador Dali, William F. Buckley Jr., and Norman Mailer. Bianculli does cite an early example of Trash Talk, however, when he mentions *The Joe Pyne Show*, a syndicated talk show from Los Angeles on which the host regularly referred to his audience as "meatheads." (Archie Bunker later would apply the epithet to his son-in-law on *All in the Family*.)

Bianculli says the true forerunner of today's Trash Talk probably was *The Morton Downey Jr. Show*, which started in 1988 and ended in 1989. Like Mike Wallace on *Night Beat*, Downey encouraged confrontation, but unlike Wallace, Downey aimed for the jugular of lowest-common-denominator appeal. Downey also appreciated the value of a vocal, hostile audience. "Downey was a TV showman who knew just what he was doing, but his studio audience was much less controlled," Bianculli observes. "It was more like a horror-movie mob, minus the torches."

The first big Trash Talk show was *Geraldo*, which began as a syndicated program – Trash Talk always starts in syndication – in 1987. In his early years with ABC, Geraldo Rivera was a serious television reporter, but he became a showman when he got his talk show. At last report he was back being serious again, having abandoned his talk show to work as a news reporter for NBC for something like $4 million a year.

At the time of Geraldo's early rise in the late 1980s, *The Phil Donahue Show* was the big talk-show success. It started as *The Phil Donahue Show* in 1967, from Dayton, Ohio, then moved to Chicago where it was syndicated nationally. In 1974, the title was changed to *Donahue* and continued this way until 1996, by which time it had moved to New York – a remarkably long run. Bianculli has many nice things to say about *Donahue*. In *The Dictionary of Teleliteracy*, he writes: "By bringing his microphone into the studio audience, and opening the phones to callers watching the live show at home . . . Donahue was an early champion of the 'national town hall' concept, as well as one of the first coast-to-coast travelers on the interactive TV superhighway." Bianculli also points out that Donahue reconfigured the relationship between politics and TV. It was on Donahue's show in 1992 that Jerry Brown and Bill Clinton were allowed unmoderated debates.

About the time Donahue was getting going in Ohio, Oprah Winfrey was starting to makes noises on the talk-show circuit. From 1977 to 1984 she co-hosted a local show called *Baltimore Is Talking*, then moved to Chicago to do a morning talk show. Soon she was getting better ratings than Donahue in Chicago, which prompted Donahue to hightail it to New York. Winfrey went national in 1986 with *The Oprah Winfrey Show* and soon dominated Donahue on the national scene as well.

Oprah reigned supreme nationally until Jerry Springer challenged her during the 1997–98 season. Springer, however, continues his feckless, self-deprecating ways, telling *Playboy* magazine in July 1998: "Thirty years from now people will remember Oprah and the impact she's had on our culture and on television. I'm a blip on the screen in terms of TV history . . ."

When Winfrey launched *The Oprah Winfrey Show*, Geraldo Rivera needed to get noticed, fast, so he opted for studio clashes, once getting his nose broken when an angry guest hurled a chair at another guest. *Geraldo* spawned several imitators, among them *Ricki Lake*, which started in syndication in 1993, which in turn inspired *Jenny Jones*. The most infamous talk-show escapade ever has to be the time *Jenny Jones* ambushed a male guest by having a "secret admirer" appear on the show in a taped confrontation. The guest was twenty-four-year-old Jonathan Schmitz, and the secret admirer was Scott Amedure, a gay male. Schmitz was expecting a female secret admirer and was shocked and humiliated when it turned out to be Amedure. The stunt so angered Schmitz that after the taping he drove to Amedure's house and killed him with two shotgun blasts to the chest. The local sheriff described the killing as "a sad commentary on how individual lives can be altered by the quest for Nielsen ratings." Schmitz eventually was convicted of second-degree murder and *The Jenny Jones Show* was sued for $25 million. The "Secret Crushes" episode was never aired.

Bianculli does not like *Ricki Lake* or *Jenny Jones*, but has mixed feelings about *Geraldo*. In the early 1990s, he says, Geraldo "became as shrill and overzealous as a carnival barker. . . ." Then, perhaps because he got weary of the freaks or because he became genuinely obsessed with the intricacies of the O. J. Simpson affair, Geraldo suddenly got serious in the mid 1990s. He continued his daytime trash talk, but launched a new evening show, *Rivera Live*, on CNBC. Bianculli calls *Rivera Live* "one of the best and most thoughtful sources . . . for discussion of the legal and social ramifications of the Simpson case."

No Hug-and-Make-Up

The most heinous sin of all on Trash Talk TV is: silence. What causes the producers to panic is when a guest doesn't "act" or "react" (read: sob, curse, spit, hit, kick). On one *Geraldo* show, two sisters, Leona and Stephanie, appeared to tell their story, which begins with Leona and her husband inviting Stephanie to move in with them. As the show progressed it became clear that Leona's husband is the father of Stephanie's daughter. This we deduce when Stephanie says, "My sister's husband is the father of my daughter." But the remark caused some confusion on the set, which almost stopped the show in its tracks. Everyone, including Geraldo, huddled to make sure they understood the situation. All this was captured on the *Newsworld* documentary *Talked to Death*.

The problem really began when Stephanie would not react to Leona's accusations. Stephanie just sat in her chair on the stage, smiling. The outraged Leona yelled and stomped, accusing Stephanie of stealing her husband, trying to poison her, demeaning her at work. Stephanie just smiled. The producer used his headset phone to call his assistant backstage and ask her to come out at the break to talk to Stephanie and get her to do something, say something – anything. The assistant producer came out at the break and talked to the two sisters, then returned backstage to anxiously watch what happened. When the sisters started yelling at each other, the relieved assistant muttered "Thank you, thank you." At one point the videographer asked the assistant producer if she wanted a "resolution" on air. The assistant producer said: "Do I have to have a resolution on air? No. Would I like to have a resolution on air? Yes."

Meanwhile, Stephanie went quiet again. This time a desperate Geraldo himself walked over to Stephanie, pulled her to her feet, and in his best avuncular manner asked what she was feeling. It did not take long for Stephanie to break into tears, which made everyone happy.

Trash Talk is popular in Canada, but there are few, if any, homegrown examples. The closest might be *Camilla*, shown during daytime on CTV, with actor Camilla Scott as the host. It uses the same format as *Springer* – guests, a revved-up audience – but it tends to be rather innocent, only mildly prurient, a saccharine version of Trash Talk. A topic might be "Why Can't I Find My Prince?" If, say, a young woman is suffering the scourge of anorexia, the "expert" on the show suggests, "Why doncha just start eating, then everybody will love you again." The audience, of course, applauds the sage advice and Camilla, reeking of insincerity, flashes an all-is-right-with-the-world smile as the show goes to commercial.

Daytime talk shows offer extremes of content and taste, with *Oprah Winfrey* and *Jerry Springer* at opposite ends of the scale. Oprah tries to make her audience and guests feel good about themselves, to be the best they can be. Springer could care less and does everything to exploit the shock value of human degradation and misery, wrapping it in smarmy platitudes.

In between these two extremes are a number of other daytime talk shows. While Oprah and Jerry are on top of the ratings, *Montel Williams* and *The Rosie O'Donnell Show* are not that far behind. Montel Williams, a former naval intelligence officer, went on air in 1991 after working as a motivational speaker. Rosie O'Donnell, a film and television comedian, began her show in 1996. Her audience and guests come bearing gifts including pastries, Twinkies, stuffed animals, and a basket of corn. Critics, like *Newsweek*'s Rick Marin, writing in the July 15, 1996, edition, believe Rosie should be praised for ". . . singlehandedly saving daytime TV from itself. She's taken the trash out of talk by making nice, not nasty." Nice was in and, surprisingly, it was commercially successful.

The 1998–99 TV season brought two new but very different afternoon talk shows. *Donny and Marie* saw the return of the Osmonds to television. On October 2, 1998, Marie told *Entertainment Weekly*: "We're only limited by imagination, creativity, and anything we want. There's no way to know how things will work out, though." The winsome pair intend to focus on "human-interest guests with heartwarming stories." Why? In an October 1998 *Broadcast Week* interview, Donny told critic Shirley Knott that viewers are looking for "nice." "Something that is a little more lighthearted. People have had it with seriousness. So we're filling a void that seems to be out there." And Marie adds: "We want people to come on the show and have a good time."

The other show? Roseanne is back in her own talk show. *The Roseanne Show* would like to be all things to all people. Her show swings widely from the outrageous – the Big Butt Fashion Show – to the serious – advice to unwed mothers. Sometimes it all comes together, perhaps because Roseanne has turned out to be a good interviewer, but this may not be enough in the competitive world of daytime talk.

Rosie and Roseanne were both stand-up comediennes and actors before taking on their talk shows. Donny and Marie were singers. All three shows bring with them a ready-made audience who now wants to see them in another role. To some extent, though, perhaps each host is imprisoned in an old role. (Roseanne fated always to be the loud-mouthed large woman?) But they do have a chance now to show another side of themselves to their public.

Show Me More

After a recent presentation on talk shows, during which I showed three brief excerpts from *The Jerry Springer Show*, someone came up to me and said, "When you showed the first excerpt, I was disgusted. When you showed the second excerpt, I was interested. And when you cut off the third excerpt, I was disappointed we couldn't see more." What is it about these shows that causes this kind of reaction? It could be that, as Philip Marchand pointed out in the *Toronto Star* on January 4, 1997, "No matter how bad one has been behaving during the day, one can watch these people and still feel oneself to be, by contrast, a valuable and attractive member of the human race."

The Jerry Springer Show covers a range of lurid topics, such as "I'm Pregnant by a Transsexual" and "Teens Having Sex with Their Stepfathers." Another topic was "I Slept with 251 Men in Ten Hours." A sixteen-year-old girl appeared onstage wearing sunglasses to disguise her identity because she wanted to tell how she buried her newborn baby alive in the backyard.

The gasps are audible, the shock authentic (and marketable) and the hypocrisy thick as molten asphalt. The most common explanation for not punching the channel-changer on Trash Talk TV is, "I want to see what happens next." Springer himself harbours no illusions on any special magic he or his show might possess. In the *Playboy* interview, when asked how he became so famous, Springer ingenuously explains: "The job I have requires no skill. Anybody could do what I do. I'm lucky I have the show. I have no particular talent in this area."

Whenever I catch a segment of *Jerry Springer*, when some enraged, inarticulate guest takes a poke at another guest, I am reminded of an encounter, perhaps apocryphal, between the writers Gore Vidal and Norman Mailer. The two men, who do not like each other, found themselves side by side by the canapes at a party in New York. One thing led to another and Mailer suddenly decked Vidal, knocking him to the floor. Vidal slowly got up, brushed himself off, then calmly said to Mailer, "Oh, Norman, there you go again . . . at a loss for words."

There are times when even the producers of Trash Talk TV sense they may be going too far. This happened in May 1998 on *Jerry Springer* on the show about a man who was "married" to his horse and wanted to discuss bestiality. The show was taped, the horse appeared onstage, but at the eleventh hour the producers replaced it with an episode titled "Past Guests Do Battle."

Guests on *Jerry Springer* sign forms stipulating that if they are not what they say they are, if they are perpetrating a hoax, they are liable for damages and the production costs of the show. The hoax the producers worried about happened when four Canadian guests appeared, purporting to be a husband and wife, their babysitter, and the babysitter's boyfriend. After some prompting from Springer, the "husband" confessed to the "wife" that he had been having a sexual liaison with the "babysitter." Turned out all four guests were members of a comedy troupe from Toronto and it was a put-on from start to finish. The comedians face an $80,000 lawsuit.

Jerry and Oprah

It is interesting and worthwhile to understand who these talk-show people are, where they come from, and how they got to do what they do. This is one good starting point to examine just how these shows construct their reality. Invariably you find that hosts started out as ordinary, even low-key and earnest, journalists and broadcasters, whose careers could have gone in any number of directions – then something happened. A friend, who works behind the camera on a popular Canadian television show, calls it "the television disease." He says sometimes you can see the transformation, as if the individual, man or woman, suddenly breaks out in a rash. It happens after a few appearances on camera, followed by some requests for an autograph, perhaps then the obsequies of an overly solicitous maître d'. "Often they're really nice people, then they become monsters."

Jerry Springer, as seen in his show, could be easily dismissed as a shallow, self-important, shameless, pompous, hypocritical clown. But in person, and at public appearances, he comes across as quite likable, self-deprecating, and a performer who is in on the joke. He has been a lawyer, politician, and journalist. He once admitted to having sex with a prostitute and resigned from the Cincinnati City Council, only to be elected later as mayor. It was an accomplishment for Springer, as his background was left-of-centre liberal and Cincinnati is a rather conservative, right-of-centre place.

Springer was born in London, England, after his parents had fled the Holocaust, which claimed the lives of his grandparents. He worked for Senator Robert Kennedy during his presidential campaign in 1968. He launched his broadcasting career in 1982 as a political reporter and commentator on Cincinnati's WLWT-TV, eventually becoming the anchor of Cincinnati's top-rated news show. He won seven Emmys for his nightly television commentaries. When he first became a national talk-show host, Springer's topics were safe for family viewing, involving such issues as "Grandparents Raising Grandkids." Problem was, hardly anyone watched. Facing cancellation, he started to juice up the show with topics such as, "My Girlfriend Is a Call Girl" and "My Boyfriend Turned Out to Be a Girl." He let his hair grow, started mocking his guests ("Go to your room!"). And his star began to rise.

Oprah's star had ascended first. Every year, *Entertainment Weekly* publishes a list of the 101 most powerful people in entertainment. Power includes popularity but much more. As *Entertainment Weekly* says: "Our definition also includes the incalculable: range, clout, the speed with which people return your calls." On top of this list for 1998 is Oprah Winfrey, the first woman and African-American to be in that position.

The Oprah Winfrey Show reaches 33 million viewers a week in the U.S.A. and millions more in the other 132 countries which show it. Her show generates approximately $300 million a year and *Forbes* places her personal wealth at more than half a billion dollars.

When the show was launched in 1985 it was similar to many talk shows of that time. Oprah was seen as the female Donahue. In 1994 she renounced Trash Talk TV and now scatters celebrity interviews within her shows and urges viewers to become better people. Her topics are less likely to be controversial and more likely to be about subjects like anorexia and planning for old age. Yet even now she is not without her critics.

It is the feeble and faked depiction of authenticity, the contrived illusion that we are witnessing real human interaction, real emotion, that accounts for much of the popularity of Trash Talk TV, even the ones that, like Oprah's, aspire to a higher ground. Rick Salutin, in his weekly column in *The Globe and Mail*, describes an *Oprah Winfrey* segment he caught one afternoon that dealt with "healing relationships with fathers." A young father on stage was suing for access to his son, who was in the audience with his mother, the man's ex-wife. As Salutin points out, the mother's disappointment with her ex-husband is because he had not been there for his son when he should have been. On stage, with the father, was a family therapist, who sympathized with the mother but urged her toward reconciliation. The father expressed vague regrets. And from the audience a man arose, confessed his hatred for his own father, a hatred, he said, that lasted beyond his father's death, yet he had eventually forgiven him. He urged the mother to see that a relationship with the father was good for their son.

Salutin concludes: "Speaking solely of my own reactions, most of it felt forced and fake. The penitent dad looked like he was suppressing nuclear rage. The therapist seemed far too happy about being on *Oprah*. And the oh-so-feely audience guy sounded desperate for approval, which he got when Oprah named him her 'angel for today.' Each seemed to me, under a cover of self-exposure and honesty, false and deeply inauthentic – with the exception of the tight-lipped, angry mom, who alone was not bursting with desire to communicate her feelings. . . ."

On the other hand, it is not difficult to find good things about Oprah's program. Speaking at the ceremony where she received an Emmy for Lifetime Achievement, Phil Donahue told Oprah: "More than a great star, you are a twentieth-century political figure. Your good works have touched us all." Among these works would be Oprah's on-air book club which aims to get Americans reading. Once a month she chooses a book for her audience to read – and her audience is substantial. A month later she invites the author on the show to discuss the book over dinner, the impact of which makes an instant best-seller of any book she chooses. Oprah also insists that publishers make the book available in inexpensive paperback editions and donate 10,000 copies of each book to libraries.

In 1997 she launched the Angel Network, which Christopher John Farley, writing in *Time* for October 5, 1998, describes as "an on-going campaign to spur her viewers into good works like building houses for needy families, volunteering at local schools, and saving spare change to fund college scholarships." Her more recent shows contain a "Remembering Your Spirit" segment which offers spiritual advice.

Kate Filion, in an April 1996 article in *Saturday Night*, defended *The Oprah Winfrey Show* when she wrote: "Beneath the crassness and cynicism, many of the shows are genuinely dedicated to consciousness-raising about the horrors of domestic violence, racism, gender discrimination and child poverty. Oprah has probably done more than any other person on this planet to raise public awareness of child abuse." Perhaps it is her own history of being abused and a drug user and of fighting a weight problem that makes her so empathetic to guests, audiences, and viewers alike. That and the fact that she looks and sounds like much of her audience in the U.S.A.

The Good News

Is Trash Talk TV just harmless fun? Or a writ-small version of the same impulse that motivates others to write tell-all autobiographies, exploring their abused lives, their alcoholism, their crimes and misadventures, their salacious errors and excesses? Think of famous movie stars whose careers began on the casting couch. Perhaps "fame" and "celebrity" are the wrong words; maybe all the guests want is "exposure." Maybe they truly believe that a guest spot on *Jerry Springer* could lead to enduring fame, real fortune, or, like the Brando character in *On the Waterfront*, maybe they believe twenty-five seconds of national exposure on TV could make them a "contendah." After all, ordinary mortals become renowned anchorpersons simply because they have good hair, a pleasing facial-bone structure, and an ability to read. Or maybe it's something entirely new, as if the TV camera emits some magical, life-enhancing rays that make dreary, anonymous lives less dreary, less anonymous.

Kate Filion, writes: "If memory serves, many of those now decrying the tastelessness of going public with one's private pain spent decades touting the wisdom of letting it all hang out and will in all likelihood still be self-actualizing when they are hooked up to respirators. When the bourgeoisie looks at the human potential movement in the funhouse mirror provided by talk shows, it doesn't like what it sees. Hence the rephrasing of that classic credo: *'I'm OK, you're . . . in bad taste.'*"

When Trash Talk TV came under bitter attack in the mid-1990s, the magazine *Entertainment Weekly*, its intent doubtless ironical, argued that these programs were not without virtue. They were models of cultural diversity; they led the way in breaking down television taboos; in the Puritan tradition, they encouraged sinners to publicly recant their transgressions; they cheerily encouraged their audiences to consider how much better off they were than the program's benighted guests; and finally, they offered a snug refuge for washed-up celebrities. Burnt-out stars who used to fill in on *Hollywood Squares* and make guest appearances on *Murder, She Wrote* could get their egos boosted by exchanging meaningless banter on a talk show.

Finishing Off the Nights

Television talk shows are first and foremost narcoleptic. But they are also the synthesis of everything that is wrong and mostly rightly despised about television. They are hosted by sycophantic clowns and pander to the postliterate, intellectual underclass that has always been the most desirable demographic of television hucksters. Talk shows thrive because they are cheap to make, easy to produce, and are the ultimate "infomercial," selling celebrities, movies, TV shows, records, comedy acts, models, and most of all the products. . . .

– John Haslett Cuff, *The Globe and Mail*, May 28, 1992

On September 27, 1954, when Steve Allen debuted as the host of NBC's *Tonight Show*, he made a prophecy: "I want to give you the bad news first. This program is going to go on forever." Forty-five years later and one of the longest-running shows on television, *The Tonight Show* might just fulfil that prophecy. Steve Allen is credited with setting the format for the late-night talk show – the opening monologue, the announcer-sidekick, the couch and desk arrangement, some outdoor segments, performances by people with strange talents, and, of course, casual talk with celebrities. When Allen left the show in 1957 to spend more time on his own prime-time show, he was replaced by the unpredictable Jack Paar. Given to emotional outbursts, Paar also conducted brilliant interviews with people like Fidel Castro and Robert Kennedy.

Paar quit in 1962 and the new host, Johnny Carson, was to remain for thirty years. Years later, Carson's name was linked to that of Walter Cronkite. Both of them outlasted any other television personality. Both of them were highly respected by the viewers. The popularity of *The Tonight Show* was amazing under Carson. The show was watched nightly by some 8 million viewers. In 1992, Carson retired and Jay Leno took over.

And then the battle was on between NBC's *The Tonight Show* with Jay Leno and CBS's *Late Show with David Letterman* which debuted August 30, 1993. For the first two years, Letterman's show drew more viewers than Leno's. And other late-night talk shows hosted by the famous and would be famous arrived on the scene. Some stayed, most left – Arsenio Hall, Whoopi Goldberg, Chevy Chase, Dennis Miller, Conan O'Brien.

These shows have been imitated around the world but it is important to remember, as Don Gilmor, writing in *Saturday Night* in September 1998, points out: "The late-night talk show, as defined by Johnny Carson and exemplified by David Letterman and Jay Leno, is an American Creation. It has a peculiarly American energy, driven by false enthusiasm and a cultural preoccupation with celebrity."

These late-night talk shows are the stuff of dreams. What are most of us doing at that time of night, usually after 11:30? We've watched the news, set the alarm, put out the cat, checked on the kids, read for a bit, and are now getting ready to turn out the light. The "real world" most of us live in is coming to a close. We've been fawned over by Regis and Kathie Lee, exhorted by Oprah, titillated by Jerry Springer, and amused by Rosie O'Donnell. Maybe it's time to give talk a rest. But the constructed "media world" is far from over for the day.

Perhaps a realistic final note about TV talk shows comes from the fictional talk show *The Larry Sanders Show*, which started in 1992 and had its finale at the end of the 1997–98 season. In his *Dictionary of Teleliteracy*, David Bianculli shows that he clearly is a fan and admirer of both Garry

Shandling, who plays the fictional Larry Sanders, and the smarts of the show itself. "The stories are so intelligent, believable, and close to the bone that the show has become one of the hottest guest-shot tickets of the nineties. . . ." No pandering here, Bianculli notes, as *The Larry Sanders Show* assumes viewers have a firm grasp of such tradepaper fodder as ratings, shares, time slots, lead-ins, superagents, affiliate clearances, contract ploys, show bookers, and mid-level network executives.

The Larry Sanders Show was fictional, and a comedy, but a comedy that teetered between two realities, the "reality" of a TV talk show and the "reality" of the world of the people who appeared in the talk show. It never underestimated the intelligence of its audience, always played up to the savvy of media-hip viewers. At its best, it often caused us to forget that here was a third reality, the reality that the other two realities were anything but real. If that sounds confusing, you have a taste of what the show did, week after week, to the viewer.

The Larry Sanders Show ended as sharply as it began. The finale is about the finale of the fictional talk show. As he walks off for the last time, the fictional Larry says what would be on the mind of any real talk-show host at the same moment. He says, "I hope we beat Leno!"

8

You Provide the Prose, I'll Provide the War:
Television News

~

Kane's Office, Inquirer, 1898

> *BERNSTEIN: We just had a wire from Cuba, Mr. Kane... [reading]*
> *Food marvellous in Cuba – girls delightful stop could send you prose*
> *poems about scenery but don't feel right spending your money stop*
> *there's no war in Cuba signed Wheeler. Any answer?*
>
> *KANE: Yes. Dear Wheeler – you provide the prose poems – I'll*
> *provide the war.*
>
> — Orson Welles's *Citizen Kane*, 1941

Supposedly based on the real life of newspaper mogul William Randolph Hearst, *Citizen Kane* was controversial and innovative. The above quotation is supposed to have been taken from a conversation between Hearst and one of his reporters in Cuba.

We are watching the news on television. The last item is a "soft" piece, something that might appear on CTV's *The Friday File.* We see a field of trees in Switzerland as a familiar, authoritative voice tells us that the recent warm weather has produced an excellent crop of spaghetti in the Swiss Alps. Peasants in traditional costume cut spaghetti from the trees and lay it in the sun to dry. The voice tells us that the fine weather and the absence of the "spaghetti weevil" have contributed to a bumper crop this year and, better still, the spaghetti has grown to a uniform length.

Whenever I show this clip there is a fluttering of hesitation from the viewers, then someone laughs and soon the room fills with laughter. But some are thinking: Does spaghetti grow on trees? Maybe in the Swiss Alps ...

maybe – where does spaghetti come from? If I showed the same clip to a group of children in Grade 4 or 5 I am sure most of them would believe spaghetti grows on trees. Why? Because the clip, a black-and-white item from an old BBC news show, cleverly uses all of the basic elements that have made television our most "trustworthy" source of news.

Let's look at these basic elements:

- *The Voice of Authority.* The voice was that of the BBC's Richard Dimbleby, for British viewers their most trusted commentator, the equivalent of Walter Cronkite or Dan Rather in the United States, or Lloyd Robertson or Peter Mansbridge in Canada.
- *Seeing Is Believing.* We see the spaghetti trees. We see people cutting spaghetti from the trees. We see the strips of spaghetti, all of uniform length, drying in the sun.
- *Believable Details.* In this case, the "spaghetti weevil," which this year mercifully didn't attack the spaghetti crop. An authoritative voice, a "scientific" term. It must be true. (They could have shown a close-up of any weevil munching on anything.)
- *Background Music.* Most viewers of television and movies, whether they are watching fictional dramas, documentaries, or commercials, pay little attention to the music, yet it is of vital importance. For *The Spaghetti Tree*, they used background music of the type associated with authentic travel items. Sometimes we hear "happy" music, "sad" music, or "The monster is coming" music – anything to lull us into a mood to believe what we are seeing.
- *Local Colour.* The people cutting and gathering the spaghetti are wearing peasant costumes, using farm tools, and at the end the spaghetti is served in traditional bowls to a happy crowd of people at outdoor tables for the traditional feast on the first day of harvest in surroundings that look like the Swiss Alps.

The clip originally ran on the BBC newsmagazine show *Panorama* on April 1, 1957. At the end of the item, Dimbleby appeared on camera to inform the viewers that he – and they – knew very well that spaghetti did not grow on trees but that it grew on the walls of the mines in North Wales.

But what if it wasn't shown on April Fool's Day? And what if it was not a film about the spaghetti harvest but about the Gulf War? Or the riots in Los Angeles in 1992 following the Rodney King verdict? How would you know if what you were seeing and hearing on television was accurate if you had no other sources of information? In their 1992 book *How to Watch TV News*, authors Neil Postman and Steve Powers tell us that "anyone who is not an avid reader of newspapers, magazines and books is by definition unprepared to watch a television news show . . . Anyone who relies exclusively on television for his or her knowledge of the world is making a serious mistake."

Any discussion of television news must always consider the basic fact: TV news is a commercial enterprise whose purpose is to make money as well as to inform. In *How to Watch TV News*, Postman and Powers, who really do not think much of TV news, suggest that viewers should be aware of three things. First, that American television is an unsleeping money machine. Second, while journalists pursue newsworthy events, management often make decisions based on business considerations. Finally, decisions on the form and content of news programs often are made on the basis of information about the viewer, the purpose of which is to keep viewers watching so they will be exposed to commercials.

Postman and Powers cite an example from television coverage of the student uprising in Tiananmen Square: the image of a lone student standing in front of a tank, as if stopping it from going forward. Media critic Jay Rosen says this image suggests that power comes to those who face the barrel of a gun, providing that a camera is recording the act and the act is witnessed by a vast audience. The image of the student in front of the tank is unforgettable, but as Postman and Powers point out, if that is all you knew about the student uprising you did not know very much. You need more information. Who rules China? What rules do they acknowledge? What is the ideology behind the rules? How did the students interpret democracy and freedom?

The image is not enough.

Television networks rarely showcase strong television analysis. Nor are they very willing to discuss the techniques they use with cameras, lighting, sound, music, dubs. Most major newspapers have television and film critics. They often will gleefully report in detail the foibles of their electronic cousins, but how many newspapers have newspaper critics? The best we can hope for are strong letters to the editors correcting inaccuracies, and newspapers willing to print them. Or more movies like *Wag the Dog*, *Pleasantville*, and *The Truman Show* that convey what all television producers know about the clever tricks and spins that are part of everyday news coverage.

Studies show that 80 per cent of Canadians trust television news and believe that what they see on the tube is the truth. They trust television more than newspapers. I could tell you that television and print news is distorted and biased, with examples, but that would be distorting the situation, "media bashing" rather than media education.

My emphasis here is on national evening newscasts, not local news. Local news tends to have the same format, with three or four people sitting at a horseshoe-shaped table, the father-figure anchorman (usually a man), the weather person (an attractive woman or an ordinary-looking fellow trying to do stand-up comedy), and a sports reporter (an Uncle-Bob character who talks loud and dresses louder). They all get along fabulously, nobody's ever in a bad mood, though after reporting that someone's house burned to the ground they manage a flicker of that's-a-darn-shame before moving on to the feel-good piece that ends the show. The marketing strategy seems to be to bring nice, jovial people into your house at suppertime, providing your house isn't the one that has burned to the ground.

A notable exception in Canada is *City Pulse News*, the news program of Citytv in Toronto (owned by CHUM Television, which also runs The National cable stations Space, Much Music, MuchMoreMusic, and Bravo!). When Citytv started this format thirty years ago it was considered revolutionary. It showed the entire newsroom, behind the cameras, editors working on stories, people pushing cameras over the floor, directors cuing on-air people. The anchorpersons walked around, microphones strapped to their heads. They did more live coverage than most, wandering from the static studio, using reporters with handheld videocams. The City Pulse format has spread to many stations across Canada and into the United States and other countries. It looks more exciting and up-to-the-second, but does it make for better, more accurate news? Or perhaps it is another illusion?

Setting the Agenda

The National Media Archive describes itself as "a Computerized Database of Canadian National Television News." It is part of The Fraser Institute, regarded by many as an ultra-conservative think tank, but when it does surveys of television news it does them with diligence. In a report on the television news of 1997, it began by stating that Canadians, when asked to rank newspapers, television, and radio, indicated that television is their primary source of information about public policy. The National Media Archive logged 3,477 stories on CBC and 5,410 on CTV during 1997, identifying the main theme of each story, and the region or country on which the story focused.

In its conclusion, The National Media Archive noted some interesting points about coverage on CBC and CTV. The public may rely on television for its news about public policy but ". . . Canadian television news focuses a relatively small proportion of its news agenda on substantive public policy issues. Governance issues – the public policy side of government – were the second most reported type on CBC, and the third most reported issue type on CTV. Political coverage, that is, news focusing on The Nation's leaders and their strategies and tactics, comprised the primary news agenda item for both networks at 21 per cent of CBC and 18 per cent of CTV's entire news agenda."

Second, CBC gave more substantial coverage to public policy issues while CTV tended to focus more on the "trivial side" of the news. Finally, it was noted that not all the news in 1997 was bad news. Only 7 per cent of CBC's and 5 per cent of CTV's coverage was about war and conflict. Clearly stories about murders were the most reported crime stories, yet CBC only gave 8 per cent and CTV 9 per cent of their total news time to crime reporting.

In the Beginning

Television shapes the way we perceive events, and in so doing it often affects those events themselves. Anything that happens without the presence of the TV camera has become the visual equivalent of the tree falling in the forest. Did it make a sound? Did the event take place?

– Michael Winship, *Television*

TV news has placed us front and centre at events we would otherwise only hear or read about; political conventions and presidential inaugurations, the Los Angeles riots and the Vietnam War, the resignation of Richard Nixon and the horror of the Oklahoma bombing, the trial of O. J. Simpson and the scandals surrounding Bill Clinton, the wedding of Princess Diana and her funeral, Neil Armstrong's walk on the moon and the tragedy of the *Challenger* disaster. TV news can take us almost anywhere in the world in seconds.

It was not always that way. When network news came on air in the late 1940s, it consisted of an announcer reading from a script. There were few, if any, visuals. Early television news was no more than televised radio news.

Although TV news basically remained confined to a studio until the mid 1960s – cameras were too bulky to move around and both jet travel and satellite technology were just beginning – the 1950s saw some superb television journalists. Among them were Edward R. Murrow, Walter Cronkite, Chet Huntley, and David Brinkley.

NBC was the first nightly news out of the gate on February 16, 1948. Then, on February 14, 1949, John Cameron Swayze became the first star of TV news. His show, *The Camel News Caravan*, was the first TV news program to show newsreel footage, and in 1954 became the first to broadcast in colour. *The Camel News Caravan* became *The Huntley–Brinkley Report* on October 29, 1956, co-anchored by veteran newsmen Chet Huntley and David Brinkley. The show ran for almost fourteen years remaining consistently in the top spot. When Huntley retired in 1970, the program was renamed *NBC Nightly News* with David Brinkley and John Chancellor. They were succeeded by co-anchors Roger Mudd and Tom Brokaw in 1982, with Brokaw becoming sole anchor in 1983. When the Berlin Wall opened, Brokaw was the first network anchor on the scene.

CBS entered the TV news field on May 3, 1948, with *Douglas Edwards with The News*, a title it kept for most of its run. In the forty-one years that followed, CBS has had only three other anchors – Walter Cronkite, Connie Chung, and Dan Rather. Cronkite, who succeeded Edwards in April of 1962, came from print and radio news. During his coverage of World War II, he was chosen to cover the Normandy invasion by air, the only reporter so chosen.

Cronkite was more than a reporter. He had a strong influence on many of the events that shaped the U.S.A. in the 1960s and 1970s. It is his coverage and commentary during the days following the assassination of John F. Kennedy that we remember. But possibly most significant of all was his coverage of the Vietnam War following the 1968 Tet offensive. His reports were watched by millions across the United States. His February 27, 1968, report became a turning point in convincing Americans that the war was wrong. Cronkite, who seldom made any editorial comment, said: "To say that we are closer to victory today is to believe, in the face of the evidence, the optimists who have been wrong in the past . . . the only rational way out then will be to negotiate – not as victors, but as an honorable people who lived up to their pledge to defend democracy and did the best they could."

In 1974, the people of the United States voted Cronkite their most trusted newscaster. Cronkite retired as anchor at age sixty-five in 1981. He returned to cover special events, most recently to CNN as co-anchor to cover John Glenn's return to space in October 1998. Cronkite's successor was Dan Rather who, after a period of co-anchoring with Connie Chung, was named sole anchor in May 1995. The show was retitled *The CBS Evening News with Dan Rather*.

On October 12, 1953, ABC came on air with *ABC World News* hosted by John Daly. From Daly's departure in 1960 until 1983, many anchors came and went. Among them were James C. Hagerty, who had been Eisenhower's press secretary, John Cameron Swayze, who had anchored *The Camel News Caravan*, and Peter Jennings, a twenty-six-year-old Canadian when he arrived in 1965. Jennings left in 1967. In 1976, CBS made Barbara Walters an offer she could not refuse and, leaving NBC's *Today* show, she became co-anchor with Harry Reasoner. July 1978 brought a new title – *ABC World News Tonight* – and a new format. The anchor system was replaced by four news desks: Frank Reynolds in Washington, Peter Jennings in London, Max Robinson in Chicago, and Barbara Walters in New York. In 1983, Peter Jennings took over as sole anchor and, by the end of the 1980s, had helped take CBS to the top of the ratings for network news.

These comings and goings have been significant because millions of viewers look to these newscasters for guidance, reassurance, and insight into what they take to be the real world. In addition, the news reports are seen as valuable both for the advertising they draw directly and the prestige they lend their respective networks.

What's News in News?

TV news has come a long way from its start as televised radio. The authoritative newscaster symbolized by Walter Cronkite represented television news at its finest. It's unlikely that any reporter will ever again enjoy such status. As technology gives us more and better images faster than ever before, the TV producer who chooses them is replacing the TV journalist as the one determining what we perceive as news. Also, as Steven Stark points out in *Glued to the Set*, Cronkite was very much "part of an era when paternalism was still acceptable and authority figures had more authority. After the experiences of Vietnam and Watergate, which he helped present to the American people, the public grew not to trust *anyone* anymore . . . This new, atomized world of television would combine with a new, skeptical America to ensure that there could never again be another Walter Cronkite."

Who? What? Where? When? Why?

Every newspaper reporter should answer the questions, Who? What? Where? When? Why? And should do it in the first paragraph as nearly as possible. This is the first and greatest commandment in the matter of journalistic style and the penalty for breaking it is the wastebasket and swift oblivion.
– Robert Karl Manoff and Michael Schudson, *Reading the News*, 1986

In journalism, these "five Ws" come from an era when "news" meant print news – before radio, long before television. This advice to reporters, now nearly a century old, has become not only the first commandment but the second nature of American journalism.

My colleague O'Malley thinks Manoff and Schudson must have been writing in jest, or with heavy irony. He regards the rule of five Ws as "one of those earnest dictums that accounts, more than anything else, for making most newspapers as dull as they have become. So many talented newspaper writers have squirmed under the duty of cramming these answers into the first paragraph, but the dictum continues, passing from one dreary journalism class to another. No matter that a radio news item might begin with a telling quote, or a television news item with a shot of an airplane exploding on a runway."

O'Malley suggests if you want to go back to the glory days of print reporting, then go *way* back – fifty or one hundred years ago – to see how this "first commandment" of journalism was adhered to by some rather noteworthy "reporters," like Victor Hugo and Ernest Hemingway.

Ernest Hemingway, who began his newspaper reporting career with the *Toronto Star*, reported from Spain in April 1937 to *The New York Times*, demonstrating the sparse, vivid style readers later would encounter in *For Whom the Bell Tolls*:

"MADRID, APRIL 24 – The window of the hotel is open and, as you lie in bed, you hear the firing in the front line seventeen blocks away. There is rifle fire all night long. The rifles go 'tacrong, carong, craang, tacrong,' and then a machine gun opens up. It has a bigger caliber and is much louder – 'rong, cararibg [*sic*], rong, rong.'"

O'Malley's dictum for journalists would be: "Go out and see something, listen to something, then come back and tell us what you saw and heard."

But now, for television, I'll use "the five Ws" as a framework to discuss television news.

Who?

We want the best person, period – and Canadians are hardly exotic . . . Canadians do more with less.

        – David Westin, President ABC News (*Maclean's*, June 22, 1998)

Herber Gans, in his 1980 book *Deciding What's News*, explains that people who make the news fall into two distinct categories: Knowns and Unknowns. The Knowns come from the political, economic, social, and cultural elites. The Unknowns are ordinary people. Not surprisingly, Gans found that the Knowns make national news programs four times more often than Unknowns. He also concluded that television news is primarily about people, Knowns and Unknowns, and that less than 10 per cent of the stories he observed on television were about abstractions, objects, and animals.

Despite their considerable energy and best intentions, few reporters witness events firsthand. Usually they rely on what others tell them, often those involved in events or eyewitnesses to it, or knowledgeable "sources" or "contacts" the reporters have cultivated. News reporting is supposed to be "objective," which is usually interpreted to mean that reporters try to keep themselves out of the story as much as possible. The merits of "objective journalism" are a constant source of discussion at journalism seminars.

For years it was conventional wisdom that a reporter should never use the personal pronoun. But, more recently, others have argued that the reporter can never really remove himself or herself from the story. In their view, use of the personal "I" simply demonstrates the truth that the reporter always puts a slant on what he writes, by the selection of images and quotations, by their placement in the text, by the words that he or she uses to describe people and events. The reporter constructs reality and the reader negotiates its meaning in the interpretation of the story. As the third key concept reminds us, we all bring our backgrounds, life experiences, education, and biases to whatever we encounter.

News is not reality. Every news item on television – and other media – is carefully constructed, a mixture of image and sound that has been assembled to tell a story that will capture the viewer's attention. The significant "who" in this context is the "who" that makes these decisions, chooses these images and sounds, and presents this perspective to us on a daily basis. It is someone like you and me, the only difference being that this someone happens to be working in the media. He or she has nighttime fears, indigestion, worries about the kids, car troubles, and occasional bursts of happiness. On average, "they" are us.

Those in control of the media – such as owners, publishers, editors-in-chief – set the agenda for the people who work for them, who in turn set the agenda for the consumers of news. The written and unwritten directives set in place by those who control the media have a major influence on the way stories are presented. In an article in *The Nation* in June 1998, Arthur Kent, a former news correspondent for NBC, wrote: ". . . only recently, because of takeovers by corporations inexperienced with, or hostile to, responsible journalism, have the news divisions of ABC, NBC, and CBS come to be managed solely as profit centers. As any statistical or anecdotal sampling of program content demonstrates, the quest for ratings now outweighs virtually all traditional editorial ideals of broadcast news, such as practicing restraint instead of sensationalism and establishing, each day, a responsible balance between domestic and foreign coverage." In order to make money, TV news must above all be entertaining. This is why TV pays big money to good, experienced, and respected journalists, luring them from the dull responsibility of journalism to the bright lights and fast lanes of entertainment.

An Associated Press story in July 1998 reported that NBC *News* agreed to a new contract for broadcaster Tom Brokaw that pays him $7 million a year. A new contract for Geraldo Rivera reportedly was for $30 million over six years. Katie Couric, the host of *NBC News Today*, had her salary tripled to $7 million.

The reason for the big money is simple: ratings. Shows like *Today* and *Nightly News* and *Dateline NBC* have been regularly whomping their competitors. All of which prompted Robert Lichter, director of the Washington-based Center for Media and Public Affairs, to remark: "This doesn't blur the line between news and entertainment. It reminds us that there is no line. Journalists don't make big bucks, entertainers do. So smart journalists become entertainers."

A celebrity has power. Stars usually get what they want. They know their star appeal gets higher ratings, and higher ratings bring in more money, so why shouldn't they get a good chunk of it?

An interesting example of the power of celebrity occurred in the summer of 1998 in the aftermath of an embarrassing news fiasco on CNN the month before. CNN's magazine show, *NewsStand*, reported that U.S. commandos used Sarin nerve gas on American defectors in Laos as part of "Operation Tailwind" in the 1970s. The program caused a sensation and was given greater credibility when *Time* followed up with a story based on the facts uncovered by *NewsStand*. Alas, CNN retracted the story two weeks later after a legal review determined that the claims made on *NewsStand* were not supported by evidence. CNN's top military analyst, retired Major-General Perry Smith, resigned in protest, calling the *NewsStand* report "sleazy journalism."

Ted Turner, the founder of CNN, said the incident was one of the worst moments of his life. "This is a terrible embarrassment to all of us at CNN," he told reporters at a meeting of the Television Critics Association in

Pasadena, California. Then, citing an article he had read in the *Columbia Journalism Review*, Turner went on to say: "There's a lot of trivialization, a lot of overemphasis of Princess Diana's death and Monica Lewinsky. We're doing a disservice to our readers, our country and to the future of humanity if we don't deal with the important media issues of our time and of the future, and just deal with tabloid journalism." According to Chris Dafoe in *The Globe and Mail*, who attended the meeting in Pasadena, Turner singled out local television news as the worst offender. "There's nothing but one fire, one killing . . . so little substantive," Turner said. "And then at the end . . . they'll tell some little slice of life story, you know, to keep you from blowing your brains out."

Meanwhile, back at the station, heads rolled. Pam Hill, the producer of *NewsStand*, was forced to resign. April Oliver and Jack Smith, the story producers responsible for the story, were fired. But it was Peter Arnett, the star reporter who made such a name for himself and the CNN network when he covered the Gulf War from inside Iraq, who had hosted the *NewsStand* episode, thus bringing to the story his credibility and considerable celebrity. Of all the main players, Arnett was the only one who didn't get fired. CNN did not exactly rush Arnett back on the air but they kept him on staff. His next appearance on CNN was four months later.

Arnett's name appeared as a byline on the 2,000-word nerve-gas story in *Time* (*Time* is CNN's partner at Time Warner) but Arnett insisted he did not contribute "one comma" to it. However, he certainly allowed both CNN and *Time* to use his journalistic credibility and reputation to "sell" the story on television and in the magazine. Arnett explained his *Time* byline as something he agreed to do for "marketing reasons."

On the matter of CNN's nerve-gas story and Peter Arnett, and the larger issue of celebrity journalism and journalism-as-entertainment, Frank Rich said in a column in *The New York Times*: ". . . even if he only 'read the script' on camera – lending his face, voice, prestige and Pulitzer-Prize-winning credibility to its words – does that absolve him of responsibility for its contents, like an emcee on a quiz show? Is he really still a journalist, or does he just play one on TV? And if he just plays one, does that mean TV news stars should be less accountable for what they lip-sync than Milli Vanilli?" On the matter of TV's lust for ratings, Rich added: ". . . there's nothing wrong with high ratings for TV news – or high circulation for newspapers and magazines. If you don't make a profit, you're out of business. But which business is it – journalism or showbiz?"

There has been a lot of this recently. Patricia Smith admitted to inventing people and quotations in her *Boston Globe* newspaper columns. Stephen Glass, a reporter with *The New Republic*, was fired for fabricating material in his articles. Television reporter Cokie Roberts admitted she filed what looked like a live report from the White House when in fact she stood in a studio wearing an overcoat while wintry shots of the White House were projected on a blue screen behind her.

The chickens might be coming home to roost. A *Newsweek* poll released in the summer of 1998, after the CNN goof, showed that for the first time ever more than half the American public (53 per cent) consider news reporting as "often inaccurate." More telling, the same poll said that 77 per cent of those surveyed believe journalists are more concerned about ratings and profits than they used to be. And more than 75 per cent, two out of three surveyed, say the news business has "gone too far in the direction of entertainment."

Meanwhile, the dismissed producers of the nerve-gas story on CNN said they will stand by the story, which means they believe it was accurate. Time will tell.

But, they are stars. And here in Canada we have had our own dynasty of news anchors from Lorne Greene during World War II to Stanley Burke, Knowlton Nash, Peter Mansbridge, and Lloyd Robertson. At the eleventh Gemini Awards held in Toronto on May 1997, three familiar figures walked onstage dressed in white ties and tails and stood before music stands, a fun takeoff of The Three Tenors: Luciano Pavarotti, Jose Careras, and Placido Domingo. A voice announced, "Ladies and gentlemen, the Three Anchors!" The CBC's Peter Mansbridge (an anchorman "discovered" when someone heard him announcing flight arrivals and departures at an airport in Churchill, Manitoba) narrated the plot of *The Barber of Seville* as a two-line news item. Knowlton Nash, Mansbridge's predecessor at the CBC (as *Maclean's* reported) "reduced the libretto of *Carmen* to a routine homicide report." CTV's Lloyd Robertson, twirling a white handkerchief to the bars of *I Pagliacci*, won a roar of approval when he announced: "A clown cried today. No Canadians were involved."

Lloyd Robertson, Peter Mansbridge, Peter Kent, Tom Brokaw, Peter Jennings, Dan Rather: some of their faces are as familiar to us as members of our own family. They may indeed be celebrities – Ted Baxter certainly considered himself the celebrity in Mary Tyler Moore's newsroom, as did Jim Dial on *Murphy Brown* – but more than their personal fame is at stake. A *Maclean's* magazine story on the television industry and the phenomenon of the "anchorman" observed: "Ratings and millions in ad revenue ride on the inflection of authority in their voices and how viewers feel about their countenances or tailoring. They're very important icons of a network's identity and integrity."

More than 80 per cent of North Americans get their news from television and we have come to trust these anchors to be our guides through the dizzying information-overload that comes at us from all directions. (Trying to cope alone with this bombardment of information, as one media observer put it, is "like trying to drink from a fire hose.") At the end of the day we are content to sit and watch our favourite anchor, as the *Maclean's* article said, "frame reality into a 22-minute sampler of digestible sound bites, unsullied by passion or discernible opinion."

And what about anchor*men?* Why such inordinate representation of male anchors when women are doing so well in so many other corners of the media? In the United States and Canada networks use women to moderate political debates, cover elections, report on wars and famines, but men remain in the dominant position at the anchor desk. Barbara Walters and Connie Chung served as co-anchors on ABC and CBS respectively, but they never got to anchor on their own. In Canada, at the CBC, Pamela Wallin served for a time as co-anchor with Mansbridge, but it did not last long.

Some viewers still have "a father knows best" mindset, meaning it feels more natural for a father-figure anchorman to be telling us what happened in the world today. After all, is not hoisting an "anchor" man's work? I've heard, too, that the proper image for an anchorman is "believability," which explains why it is not always necessary, or even desirable, that the man be attractive. Few ever swooned gazing upon the grandfatherly countenance of Walter Cronkite, but people tended to believe him. A friend paraphrases an old truism about sincerity, saying: "If you can fake believability you've got it made." A woman who works in television said she once heard someone refer to the anchor desk as the "actor-desk," after which she was never able to regard it in any other way.

Worth noting, too, how acceptable Canadians seem to be on American television as anchors. ABC employees joke that their call letters stand for "America By Canadians." The two best-known are Peter Jennings at ABC and Morley Safer, who has co-hosted CBS's *60 Minutes* for nearly thirty years. Is it the "neutral" Canadian accent? Or do Canadians look more honest, trustworthy – believable? Do Canadians convey a more reliable perspective because Canada is not a super power? Perhaps Canadians are better trained, perhaps better seasoned, like baseball players having apprenticed in the minor leagues before making it to the majors (what the players call The Show).

But anchors, male or female, could be on their way out. Consider that we now inhabit a 500-channel universe where news is available not on an hourly basis, but every hour twenty-four hours a day, seven days a week, locally and nationally. Ontario's *Cable Pulse 24*, run by CHUM Television, uses a split screen to cover news, weather, traffic, and sports all at once. No waiting for the evening news when you can punch in any time day or night for an update. Right now, this looks like the wave of the future and the authoritative anchorman may be a thing of the past. Perhaps the frayed nerves caused by information overload and millennial anxiety will make us yearn again for the return of a calm, believable Cronkite.

What?

The very idea of trying to cram the entire world into twenty-two minutes is a little ludicrous. TV news is, after all, like a newspaper that has only one page – the front page.

— Robert Goldberg and Gerald Jay Goldberg, in *Anchors*

What is television news? The notion that "news" – print, radio, TV – is simply a mirror reflecting reality is a huge conceit. All media products are constructions of reality. What we see as "news" is not a reflection of reality, but a re-creation of what actually happened. A stationary camera trained, say, on Niagara Falls does not convey the reality of the waterfall. It's a version of reality as seen from a single location. It has a focus, an angle, a perspective.

This can be especially true in coverage of political events. When I first saw a political convention on television back in the 1950s, what I was watching, though I did not know it at the time, was "gavel to gavel" coverage of a true expression of democracy. I don't think that the same thing can be said of any recent political convention. These gatherings have become carefully staged media events, of which every aspect, from what takes place to the time it is broadcast, is carefully contrived.

With television news the construction may include images and sounds recorded at the event itself, either from the perspective (POV) of the videographer, or of the director who gives the instructions. The news construction may include a news anchor's comments either on camera or as a voiceover. It could be a man's voice, a woman's voice, a calm voice, an excited voice, a cynical voice, a recognizably authoritative voice (like Richard Dimbleby narrating *The Spaghetti Tree*). It could include special effects, graphics, animation. Every element has a purpose. Every element is intended to elicit a particular response from the viewer.

All sorts of questions should be asked by viewers watching TV news. As Neil Postman exhorts us in *Amusing Ourselves to Death*: "Ask questions, break the spell." For instance, why did they choose a low angle in this shot? Low angles, shooting upward at a subject, makes the subject look powerful, in charge – sometimes menacing. Or a high angle, shooting down on a subject, which tends to make the subject look less powerful, even insignificant. Professional news reporters and anchors know this as well as they know their allergies and favourite desserts. They know their own good angles and their bad angles. They know the value of being on good terms with the person operating the camera, or the person directing the person operating the camera. And if they know this, surely it follows that, if they wished, they could make someone look less good in front of the camera – or more significant, or insignificant.

If a topic under discussion is controversial – let's say abortion – do we hear from only, or mostly, those in favour of abortion, or those against abortion? Are those against abortion depicted as hesitant, nervous, poorly educated? Or arrogant bullies? If the segment is taped to be shown later, who selects the parts to be shown and the parts not to be shown? On what criteria? Is this person a pro-abortionist, an anti-abortionist, or someone who would rather be singing in a barbershop quartet?

Sometimes the media appear to agree about what constitutes news. (This, in itself, is revealing.) Equally interesting: occasionally an item is treated as news by one media outlet but not another. Obviously, someone is making a selection and the items included may tell us something about that individual – and the firm that issues the paycheques. All we can safely say is that what appears on TV news isn't necessarily what the news must cover but what the news wants to cover. Of course, differences may have simple explanations too. One station may just happen to have excellent visuals (a fire, a car crash, a tornado) that the other station doesn't.

Since 1976, a media watchdog in the United States called "Project Censored" has been exploring whether there is a systematic omission or under-reporting of certain issues in the national media. In 1993, "Project Censored Canada" was formed to perform the same service north of the border. Project Censored Canada defines censorship as the "suppression of information, whether purposeful or not, by any method – including bias, omission, under-reporting, or self-censorship – which prevents the public from fully knowing what is happening in the world."

According to the Associated Press, the top story in the United States in 1993 was "The Flood of 1993." That same year, Project Censored declared that the top "under-reported story" was "The U.S. Is Killing Its Young." Project Censored based this on a study by the United Nations' Children's Fund, which revealed that in 1993 the United States was the most danger-ous place in the world for young people because nine out of ten young people murdered in industrialized countries that year were murdered in the United States.

Other reasons why some stories do not get reported on television news:

- They are not "flashy" enough to keep people watching.
- They are not in the best interests, financial or otherwise, of the owners, shareholders, or advertisers.
- Investigative stories are more expensive than mere reportage.
- They are considered "too complex" for the general public.

A story of global importance that almost didn't make it was the 1984 Ethiopian famine. In 1983, reporter David Kline travelled to Ethiopia and returned with footage of emaciated adults and children starving to death. CBS, NBC, and PBS all turned him down. Kline then wrote a story of his visit to Africa and the dying people and was turned down by most mainstream magazines. *The Christian Science Monitor* finally published it but the story received little attention. Early in 1984, an ABC television correspondent in Rome learned that millions were dying in Africa because of the severe drought. He asked to go to Africa to do the story but was told the assignment would be too expensive.

Later in 1984, a BBC television crew in Ethiopia captured the stark reality of children starving to death. There was an instant, global response to the BBC story, which was carried on television networks around the world. It has been estimated that the lives of seven million Ethiopians were saved by money raised from sympathetic viewers. Much of the credit for this is due to rock musicians who contributed their moral and vocal support, starting with the British song "Do They Know It's Christmas?" This was followed by the American "We Are The World" and the Canadian "Tears Are Not Enough."

Sports Night, a sitcom about sports news reporting, tackled the question of what doesn't get reported from an ethical point of view. A young female reporter had been sent to do a pre-interview with a football player who had been jailed for beating his girlfriend. The football player sexually assaulted the reporter. The producer of the show – a woman – could convince the reporter not to press charges so that they could use the incident as leverage to get the football player to talk about the attack on his girlfriend. Although the producer initially decides to go with this in order to scoop the other network news shows, she backs down at the last moment and cancels the interview. The reporter then brings charges against the football player. It would be nice to believe that this is what would happen not only in the "media world" but also in the "real world."

Knowlton Nash, veteran journalist and former anchor of CBC's *The National*, in his book *Trivia Pursuit* points out that journalism's problems are caused by what it deals with – "its current obsession with immediacy, with the pursuit of trivia, with entertainment and gossip." And it deals with these because they bring in money. TV news is a business and Nash quotes Canadian communicator Harold Innis: "The type of news essential to an increase in circulation, to an increase in advertising . . . was essentially that which catered to excitement."

Where?

> *Journalists construct images of neighborhoods and cities, of the nation and the world around it, and even of the universe, images which for many of us constitute most of what we know about the world beyond our immediate circle of experience.*
>
> – Daniel C. Hallin in *Reading the News*

Most news stories begin by telling us where. A plane crashed. Where? Near Peggy's Cove, Nova Scotia. The prime minister holds a news conference. Where? Beijing. But the answer to *Where?* gives us other information. In his book *Reading the News*, Daniel C. Hallin lists five ways in which place provides information about a story.

1. *Place as Authority.* Authority can be instantly established if, say, the newsreader announced that the prime minister is speaking from Ottawa, or the president from the White House.

2. *Place as Useful Information.* The sports announcer tells us that the Blue Jays will play their next game in Boston.

3. *Place as Social Connection.* When Elvis Stojko skates in the Olympics and we are told that his hometown is Richmond Hill viewers in that town somehow participate in a distant happening.

4. *Place as Setting.* Lake Louise, Tuktoyaktuk, the Champs Élysées, war torn Bolivia. The setting can suggest adventure, tranquility, luxury, danger. The reporter may – apparently – be risking life and limb to find the truth, or taking his ease while speaking from a hotel room beside the mini-bar. It is important to remember that one person's "far away" is another person's "here."

5. *Place as Subject.* Consider Toronto's recent bid to host the 2006 Olympics. The visuals could be designed to make Toronto look wonderful (perhaps a handout from those working for Toronto's bid) or they could depict, say, homeless people to suggest the money could be spent on something worthier. Again, news anchors are often flown in to the site of a disaster or war or funeral – the Swissair crash off Peggy's Cove, Nova Scotia in the fall of 1998, or the funeral of Diana, Princess of Wales, in London, or the great flood in Winnipeg. At such times, the

anchor's presence makes the place itself the subject of the report and gives it importance. A reality is constructed that would not exist if the anchor remained in the studio.

The obvious value of *Where?* is the way it can give us context, connect us to the world and our community, what McLuhan meant by "the global village." "Journalists not only tell us where a particular event took place, according to Hallin, they also tell us where we are in a more general and much more important sense."

Who can ever forget the first pictures from the moon, the ethereal beauty of our earth seen from the moon? Surely an instance of the image of place as life-changing experience.

When?

All the reporters in the world, working all the hours of the day, could not witness all the happenings in the world.

– Walter Lippmann

Manoff and Schudson, in their book *Reading the News,* say the reporter's ideal answer to the question *When?* is "Just an instant ago, so recently that no one else even knows it happened."

Possibly few people really care whether CBC or CTV or Global or ABC or CNN gets a story first. The only people who care are the news people themselves, as if they are in a personal and deadly competition with everyone else in the business, including their colleagues. This does not always serve the best interest of the consumer of news, who, given the choice, surely would prefer accuracy over speed.

Another part of *When?* applies to that most artificial and arbitrary sacred cow in journalism known as The Deadline, especially in electronic journalism. Much of our news today comes from public officials, in carefully prepared press releases, at staged media conferences. If the news is good, its release is managed for maximum exposure. If not so good, the "news" can be delivered into benign obscurity by waiting until after The Deadline.

Why?

> *Americans are no longer clear about what news is worth remembering or how*
> *any of it is connected to anything else . . . We know many things (everything*
> *is revealed) but about very little (nothing is known).*
>
> – Neil Postman and Steve Powers, *How to Watch TV News*

Why? This is what most of us want to learn from news stories, and usually it is what we never find out, probably because too much emphasis is placed on the other questions. On a twenty-two-minute news show, there is no time to go into the complex details of *Why?* It costs a lot of money to get into the *Why?* And it's likely to require more words than visuals – the dreaded talking heads. Viewers might start channel-hopping, looking for more *Who? What? Where?* and *When?*

And so, "If it bleeds, it leads." The top story must grab the attention of the audience: a raging fire, a murder, a violent clash on a picket line, a scandal in high places. You don't lead off with a background piece on the Crow's Nest Freight Rate. You don't lead off with a story on the biggest watermelon grown in Huron County (though you might end the newscast with it). You grab the viewers' attention and, when you have it, move quickly on to another item, and then another before they lose interest or push the remote.

Early in 1998, the story broke about the affair between Monica Lewinsky and President Clinton. The *What?* was the tryst itself, between a young political intern and the president of the United States. The *Where?* was fascinating: The White House. Nobody much cared about the *When?* The other details were much more titillating. *How?* Yes, the logistics were interesting, considering the elaborate security measures one expects surround the chief executive officer of the most powerful nation on earth. *Why?* Boys will be boys, even Good 'Ol Boys from Arkansas? Political gain on young Lewinsky's part? Power as aphrodisiac?

CBC-TV dealt with the Lewinsky/Clinton affair in June 1998, focusing on how the U.S. media covered the scandal. According to studies used in the CBC account, nearly 70 per cent of television viewers in the United States considered the coverage of the Lewinsky/Clinton story excessive, a "media feeding frenzy." Most viewers also believed that the frenzied coverage had more to do with ratings than the public's need to know. And even less to do with what people said they wanted to know. A survey running in October 1998 on *The Hollywood Reporter* web site found that 55 per cent of Americans preferred to watch a soap opera over any presidential impeachment hearings.

The CBC show dug deeper, daring to probe the *Why?* of the matter, going back to the Watergate scandal, the investigative journalism of reporters Bob Woodward and Carl Bernstein, which eventually led to the resignation of President Richard Nixon. Turfing a president out of office has more journalistic cachet than getting the goods on the local dogcatcher, even the local mayor. The tough, persistent, aggressive, and obviously accurate work of Woodward and Bernstein brought new respect to journalism when it needed it. The success of the Woodward/Bernstein investigation spawned a new generation of reporter-sleuths hot on the trail of scandal in high places, reaching full circle twenty-five years later with the Lewinsky/Clinton scandal.

On the CBC show, TV news reporters argued that even if people don't want to know about something like the Lewinsky/Clinton scandal, it *is* news and must be reported. However, the CBC's own reporter, David Halton, suggested otherwise. "In an age of instant deadlines," he said, "the truth is often the first casualty." I wonder how reporters reacted when they found out that polls taken in July of 1998 showed that 58 per cent of Americans had a "favourable" impression of President Clinton while 69 per cent had an "unfavourable" impression of Monica Lewinsky.

There is great pressure on networks to get the story first, get 'em hooked, then follow up quickly with new details. Reporters now have access to the Internet, a rich source of unverified gossip. There was an Internet story about Monica Lewinsky keeping a semen-stained dress after one of her encounters with Clinton. *Let's go with it,* say the news media. *If we don't, someone else will. If it's not true, we'll get another story out of the denial.* When *Who?* and *When?* overtake *What?* and *Why?* the real casualty becomes responsible journalism.

The competition among TV news-gatherers and reporters is much fiercer now than ten or twenty years ago. In the mid 1980s in the United States, ABC, NBC, and CBS had the attention of 80 per cent of viewers. By 1998 they had less than 50 per cent of the viewers. This dwindling viewership had a tremendous impact on the corporations who own the networks.

It resulted in increased pressure to maintain and increase ratings, which in turn gave more emphasis to news-as-entertainment. Coverage of foreign news plummeted, dropping by 30 per cent in the ten years up to 1998. The line between tabloid journalism and solid reporting has become increasingly blurred, with more stories on individuals than institutions, issues, and ideas.

There has been a small backlash, predominantly in the southern United States, from TV news stations that report only "good news" stories. No murders, rapes, wars, economic crises, or natural disasters – just feel-good, happy stories. Some might argue such stations are addressing an imbalance, giving viewers a choice, but the result is as damaging to the reputation of journalism as the scandal-mongering, media-frenzied folks who bring us the latest episode of the Lewinsky/Clinton affair, from any source, reliable or unreliable.

An editorial in the September 5, 1998, edition of *The Globe and Mail* sums up: "We also know that TV plays to its strength: pictures. The more visually arresting the pictures and the scenes, the more compelled we are to watch. So when the TV lineup editors are forced to choose between showing us discussion or devastation in our society, devastation wins out, even if its impact on our lives is more remote than the debate we need to see."

But there is a place on television that tries to give us the *Why?* The programs we call "newsmagazines" have their roots in the *See It Now* series hosted by Edward R. Murrow from 1951 to 1958. Their analysis ran the gamut from spending time in Korea learning about the people and the culture during the Korean War to the famous shows attacking McCarthyism. By 1997, ten hours of prime-time television were devoted to newsmagazines, from *60 Minutes* (1968) to *Dateline NBC* (1992), *Primetime Live* (1989), and *20/20* (1978).

Canada has its own newsmagazines with CTV's venerable *W5*, now in its 32nd year. The CBC has both *The Journal*, which, when it began in 1982, made CBC the first North American network to have a daily prime-time newsmagazine, and *the fifth estate*, now in its 24th season.

Some critics say that behind each newsmagazine is a failed drama. When a drama fails, it is cheaper to replace it with a newsmagazine, which costs about $400,000, a third of the cost of a new drama series. Newsmagazines also serve as great counter-programming tools. Why risk a new drama against something that you know will beat it in the ratings? Also, some news-magazines are deliberately scheduled against something like *Monday Night Football* to provide an alternative for those who don't like sports.

Still, newsmagazines do go into the *Why?* of a story. And they are popular (they consistently finish in the top twenty at the end of the year). A recent survey showed that 51 per cent of their audience believe them to be truthful.

All the News All the Time

In the mid 1980s a group of executives at CBS were discussing Ted Turner's CNN, the all-news network that was launched June 1, 1980. Their comments were not favourable. A few years later they were eating their words. As one of these executives, Jon Katz, wrote in *Rolling Stone* in September 17, 1998: "Turner's CNN hit broadcast journalism like one of the SCUD missiles fired during the Gulf War – seen live via cable. CNN was a stunning idea, a slap in the prosperous faces of the three network-news divisions, a radical challenge."

Today we have not only CNN but also CNBC, MSNBC, and Fox News Channel in the U.S.A.; and in Canada, CBC's *Newsworld* and *RDI*, as well as CTV's *News 1*. They offer us news in every conceivable format. They have ensured that never again will the regular broadcast networks dominate TV news. But in the United States the question is whether or not all news channels can survive. Last year, CNN's audience dropped 5 per cent. On any given day some thirty-four million people in the United States watch professional wrestling. But only 376,000 households tune in to CNN, while Fox News manages to reach 36,000. Cable news is a medium which has never fully realized its potential.

Cable news is, in turn, challenged by news on the Internet. Internet news is of many different kinds. Famous newspapers from around the world as well as television news programs have many of their items posted on the Internet for instant access at any time. In October 1998, Canadian Press introduced *Command News* which would "bring the power of real-time Canadian news to the corporate and government desktop . . . organizations that need to stay on top of breaking news can do so through the Internet without leaving their desks." Basically this means that anyone can access the same source of information used by Canadian newspapers, radio, and television stations to find out what is happening.

Something new and different is the provocative *The Drudge Report*, run by thirty-one-year-old Matt Drudge out of his shabby Los Angeles apartment. What shot him to prominence was his revelation that although *Newsweek* had the Clinton and Lewinsky story it was sitting on it. Millions of people visited his web site for details and the major news sources then felt compelled to report the story themselves. Although Drudge is not always correct, he has called attention to a fundamental question about television news – is media power too concentrated?

People who give us the news on TV aren't much different from us. Being on TV gives their opinions more exposure, not more validity. As Peter Jennings urged when speaking about both TV and print news: "Viewer, reader, listener – beware. Be critical!" Watch carefully, think critically. And keep an imaginary custard pie within pitching distance.

9

Television Gives Good Grief: From JFK to Diana

∽

*What we witnessed with the death of Kennedy was the triumph of tele-
vision; what we saw with his assassination, and with his funeral, was the
beginning of television's dominance of our culture – for television is at its
mesmerizing best when it is depicting the untimely deaths of the chosen
and the golden. It is as witness to the butchery of heroes in their prime –
and of all holy-seeming innocents – that television achieves its deplorable
greatness.*

— John Irving, *A Prayer for Owen Meany*

For many people nothing is real unless they see it on TV. And over the
past forty years there have been many momentous events we have witnessed on TV that have held us hostage, transfixed, for days and weeks.

The assassination of John F. Kennedy on November 22, 1963, at 1:40
P.M. Eastern Standard Time, followed by the days of grieving, culminating
in the magnificent state funeral, demonstrated McLuhan's concept of television making a community of the world. McLuhan must have been as
stuck in time as the rest of us, knowing exactly where he was and what he
was doing when news of JFK's assassination sounded around the world. As
well, as Michael Winship points outs in *Television*, "It was during those
days that all of us suddenly realized the importance and power of network
news. It kept us in instant touch with what was going on and allowed us to
share in a period of national sorrow and healing."

In 1997, television reported the death of Diana, Princess of Wales, in
Paris, and the public, global grieving that followed. Mother Teresa died

soon after, and her funeral also received global attention, but nothing like what Diana received – so young, so pretty, so tragic.

Ever since the Kennedy–Nixon debates in 1960, I have been fascinated by the way in which television deals with momentous events. What happens when television brings us together to witness confrontation, to share sorrow, to go through a mourning process, or to celebrate Olympic victories? There is a shared history here. But – the question should be asked – how are such events chosen and what impact does the massive television coverage have on audiences?

According to Edward Wakin, in his excellent book, *How TV Changed America's Mind*, "Television changed the face and pace of politics. It changed attitudes towards war. It magnified heroes and exposed villains. It brought confrontation into the living room. It also opened eyes by calling attention to situations that otherwise would have remained out of sight." And at the same time television has changed how we see ourselves and our world. Using thirteen events from Wakin's list of twenty-nine such events, and adding the death of Diana, I want to look at how television made a difference.

1. The Nixon–Kennedy Debate

On September 26, 1960, seventy-five million Americans watched a live television debate carried on all three networks between two presidential candidates: Richard Nixon, the Republican who had served two terms as vice-president, and John F. Kennedy, a relatively unknown junior senator from Massachusetts. It should have been an easy victory for the dogged, hard-working, experienced Nixon, but it turned out to be a surprise win for young, charismatic Kennedy.

In fact, on radio, many listeners thought Nixon had won. He appeared to have outpointed Kennedy, if one were to judge only by what was heard – not by what the camera had seen. The camera had seen a sneaky-looking, sweaty Nixon, and a cool, witty, handsome, confident Kennedy. The crucial difference is that Kennedy's advisors somehow knew the impact television would have, and Nixon's did not.

Television taught politicians that how they looked could be as important, if not more important, as what they said. It was a portent of things to come.

2. Vietnam: The Living-Room War

Nine thousand miles from home, the United States in the 1960s and early 1970s engaged in a vicious, inconclusive war in Vietnam. Unlike the war in Korea, when filmed footage of the fighting took a week to get back to the United States, by 1967 Americans were able to watch the war in Vietnam from their couches every evening, the footage now carried by satellite. The deaths and cruelties became a staple in the lives of Americans after dinner, even during dinner. In 1914, it was easier to ignore World War I, halfway around the globe from you, than it was, in 1968, to ignore someone being bombed while you watched from your living room. Television made the difference.

In 1968, Walter Cronkite, voted the most trusted person in television news, visited Vietnam to check things out on his own. What he discovered was the opposite to what his government had been telling him. He reported this, not only on the evening news, but on a special prime-time show on the war. President Lyndon Johnson watched Cronkite's report along with the rest of the United States and responded by saying that if he had lost Cronkite's support, he had lost the support of the country. A month later, Johnson called for peace talks to end the war. Many other factors were involved, of course – student demonstrations, growing congressional opposition, a new youth culture – but a case can be made that it was television that ended the war.

3. The Kennedy Assassination

On November 22, 1963, I was in Spokane, Washington, coming out of a philosophy class at Mount St. Michael's where, along with 120 other young Jesuits from Canada, Oregon, Washington, and California, I was studying for the priesthood. In those days, the only television we were allowed to watch was the evening news. This time, however, the rules were relaxed, and for the next four days we Jesuits watched something unique on television: the death of a president, the mourning, the grief, the funeral. My colleague O'Malley was then a young reporter in Winnipeg. He remembers having bought a new de-icing spray that same day and was delighted at how effectively it cleared the windows of his car in the parking lot. Waiting for the elevator to take him to the newsroom, he encountered the editor, agitated and red-faced and not the least interested in his new de-icing spray. Only when he reached the newsroom himself did O'Malley learn of the calamitous event in Dallas. He was dispatched to Portage Avenue for man-in-the-street interviews. Years later it occurred to him that many people's most vivid memory of the Kennedy assassination would be of their own response to his question: "How do you feel about President Kennedy's murder?" One woman fainted.

It was Walter Cronkite's voice, breaking in on *As the World Turns*, that broke the news to Americans that their president had been shot. Soon after, Cronkite went live on television to announce the death of Kennedy.

America came to a standstill. Television did what it had never done before; it took all commercials off the air and for four days covered the events as they happened. Network coverage was immense. NBC devoted 71 hours and 36 minutes to the Kennedy story, ABC 60 hours, CBS 55 hours. The average U.S. family watched 31.6 hours of the Kennedy story over the four days it happened.

Anchor David Brinkley referred to the event as "our first genuinely national funeral, a death in our national family attended by every one of us." More than thirty years later, Edward Wakin noted that with the coverage of the Kennedy assassination and mourning "television had just crossed a threshold. Viewing was no longer just escapism. It felt like a duty in times of national crisis. TV was the glue holding together a nation of indivisible viewers."

It was an incredible week. Live coverage during those four days, constantly interspersed with footage of the assassination, included the arrest and murder of Lee Harvey Oswald, the assassin, and Oswald's own assassination by Jack Ruby, a Dallas nightclub owner. Viewers actually saw Oswald's murder live on television.

The day Oswald was to be transferred to the County Jail from the City Prison in Dallas, federal officials in Washington urged that the transfer be done secretly – no fuss or fanfare. The local police, however, chose to announce that the transfer would take place at noon and that it would be televised live on NBC. In the chaos of that transfer, with newsmen shouting questions and cameras flashing and rolling, Ruby stepped forward and shot Oswald in the stomach. Jonathan Miller, writing in *The New Yorker* at the time, observed: "In being so inquisitive, television may have become an accomplice in the crime – may actually have jogged events in the direction they took . . . One could almost feel the lens urging Ruby out of the crowd. In fact, in the pictures, it looked as if *he came out of the camera itself*" [my italics].

Steven Stark, writing in *Glued to the Set*, noted that ". . . this was the event that legitimized television in the eyes of the public, which meant that after it was over, print would never again challenge TV as the public's primary source of information and authority." On the Jack Ruby affair, Stark adds: ". . . television changed history twice on that day – the first by literally setting up Ruby with his opportunity, and then providing America with its first dramatic, watch-it-as-it-happens national news event. From Ruby's bullet to CNN in Baghdad to O. J.'s Bronco chase, the news would never be the same as it sought to capture – and sometimes create – similar moments."

The only footage of Kennedy's assassination was shot by Abraham Zapruder, a Dallas dressmaker who used his 8mm movie camera to film the presidential motorcade. The twenty-six seconds of film were used as evidence in the investigation. In July 1998, the Zapruder footage, computer enhanced, was released to the public on a forty-five-minute video with a historical narrative and interviews, all part of a study of the filmmaking process. The startling quality of the enhanced footage shows the assassination in vivid detail and it may well change people's mind about the "lone gunman" theory.

4. The Assassinations of Martin Luther King and Robert Kennedy

Five years after the Kennedy assassination, two more public killings occurred, only two months apart. On April 4, 1968, a sniper shot and killed civil rights leader Dr. Martin Luther King, Jr. in Memphis, Tennessee. Then, on June 5, in a Los Angeles hotel, Robert Kennedy, brother of the assassinated president, was shot after he delivered a victory speech on the evening he had won the California primary. The primary selected candidates for the Democratic National Convention, which would have chosen him as its presidential candidate. He died the next day.

Television covered the rioting and looting that followed King's murder, as well as the events leading up to the funerals of both men, all carried live across North America and around the world. Wakin observes that millions of mourners attended these funerals courtesy of television. The experience became larger than life with dramatic close-ups and solemn narration. "Americans were not mourning leaders somewhere distant on a platform. They were mourning murdered husbands and fathers and seeing the tears of their wives and children. The TV experience turned political assassination into personal losses as immediate as a death in the family."

5. Walking on the Moon

Another eidetic moment brought to us by television. Where were you when man first walked on the moon on July 20, 1969?

I had just finished teaching an evening summer-school class at Loyola College in Montreal. It was still early, I knew I had plenty of time to get to a television set to watch the first person set foot on the moon. Neil Armstrong was the astronaut who stepped on to the moon's surface at 10:56 P.M. Eastern Standard Time. Nearly a billion people around the world watched him live on TV. An interesting statistic is that, while all of us who had access to television watched a man achieve what had up to then been thought impossible, the crime rate fell dramatically. People were too caught up in that moment – courtesy of television – to go out and commit crimes. The next night the crime rate was back to normal. But for one night, television, instead of being blamed for causing crime, was praised for stopping it.

President Kennedy, television's first political superstar, again had a hand in this momentous piece of television history. It was Kennedy who launched the space race with the Russians, staking it all on his prediction in 1961 that the United States would land the first person on the moon. Television captured the race, presenting it as news, but it really was some of the best propaganda ever devised to show the United States as a nation strong and trustworthy (and finally to surpass the Russians' great success with Sputnik in the 1950s).

Television eagerly covered the drama, suspense, and emotion of the race to the moon, often using Hollywood techniques, right up to that first step when Armstrong's words seemed rather grandiosely scripted ("That's one small step for man, one giant leap for mankind.") Here was Neil Armstrong, 238,000 miles from us on the moon and we saw it happen live. There would be very little that would ever again be out of television's reach.

6. The Kent State Killings

On April 30, 1970, President Nixon escalated the Vietnam War when he announced that he was sending troops into neighbouring Cambodia. Among the many protests that greeted this announcement was one that took place on May 4, 1970, at Kent State University in Ohio. National Guardsmen sent to disperse the students fired into the crowd, killing four students and wounding eleven others.

The coverage of what some called "The Kent State Massacre" was massive, but NBC chose a novel, and dramatic, way to capture the solemn horror of the event. The network used still photographs of the killings, leaving the pictures on screen for seven seconds, with voiceover narration. Then they left the pictures on the screen for a further twelve seconds, this time with no narration, music, or sound of any kind. Twelve seconds of silence on television is an eternity and NBC's presentation packed an emotional wallop.

7. The Iran Hostage Crisis

On January 20, 1981, two important stories were breaking at the same time. Ronald Reagan was being sworn in as president, and the Iran hostages – fifty-two staff members of the United States Embassy in Iran – were being freed after 444 days of captivity. CNN handled the challenge by splitting the screen and covering both events simultaneously.

The two news items actually were related in a way that was brought about by television. President Jimmy Carter had run against Reagan in a close race. Just before the election, news broke that the Iranians were offering new terms for the release of the hostages. It had been a long, ongoing saga, with television keeping the drama boiling during the days of captivity. It became an American obsession, a point of humiliation and pride.

Every night, starting in January 1980, Walter Cronkite ended his nightly newscast with: "And that's the way it is on _____, the ___th day of the hostages' captivity." If the hostages could be released before election day in the United States, the television coverage would almost certainly mean victory for Carter. Unfortunately, for Carter, negotiations broke down and instead of a timely and welcome hostage release, TV went all out during a crucial part of the Carter campaign to cover the anniversary of the hostage-taking.

Reagan won the election.

When Iran ultimately decided to release the hostages, news of the release was scheduled for the same day as Reagan's inauguration. Thousands of journalists travelled to Germany, the first stop for the hostages after their release. Satellite TV sent the images of the freed hostages, intercut with visuals of the presidential inauguration. The Reagan years were off to a fine start.

8. The Invasion of Grenada

This is the television story that was not to be, a major global story but one that the media were not allowed to cover because the United States government would not let them.

Over three days, beginning on October 25, 1983, U.S. troops invaded the island country of Grenada to protect a thousand American citizens working there. A pro-communist group of rebels had overthrown the government and seized control of the country.

Having been burned by the media when it was in Vietnam, the United States decided to curtail the power of the press with a news blackout. The only information reporters could get was what was handed to them by U.S. officials. Apart from this, they could only describe in general terms the mountainous, volcanic island, the surf and the banana plantations, material more suitable for travel stories than war reportage. And they had no way to verify the information handed to them by what were known as "official sources." The story thus became government censorship. Perhaps the U.S. government knew it would not look good that the most powerful country on earth invaded a Caribbean island of only 133 square miles, with a population about the size of Saskatoon's.

9. The Challenger Disaster

Chosen from among 11,000 candidates who applied, thirty-seven-year-old Christa McAuliffe joined the crew of the space shuttle *Challenger*. McAuliffe was a mother of two, a personable, well-liked school teacher who became an instant celebrity. On the morning of January 28, 1986, *Challenger* roared off into the blue with McAuliffe and six other astronauts.

McAuliffe's family were at the launch site. Millions of school children, including her own students, watched the event live on television. Part of the plan this time was for McAuliffe to teach, via closed-circuit TV, two fifteen-minute lessons from outer space. A minute after the launch something went terribly wrong and the *Challenger* exploded, bursting into flames in full view of those watching at the launch site and the millions more watching on TV around the world.

Networks preempted all other programming for five hours and that evening each network ran a prime-time special on the *Challenger* disaster. Footage of the explosion, the flames and smoke and flying debris, were shown over and over, day and night, along with the requisite visuals of McAuliffe's shocked parents.

The evening after the tragedy, President Reagan, the actor-turned-president, used his skills as a communicator to praise the crew as heroes. Speaking directly to the children who had watched the tragedy live on TV at school, he used television as a vehicle for national grief counselling. "I know that it's hard to understand that sometimes painful things happen," the president said. "[But] it's all part of taking a chance and expanding man's horizons. The future doesn't belong to the faint-hearted. It belongs to the brave. The *Challenger* crew was pulling us into the future and we'll continue to follow them." President Reagan took advantage of a prime-time audience to lecture viewers on American principles and values – the spirit of freedom, openness – when he said: "We don't hide our space program, we don't keep secrets and cover things up. That's the way freedom is and we wouldn't change it for a minute."

Oh? How would that have played three years earlier to the newshounds trying to cover the invasion of Grenada?

10. The Tiananmen Square Massacre

Sometimes TV coverage of one news event precipitates another. On May 15, 1989, a summit meeting took place between China and Russia. China's leaders had invited the world media to cover this historic meeting, the first time China and Russia had gathered for a formal tête-à-tête in thirty-one years. Cameras were positioned to capture the summit events in Tiananmen Square.

Chinese students and workers demonstrating for democracy knew a photo-op when they saw one. Aware that the world was watching, they staged a huge demonstration, really a strike, in Tiananmen Square. More than a million Chinese gathered in the square, confident that with the cameras rolling and live coverage beaming to the rest of the world the Chinese army would not dare retaliate. When live coverage ended on May 24, videotapes had to be sent to Hong Kong for satellite transmission to the rest of the world.

Things changed. On June 4, 10,000 Chinese soldiers, along with tanks, rolled into Tiananmen Square at 2:00 A.M. and three hours later a thousand young students and workers had been killed and a thousand more wounded. When the graphic depictions of the violence were transmitted to the world – not live, but soon enough – the impact was powerful and immediate: economic sanctions were imposed on China, business transactions were halted, tourists stopped coming, the Chinese economy was shaken, and the image of a liberal nation that the Chinese leaders were assiduously promoting was shattered.

The impact of the Tiananmen Square Massacre reverberated elsewhere. On November 11, 1989, after years of unrest and dissension, East Germans were allowed to travel freely to West Germany. That night, at midnight, the world watched as East Berliners and West Berliners tore down the hated Berlin Wall. TV producer Tara Sonenshine – cited in Wakin's *How TV Changed America's Mind* – commented: "It's not too much of an exaggeration to say that the German revolution began in Tiananmen Square . . . The Chinese leadership . . . understands fully the impact of television. The dramatic images of the crumbling of the Berlin Wall were barely seen in the homes of ordinary Chinese citizens." Again, TV was an important catalyst for historical change.

11. Operation Desert Storm

Now we are in the 1990s, almost forty years after Nixon and Kennedy stood before the cameras for the great presidential debate that took American politics, and global TV news coverage, down a road it had never before travelled, never imagined – Marshall McLuhan notwithstanding. In a small book titled *The Medium Is the Massage*, published in 1967 at the height of the Vietnam War, McLuhan wrote: "We now live in a global village, a simultaneous happening . . . We have begun again to structure primordial feeling, the tribal feeling, the tribal emotion. We have had to shift our stress of attention from action to reaction . . ."

This kind of TV experience was new, which necessitated learning on the run, by trial and error: from the living-room war of Vietnam . . . the invasion of Grenada . . . coverage of the *Challenger* disaster . . . Tiananmen Square . . . the Berlin Wall.

What now?

On January 16, 1991, I was eating dinner and watching the news on television when Operation Desert Storm began. As we would have said in San Francisco in the 1960s, this was a mind-blowing experience: sitting down to dinner, plate on my lap, utensils ready, turning on the TV, and suddenly – live, in colour – a war! It was as if the cameras were at the ready as the first Allied troops came ashore at Normandy. It was the first war ever started live-to-camera, as if some disembodied Steven Spielberg, perched high on a director's chair, had intoned, "Action!"

Was it coincidence that President George Bush had ordered the air assault to begin when it did, smack in the middle of prime-time? My first thought was, *This whole war has been orchestrated for television*. We had come a long way from Vietnam, from Grenada.

I was not alone. Derrick de Kerckhove, director of the McLuhan Program in Culture and Technology at the University of Toronto, must have watched the start of Desert Storm as I had, for he later wrote in *Media and the Gulf War: A Case Study by the Association for Media Literacy*, (May 1991): "We are watching this war on TV with our electronic eyelids closed, as if we were treated to a collective meditation rather than the true participatory medium. We are being denied two major reality-anchoring processes: direct perceptual evidence and historical and other contextualizing options." Another observer, among the global millions who watched the first missiles rain down on Baghdad, was P. J. O'Rourke, who later wrote in *Rolling Stone*: "This is the first globally broadcast, real-time, live-on-camera televised war. It's so televised, in fact, that increasing CNN's Nielsen ratings seems to be an allied war aim only slightly less important than degrading Saddam Hussein's command-and-control capacity."

All news came through the military. Reporters had to work in pools, small groups being allowed into battle zones, then reporting back to their colleagues. The pool reporters were closely supervised by the military, who allowed them to observe the war only from carefully selected locations. There were also constant briefings by skilled military spokespersons. The only information given was information that would assist the allied cause. Videotapes released showed flawless bombing runs, with no civilian casualties. Reporters who tried working outside the pools were arrested.

No matter what was actually happening, we were given, courtesy of the military, "media reality." The truth now consisted of words and images, TV's mainstay. Consider the choice of words used to describe Operation Desert Storm. Hussein's military was "a war machine," the allied forces were simply called "the army, navy, and air force." They resorted to "censorship," we adhered to "reporting guidelines." They used "propaganda," we used "press briefings." At the height of Operation Desert Storm, *The Guardian Weekly* printed a lexicon:

They:	*We:*
Destroy	Take out
Kill	Eliminate
They launch:	*We launch:*
Sneak missile attacks	First strikes
Without provocation	Preemptively
They are:	*We are:*
Brainwashed	Professionals
Paper tigers	Lionhearted
Cowardly	Cautious
Blindly obedient	Loyal
Ruthless	Resolute
Their missiles cause:	*Our missiles cause:*
Civilian casualties	Collateral damage

What about the images? At the beginning we saw a still photo of CNN's Bernard Shaw and heard him say, "The skies over Baghdad have been illuminated." There were unforgettable visuals of the Baghdad sky lit up by tracer bullets, the video-game destruction of Iraqi targets as seen by the bombers' remote cameras, familiar TV reporters wearing gas masks, stunned looks on the faces of the prisoners of war, desert scenery that looked more like *Lawrence of Arabia* than a 1990s battlefield.

Mostly it was a war of voices. Government censorship on both sides and inaccessibility to the battlefield forced TV news to rely heavily on maps, charts, press briefings by the military and talking-head experts, simulated animations of what might be happening, and repeated shots of jet fighters taking off from aircraft carriers. The networks added their own graphic intros to their nightly reports, with rousing military theme music to mask the lack of any significant live coverage.

Not much mention has been made of the role of advertisers in Operation Desert Storm. They were there from the start, as soon as the first U.S. troops landed in Saudi Arabia. Flag-waving "corporate donors" pitched in, dispensing freebies to the troops. A partial list (from the January/ February issue of *Mother Jones*): 60,000 cases of Coca-Cola and Pepsi-Cola; 22,000 cases of Anheuser-Busch near-beer; 100,000 AT&T calling cards; 5,000 Sony Walkmans; 60,000 Polygram cassette tapes; 40,000 Calvary wrist compasses; 1,000 Rawlings high-visibility footballs; 10,000 cartons of Marlboro cigarettes. A single image of any of these products, appearing on all three networks, was worth about $250,000 in paid media time.

Any suggestion that the advertisers were exploiting a dangerous, tragic situation was downplayed or ignored by the PR people hired to handle the media. "We did what we thought was exactly the right thing to do," Coca-Cola spokesman Randy Donaldson told *Mother Jones*. "There was no known risk involved [to the soldiers] on the week we made the deliveries. Some people think it was wrong. Well, I just don't agree with that."

When Operation Desert Storm ended, forty-three days after it began, 200 allied men and women had been killed, against some 100,000 Iraqi losses. The American military was pleased with the results of the war *and* the media coverage. The disastrous images of Vietnam and the media blackout of the invasion of Grenada had been replaced by new knowledge. The U.S. military had effectively controlled the information fed to the public, keeping it uninformed of what really was happening, but happy to see how wonderfully the military performed. When the shooting stopped, when the tracer bullets vanished from the sky over Baghdad, U.S. Secretary of Defense Richard B. Cheney summed up: "TV coverage is just one tremendous piece of advertising for the United States military and for the people who serve in it."

In a series of staged, yellow-ribbon receptions, the soldiers returned home from the Iraqi battlefield triumphant. We watched hometown parades, the kisses and hugs, as brass bands played and crowds cheered. We saw some military funerals, grieving families. There were comparisons with the troops who returned from Vietnam, who were greeted with indifference, even disdain. Why the difference? Because Vietnam was a national embarrassment? Because the home team won this one? Television played an important role in conveying these impressions of both wars.

The Gulf War was also a tremendous piece of marketing for CNN. Its ratings soared by 1,000 per cent during the first three days of Operation Desert Storm. CNN maintained continuous onsite coverage from Baghdad day and night, so other networks, for an unspecified fee, often picked up and carried the CNN feed. Even the military relied on the CNN reports, as when Richard Cheney, the Defense secretary, told reporters at a briefing: "It would appear, based on comments coming in from CNN crews in Baghdad, that the operation was successful." And when the war finally ended, David Letterman quipped, "Finally we can go back to ignoring CNN."

The truth is that Operation Desert Storm put CNN squarely and conspicuously on the map of global news coverage, never to be ignored again.

12. The Rodney King Beating and the Los Angeles Riot

If George Holliday had not been trying out his new camcorder on the evening of March 3, 1991, most of us would never have heard of Rodney King. Late that night a police chase ended when a car was forced to a stop in a Los Angeles suburb. The African-American driver ran from the car, the police caught and subdued him by zapping him with a 50,000-volt stun gun.

Holliday heard the commotion, went to his balcony, and used his new camcorder to videotape the scene below: police whacking and kicking Rodney King. When it ended, King had eleven fractures in his skull, a crushed cheekbone, broken ankle, internal injuries, and possible brain damage. Holliday sold his tape for five hundred dollars to a local TV station, from which it was picked up first by CNN, then by ABC, CBS, and NBC. The entire videotaped clip ran eighty-one seconds and recorded fifty-six blows to the body of Rodney King. It was determined that within a week the clip had been viewed on TV by four out of five Americans.

When the four policemen charged with assault and extreme use of force were acquitted on April 29, 1992, the Los Angeles Riot erupted, with fires, looting, and heinous instances of brutal, random violence. The riot lasted nearly three days, during which time 44 people were killed and nearly 2,000 were injured. There was more than a billion dollars of property damage.

The Rodney King beating brought in a new era of television news coverage: that of the amateur videographer. At the time, it was estimated there were fourteen million camcorders in the United States, a number that has probably doubled since then. It constituted nothing less than the ultimate demystification and democratization of electronic journalism, a new age when anyone anywhere can be a news reporter. We can expect to see much more Holliday-type coverage. News shows specializing in amateur footage began appearing on TV soon after the Rodney King incident, picking up where *America's Funniest Home Videos* left off – police chases, domestic violence, robberies-in-progress, highway collisions, suicides, gang violence, animal attacks, natural disasters. It is as if the U.S. public wanted to take back television news from the networks.

13. The O. J. Simpson Affair

It is difficult to imagine a prime-time drama with all the ingredients for success that this "live" story had. A football star, national sports commentator, Hollywood actor. A handsome, famous, rich young man with a beautiful wife and family, a fabulous house, an adoring public. He was "The Juice" and there he was, on June 17, 1994, in his white Bronco, pursued by the police on the Los Angeles freeway, live on TV, millions watching.

O. J. Simpson was about to be arrested for the murder of his wife, Nicole Brown Simpson, and her friend Ronald Goldman. Simpson did not turn himself in, on the appointed day, and so the police were chasing him. They eventually caught him. Then there was the trial, which lasted 372 days, all of it covered live on TV. CNN ended up showing 630 live hours of the trial.

The trial had everything viewers had come to expect from a television soap opera: romance, sex, intrigue, suspense, colourful characters. Mark Fuhrman and Kato Kaelin became household names. There was the eccentric judge, the posturing attorneys, and Marcia Clark, the leggy prosecuting attorney (the real-life inspiration for Ally McBeal?).

A Gallup Poll released just before the beginning of the trial showed that 68 per cent of whites believed Simpson was guilty and 60 per cent of African Americans believed Simpson was innocent. As the poll indicated, the issue of race would be important during the trial. On October 3, 1995, more than 150 million Americans and untold millions around the world stopped what they were doing to watch television and hear the verdict: "We, the jury in the above-entitled action, find the defendant, Orenthal James Simpson, not guilty of the crime of murder."

On one level, the O. J. Simpson trial was great entertainment, for all the soap-opera reasons mentioned, but also because it made use of what television can do superbly: live coverage. We see this mostly in sports TV: the efficient use of camera positions – different and specialized for hockey, football, basketball, baseball – the use of slow-motion replays, the virtuoso skills of the technicians operating the cameras, the decision-a-second instructions from the directors, the inventive ad-libbing by "colour commentators," the real, unscripted, open-ended suspense. As Wakin points out, the televised trial became a place where the people of the United States were forced to confront issues of race, domestic violence, and the way in which the criminal justice system operates.

14. The Death of Diana

It didn't take long to see this tide of grief that just kept building and building and building and we had to follow it. I should not have been as surprised as I was by that grief, as we did play a role in creating the grief, and we created it because we created Diana . . . We felt that we were justified in feeding the public's desire to know, rather than its need to know.

– Kelly Critchon, Executive Producer for CBC's *The National*, quoted in *The Globe and Mail*, May 29, 1998

Diana, Princess of Wales, was a celebrity with all the perks and problems that go with being a celebrity. But she was also a person, a complex human being like all of us, except that she was not an "ordinary" person. Though divorced from Charles, the Prince of Wales, Diana remained the mother of the heir to the throne of England. She was many things to many people, ever since her fairytale wedding at St. Paul's Cathedral in London on July 29, 1981, but overall she became the media's darling. As with the saga of O. J., Diana's beauty, her life and adventures, seemed the ingredients of a daytime soap opera.

She was "the people's princess," the mother of the two princes William and Harry, a warm human being who seemed to care for the lowly, sick, and downtrodden: AIDS victims, cancer victims, the homeless. She made it a personal mission to rid the world of unexploded land mines. To the royal family, however, she was a problem, an embarrassment. She retaliated against her husband and his infidelities by having affairs of her own. She was more popular than Prince Charles. She seemed to be dragging the English monarchy kicking and screaming into a modern and vibrant new era.

It all came to a sudden end in Paris on August 31, 1997, when the car carrying Diana and her companion Dodi Al Fayed, pursued at high speed by paparazzi, crashed into a concrete post in a tunnel in Paris. Al Fayed died instantly, Diana died later in hospital. Unlike Diana's wedding to Charles in 1981, a wondrous fairytale gala designed for maximum impact – most definitely a planned media event – her sudden, controversial death on a summer Sunday night caught the media unprepared.

Not for long. The BBC, CBC (TV and radio), and CNN did a superlative job immediately and during the days following. The media showed us the fields of floral tributes on the lawns at the gates of palaces, the solemn hush of the streets of London, the grieving, caring faces of onlookers at the funeral procession, the evocative *clippety-clop* of hooves on cobblestones, the bell sounding, the music, the speeches. Robert Fulford summed up in his column in *The Globe and Mail*: "Television, which so often is accused of alienating and isolating people, demonstrates in a crisis that it has a unique power to create ceremonies that connect us. What the media offer is something like a wake, a shiva, a funeral parlour visitation. It's a chance for everyone to feel involved."

But through it all, no matter how it tried and despite its best manners, television reminded us again that it is and always has been show business. As for Diana's death and the long aftermath, the media had little real information to impart, but took days to impart it.

So, they resorted to statistics: 1.8 million official condolence web sites by Labour Day, $45-million worth of flowers purchased in London in a week, a television audience of one billion watching the funeral, a million observers lined up along the route of the funeral procession. There were comparisons – how Diana's death ranked with President Kennedy's, with Princess Grace's. The media looked for blame – the paparazzi who chased Diana to her death and then photographed her dying, the tabloids that paid big money for the photographs, the driver of the car, the Royal Family for being cool and distant, the media themselves. Periodically, the media blame themselves for many of the problems around us. Michael Levine, in *The Princess and the Package*, tells us that this is "their way of reminding themselves and us how powerful they are. Their self-importance is fed further by the habit of politicians, clergy, and moralists to blame all senseless acts of violence . . . on the media."

When they ran out of statistics, comparisons, blame, and *mea culpas*, the media fastened upon the rich and famous, the cult of celebrity. *Entertainment Weekly*: "It is one thing to recall that Diana was a pop princess, a royal who dished with Elton John and danced with John Travolta; the fact that she was charmed and enthralled by celebrity culture made her seem endearingly contemporary. But as one star after another tried to claim her as one of their own, it became clear that, bereft of any sense of proportion, they in fact saw themselves as similarly aggrieved royalty."

All that was forgotten, or put aside momentarily, on the day of the funeral when some 2.5 billion people – nearly half the world – watched as on a warm, sunny day the cortege slowly moved through the streets of London. Television tried to let the spectacle show itself, speak for itself: the silent crowds, teary faces, Diana's sons walking with their father, grandfather, and uncles. Then the music, the pop (Elton John's rewritten "Candle in the Wind," originally inspired by the death of Marilyn Monroe) and the sacred (the choirboys of the Abbey). And the eloquent, challenging eulogy by Diana's brother, Earl Spencer, who indicted "every proprietor and editor of every publication that has paid for intrusive and exploitative photographs of her."

For the most part the networks did try not to intrude, but it was evident that American television chafed under these mostly self-imposed restrictions. They could not resist telling us what we were watching, or, worse, how we *should* be feeling. They nudged us to notice this or that celebrity in the crowd. When it came time for the respectful minute of silence (eloquently achieved by CBC's Peter Mansbridge when he simply said, "Let's just watch") ABC could hold its voice no more than . . . thirty-nine seconds. All the coverage was constructed, even the properly observed minute's silence, but the Americans could not resist constructing also how their audience should react emotionally. They kept cutting back and forth to the crowd, saying things like, "Look, that man is crying." And, "That woman is comforting him." They were telling viewers what to see, what to hear, and how to feel about what they saw and heard.

There was, no doubt, the worry of "dead air" – viewers might punch the dreaded channel-changer – but it was more the conditioned response they were after, that viewers can't be left uninterrupted to view and watch the spectacle on their own.

I liked *Entertainment Weekly*'s observation, that "what we really wanted was to be left alone, to consider our own strange affection for a mother who loved her children, a public figure to whom nothing seemed more glamorously unattainable than a private life, a woman we never knew and still somehow loved to death."

By mid October, there were more than 23,000 Internet sites on Diana. Canadian media educator and author Barry Duncan wrote,

There have been so many media/pop culture angles and journalistic ruminations that it is mind-boggling: the fairytale princess conveyed by images of the courtship and wedding of the twenty-year-old Diana; the coverage of her disintegrating marriage; the incriminating antics of her husband together with the other royals; the images of the lonely, vulnerable, victimized Diana contrasted with the celebrity-seeking jet setter who skillfully deployed the media, even staging events for them but at the same time abused by the same because of their obsessive need for sensational photographs. . . .

Of greater and more lasting importance for image making was the coverage of her charitable work – her empathy for the sick and battered

... her engaging smile that lit up every place she went. Much of Diana's power and charisma was grounded in these complex and often contradictory strands which were picked up by the media and occasionally critiqued.

Duncan cited an essay in *Time* in which the writer Lance Morrow observed: "People projected all sorts of fantasies upon Princess Diana in somewhat the way girls project little play scenarios upon Barbie dolls."

Duncan rightly drew our attention to how the audience negotiated meaning. Which of the many Dianas were each of us grieving? Duncan suggested, "Our task is to explore several of these fantasies and, where possible, show how they reveal the ways that people create their own interpretations of mass mediated spectacles."

Marshall McLuhan said "the medium is the message." As Michael Levine points out: "With Diana that was eminently true. Today's multichannel, visual media thrives on beauty, youth, and drama. Diana provided the look and the plot line to fill the media's need. Her youth and extraordinarily photogenic face made her perfect for our image-conscious age."

The extent to which the "paparazzi" were involved in the death of Diana was a major issue. The word was coined by film director Federico Fellini for the surname of the society photographer in his 1959 film *La Dolce Vita*. The man on whom the character was modelled, Tazio Sechharioli, was still alive when Diana was killed. He died in the summer of 1998, at the age of seventy-three.

What to make of *The National Inquirer*, the American tabloid with a reputation for spending big money for paparazzi photographs, suddenly staking out the high ground, not without a certain irony, by refusing to bid on the crash photographs and urging other newspapers to "shun" these pictures? It is worth examining, as well, how the Diana story was handled in other countries to see what angles were taken, and how the story remained news. Remember, too, that when it comes to covering the news, timing is all. Diana was killed on a Sunday, the day when the big papers are filled with long feature stories, many set days before. One newspaper in London carried a story that day that said, "If Diana had five fewer IQ points they would have to water her every day." Such sentiment would be anathema within hours of the tragic news from Paris.

Elton John's rendition of "Candle in the Wind" provided a powerful emotional moment at Diana's funeral. The viewers knew Elton and Diana were friends and that he had rewritten the lyrics to his 1973 tribute to Marilyn Monroe. At the end of their coverage of the funeral, CBC used the song as the sound track for a seven-minute closing summary of the day. It was no more and no less than a music video, possibly the first one ever created in such a manner. The song went on sale the day after the funeral, with all profits going to Diana's special Memorial Fund. By January 1998, "Candle in the Wind" had become the biggest-selling single in recording history, with sales of thirty-four million copies.

Other people died the week Diana died. Most had only their families and loved ones to grieve them. Mother Teresa died a few days after Diana and even her death was partly eclipsed. Her funeral, too, was carried live, from Calcutta. She and Diana were very different people, celebrities, for very different reasons, though in their deaths the good they had done was reflected in the silent crowds lining their funeral processions, sharing grief that was genuine and profound. It's interesting to ponder what the networks' motives were for covering Mother Teresa's funeral live.

Which brings us full circle to the role of media, especially television, as an agent of counselling, healing, and community, the way it brings us together as we observe the momentous rituals of happiness and sorrow, celebration and grief. Earlier I mentioned John Irving's response to the assassination and funeral of John Kennedy. In the introduction to *The Power of Myth* by Joseph Campbell and Bill Moyers, Moyers describes telling his grown children about Campbell's reaction to President Kennedy's funeral. "The public murder of a president, 'representing our whole society, the living social organism of which ourselves were the members, taken away at a moment of exuberant life, required a compensatory rite to reestablish the sense of solidarity. Here was an enormous nation, made those four days into a unanimous community, all of us participating in the same way, simultaneously, in a single symbolic event.' He said it was 'the first and only thing of its kind in peacetime that has ever given me the sense of being a member of this whole national community, engaged as a unit in the observance of a deeply significant rite.'"

On July 1, 1998, while Canadians celebrated their country's birthday, the first of many groups of people gathered at the Althorp estate near a village north of London to mark what would have been Diana's thirty-seventh birthday. Diana's ancestral home now is open a few months a year, allowing people to visit a museum and to look across a lake at the island where she is buried. There were fears that the village would be overrun with tourists, but this did not happen. A villager told CBC news that more media were overrunning the place than tourists.

The technical difficulties faced by the television crews who covered the death and funeral of John Kennedy no longer exist. Some would say that, by comparison, the funeral of Diana was almost choreographed. In many ways, television news is constantly ready for such an event. As gruesome as it sounds, there is a photographer always with the president just in case "something" happens. Someone who watched the reporting in 1963 told me: "As I remember it, however, when Kennedy was killed, the coverage had a weirdly extemporized feel to it. It was all so much more shocking." Television has changed that.

Final Thoughts: Say Goodnight, Dick. Goodnight, Dick.

~

. . . for the world, which seems
To lie before us like a land of dreams
Hath really neither joy, nor love, nor light,
Nor certitude, nor peace, nor help for pain;
And we are here as on a darkling plain
Swept with confused alarms of struggle and flight,
Where ignorant armies clash by night.
— Matthew Arnold, "Dover Beach"

W e could go out on a sombre note. Matthew Arnold's "On Dover Beach," studied by generations of students across the English-speaking world, sums up the world of television for those who have no media education – the darkling plain, confused alarms, ignorant armies clashing by night. It is our hope that media education, and this book, will help you see more clearly the world which on television "lies before you like a land of dreams" and help shed some light on that "darkling plain."

Or we could end on a whimsical note as suggested by the title given to these Final Thoughts. In the late 1960s and early 1970s there was a wonderfully satiric show called *Rowan & Martin's Laugh-In*. Hosted by comedians Dan Rowan and Dick Martin, the show was fast-paced, offering a rapid-fire barrage of punchlines and sight gags. It was a new approach to comedy on television, aimed at the electronic viewer's short attention span, an early illustration of how TV was changing everything.

"Verrrr-ry interesting," comedian Arte Johnson used to say.

And it was. It was an excellent example of comedy working *with* the medium, not merely putting vaudeville (or radio) on TV. *Laugh-In* showed that even limp punchlines and silly sight gags worked if they came at you so quickly that you forgave them because you were primed for the next limp punchline and silly sight gag.

Laugh-In took a critically comic look at American pop culture and ran for five seasons on NBC. Host Dan Rowan ended every show by telling co-host Dick Martin, "Say goodnight, Dick." And Dick would always comply, "Goodnight, Dick." That little gag sums up the amiable idiocy of a lot of TV programming. But it also suggests that the idiocy can be subverted, turned around.

What do we hope you found for yourself from this book? We hope it isn't something as unimportant as that we like *Ally McBeal* and *Law & Order*, I find *Seinfeld* boring and O'Malley enjoys it, or that we both admire the acting and writing of *Frasier* and *Due South*. We are certainly not advocating some sort of eat-your-broccoli approach to TV-viewing. We certainly are not advocating any "bash-television" or "ignore-television." Television is powerful and everywhere, but it is only a medium, in itself neither bad nor good. It's what you do with it that is important.

As for what is *not* in the book, we eventually decided to concentrate on the present and not dwell extensively on the marvellous old shows on television. But we've added some history and chatted a bit about our favourite shows. We are trying to help viewers learn how to watch the television of today and in the immediate future. They experienced the shows of the past their own way. We can't do anything about that. We can try to do something about the way viewers watch television now. It is an evanescent medium, always changing, often so quickly that what is new and exciting in September is outdated – or cancelled – the following April or sooner.

Television is not just entertainment, or news, or drama. It is not just a profit-oriented business. Sitcoms aren't just sitcoms. TV presents good values and questionable values. TV is not to blame for all the violence in the world. News can be entertainment and entertainment can be news. Television's coverage of major events has made a difference in our lives, our cultures, our world.

We decided to dwell mainly on North American television. The book is not about how British or Australian television is better than North

American television. Many viewers who have enjoyed "foreign" shows such as *The Singing Detective, Chef, Two Fat Ladies, Prime Suspect,* and *Inspector Morse* may agree that much of the television fare in North America suffers by comparison; it was not our objective to demonstrate this.

I believe that England's concerted emphasis on media education over many years has contributed to a more media-literate society. And given the symbiotic relationship between quality media and discerning viewers, this will, over time, encourage and sustain better writers, actors, producers, and directors – better television.

Len Masterman's work has had an impact on me. His emphasis, too, was on television, for the obvious reason that television is so pervasive and powerful. In his groundbreaking book *Teaching the Media,* he makes a list to explain not only why media education should be a required subject in the schools but also why it must be given "the most urgent priority." The book was published in 1985, but it remains as relevant now as it was then. Its relevance is not just for teachers and students; his reasons remain valid for each of us. The idea of "repetition" is something that I encountered in every aspect of my Jesuit training. Whenever I learned something or found something of interest, I would be sure to review – or "repeat" – what I had found. At this point, it is useful to "repeat" the reasons Masterman outlines in *Teaching the Media* for taking a critical look at television. Here are his seven reasons (the italics are his):

1. The high rate of media consumption and *the saturation of contemporary societies by the media.*
2. The ideological importance of the media, and *their influence as consciousness industries.*
3. The growth in the *management and manufacture of information,* and its dissemination by the media.
4. The increasing *penetration of media into our central democratic processes.*
5. The increasing *importance of visual communication and information* in all areas.
6. The importance of *educating students to meet the demands of the future.*

7. The fast-growing national and international pressures to *privatise information.*

There is nothing wrong with teaching people – students, parents, grandparents, whoever – how to *enjoy* television. If people can become shrewder, savvier viewers, they will be more discerning and demanding, and television must respond in kind. If you enjoy a program – a sitcom, a drama, a documentary – let the network know. With an audience educated about the media the good shows stand a better chance of surviving.

There are advocacy groups whose objective is to attack, calling people who watch television "tubeheads" and "couch potatoes," attacking advertisers, attacking the media for being addictive. While I might not disagree with some of their findings, what they do is *not* media education. The advocacy activists do nothing to champion what is good, uplifting, funny, and exciting on TV. O'Malley and I both agree with TV critic David Bianculli who wrote in *Teleliteracy*, "The best way to play an active role in improving television is to seek out, acknowledge and support its most important and impressive efforts."

O'Malley gets frustrated with me when I won't venture opinions on what is "good" and "bad" on TV. The point of media education is neither to attack nor to praise. I am not and never had aspirations to be a television critic. Media education gives people the tools to make up their own minds. Writing in *The New York Times Magazine*, September 20, 1998, Caryn James said: "Ignoring TV's complexity is a dangerous game but a pervasive one. We are bombarded by doomsday warnings about television on one side and by *People* magazine fluff on the other, with little in between that acknowledges both television's allure and its fearful impact." Being media-literate fills that gap.

I have a friend, Bill Walsh, who lives in Massachusetts just outside Boston, and who teaches high school and writes a column for the local paper, *The Billerica Minute Man*. We met at a media education workshop I conducted near his home town and we keep in touch by e-mail, exchanging news and insights. Walsh probably is the only full-time media education columnist in North America.

In July 1998, he wrote a column describing his reaction to the live coverage of the Boston Pops July 4 concert: the sound, the camera work, the direction. There were cameras and microphones in remote locations, capturing the firing of a cannon here, ringing church bells there. He was in awe of the little things as much as the big things, how microphones were instrument-specific, picking out the violins when it was violin time, trumpets when it was trumpet time, even the delicate *clink* of the triangle when it was time for the percussionist to play the triangle. There were crane-shots, audience-shots, and satisfying close-ups. Walsh watched a young violinist silently mouthing the words to "Strangers in the Night" as she played it on her violin.

At the end, Walsh concluded: "Media literacy does not change the media so much as it changes us. It changes how we perceive and appreciate the constructed reality we see and hear every day. Understanding even the basics of what goes into the creation of media events is the first step in understanding and even sometimes admiring it."

Walsh has put into a few well-crafted sentences what everyone who becomes literate about the media comes to realize. No matter to whom I am writing or speaking, it is the message I want them to get. If you understand what Walsh is saying, you are on your way to becoming part of the "well-watched society" we mentioned when we began this journey.

Appendix One: Media Education in Canada

~

Media literacy is concerned with helping students develop an informed and critical understanding of the nature of the mass media, the techniques used by them, and the impact of these techniques. More specifically, it is education that aims to increase students' understanding and enjoyment of how the media work, how they produce meaning, how they are organized, and how they construct reality. Media literacy also aims to provide students with the ability to create media products.

– Resource Guide: Media Literacy, pp. 6–7,
Ministry of Education, Ontario, Canada, 1987

1. Introduction

When a group of us wrote that definition of media education – or media literacy as we called it – and the Guidelines I don't think any of us knew just where media education would go in Ontario least of all across Canada. But it grew beyond what any of us imagined.

A book could, and should, be written on the history of the development of media education in Canada. Here are some of the highlights of that development, which has resulted in the prominent position Canadian media education now holds in the world.

As a country whose population of thirty million (there are more people in the state of California than in all of Canada) is all contained in a narrow band that stretches for some four thousand miles across a continent, we are painfully aware of the importance of communications.

Compared to our American cousins, we are considerably more advanced. All of our provinces have mandated media education in the curriculum, compared

227

with only a half dozen or so of the states. Barry Duncan, founding president of Ontario's Association for Media Literacy, argues that the launching of media education in Canada came about for two major reasons; first, our critical concerns about the pervasiveness of American popular culture, and second, our equitable, tolerant, and, until recently, progressive system of education across the country which fostered the necessary contexts for new educational paradigms.

2. The History

In Canada, secondary school film courses blossomed in the late 1960s and the first wave of media education began under the banner of "screen education." An early organization called CASE (Canadian Association for Screen Education) sponsored the first large gathering of media teachers in 1969 at Toronto's York University. Participants came from across the country. Largely as a result of budget cuts and the general back-to-the-basics philosophy, this first wave died out in the early 1970s. But in the 1980s and 1990s there was new growth in elementary and secondary school media education. And, as of September 1999, media education is a mandated part of the English Language Arts curriculum across Canada.

Canada's ten provinces and three northern territories each has its own education system. With responsibility for education resting in the hands of the provinces, there are differences in how each province deals with media education.

The Provinces of Western Canada – British Columbia, Alberta, Saskatchewan, and Manitoba

In the summer of 1991, a group met in Vancouver to form the Canadian Association for Media Education (CAME). Although most of the members are classroom teachers, other organizations are also represented, including the National Film Board of Canada, Knowledge TV Network, Pacific Cinémathèque, International Development Education Resource Association, MediaWatch, and *Adbusters* magazine. Their objectives are to educate Canadians about the media, to promote media education, and to encourage Canadian cultural expression in the media.

CAME has hosted yearly forums on media education topics. In the summer of 1994 CAME members were involved in organizing a two-week summer institute for teachers wishing to teach media education. And in the summer of 1995, CAME helped organize a credit summer course in media education at Simon Fraser

University. CAME has published two resource samplers of information and teaching strategies for teachers beginning work in media education.

In the spring of 1994, CAME signed a contract with the B.C. Ministry of Education to produce a *Conceptual Framework of Media Education.* This framework was made available to the curriculum review committees that began meeting in the fall of 1994 with instructions to incorporate suggestions for media education into all curriculum areas. It is prescribed in B.C. curricula from K to 12. The framework was also given to the Western Consortium – a group that has written a common Language Arts curriculum for the four western provinces and Yukon and the Northwest Territories. This curriculum includes a mandated segment on media education, which will differ from province to province.

And in the fall of 1996, British Columbia was the first of the western provinces to put into effect the new Language Arts Curriculum. Media education is represented in two ways. First, media education is mandated in all Language Arts courses from K to 12 as one-third of the material taught. Second, media education is part of the Integrated Resource Package (IRP) which is cross-curricular in all subjects from K to 12. British Columbia has still to develop the resources to help put into effect these changes. There is a major need to address the question of teacher training in media education. This is true of every province.

Since the early 1960s Media Education in Albertan schools has been recognized by a few "cutting edge" teachers. On a formal basis, it was not until 1981 that a Viewing Strand was recognized as one of the strands (Reading, Writing, Speaking, and Listening) of the English Language Arts Program, Grades 1 to 12. A teacher implementation monograph on Viewing at the junior and senior high levels was developed by the Alberta Department of Education and distributed to schools, but implementation was slow and fragmented with few opportunities for teacher workshops or training courses. Some school districts in Edmonton and Calgary conducted implementation activities on a short-term basis. The Viewing Strand, in practice, was not considered compulsory and therefore not well implemented by teachers.

In the spring of 1993, based on the success of a 1991 media education conference, a group of educators and media professionals formed the Alberta Association for Media Awareness (AAMA). Its goals are to promote media awareness, education, and understanding as essential survival skills for all Albertans, children and adults. Among other activities, AAMA provides forums for information, discussion, and action on media issues; prepares reaction and suggestions on media issues such as new government policy and programs; provides conferences and training sessions for teachers; maintains a resource centre; and establishes action networks.

Since 1993, AAMA has continued to promote media awareness and to organize workshops each year, but the level of activity has been modest due to significant local, provincial, and federal government financial and human cutbacks. An AAMA achievement has been to provide continuing critical and developmental input to the Western Canada Protocol (WCP) Curriculum Framework for the development of English Language Arts through the Alberta Department of Education representatives. This has resulted in major changes to the Alberta Department of Education revised English/Language Arts curriculum Grades K to 12 including: significant emphasis on media education and, for the first time, the use of the term "media text."

Mandatory implementation of the new Alberta English Language Arts curricula are scheduled for: Grades K to 9, September 1999; Grade 10, September 2000; Grade 11, September 2001, and Grade 12, September 2002. In addition, the new curricula are organized around five general outcomes, with media outcomes integrated throughout along a student outcomes basis so that student evaluation will be facilitated. A number of instructional guides and evaluation examples are under development to help teachers ensure student results. The Classroom Assessment Materials Project (CAMP) was developed for English Language Arts, and contains assessment activities and scoring criteria that include reference to media or viewing

In the neighbouring province of Saskatchewan, Mick Ellis, then Audio Visual Consultant for the Saskatoon Board of Education (and the first Canadian to obtain a master's degree in Media Education), and a group of Saskatoon educators founded Media Literacy Saskatchewan (MLS) in January of 1988. MLS goals include: to establish and maintain communication among educators; to advocate for the development and integration of media education in educational curricula; to influence educational policy-makers; to provide professional support and to maintain contact with Canadian and international media education organizations. Media Literacy Saskatchewan publishes a quarterly newsletter for its members called *Media View*.

Members of MLS have developed three programs – Telemedia, Newsmedia, Kindermedia – for use in the schools, and have also developed a media education guide extending from primary through to the end of secondary school, believing that media education should be integrated with any and all aspects of the school curriculum. In 1991, MLS became an official special subject council of the Saskatchewan Teachers Federation (STF), gaining access to all teachers in Saskatchewan through the STF *Bulletin* and allowing the funding of in-services and conferences.

Media education is a part of the common essential learnings and one of the supporting domains of the basic Language Arts structure. In core-content English courses, media studies are now required: video in Grade 10, radio in Grade 11, and print journalism in Grade 12. But there is no resource plan for these courses and it will be up to teacher initiative to develop resources for these.

Locally developed media courses have diminished except in production courses. Saskatchewan Education has mandated three options for Grade 11 English besides the required credits in English: Media Studies, Journalism, and Creative Writing. Availability of such courses depends upon student registration. Larger urban schools offer all three while smaller or rural schools tend to get registration enough for two out of three courses. While there is little in-service for all three, there is enthusiasm and a realistic attitude about ongoing updating of media studies resources by teachers. Some resources are being purchased for these courses but there is a great need for formal teacher training.

For a number of years Manitoba has had an official provincial policy on Media Education. Language Arts teachers were encouraged to integrate Media into their teaching in the Early and Middle Years by examining the messages coming from television advertising. Secondary school teachers were asked to investigate the media as part of their English courses.

Now, as part of the Western Canada Protocol group, Manitoba's new language arts curriculum has a mandated elements of media education under the title of viewing and representing. All frameworks of outcomes and standards from K to 12 make specific references to media texts and to the skills required for media education. By the end of 1998, implementation documents for all grades will be completed, as well as a list of resources. The challenge in Manitoba will be to provide formal training for teachers of the media. The University of Manitoba offered a summer school in media education for a number of years taught by Brian Murphy, President of the Manitoba Association for Media Literacy. Now the University's Faculty of Education is proposing a regular course for teachers in media education.

The Manitoba Association for Media Literacy (MAML) was founded in October 1990, the result of a Special Areas Group (SAG) Conference sponsored by the Art Educators Association of Manitoba. The role of MAML is to promote the aims of media education, in particular to assist individuals to examine the role of the media in society. To accomplish its goals, MAML sponsors presentations and workshops; assists in the development of media education programs for Manitoba schools; provides in-service opportunities; and publishes *Directions*, a quarterly newsletter.

Yukon and the Northwest Territories
Yukon and the Northwest Territories are members of the Western Consortium described above. As such they are developing media education components of their Language Arts Programs. Some teachers in these places are working on their own to introduce media education into their courses.

Atlantic Canada – Nova Scotia, New Brunswick, Prince Edward Island, Newfoundland
In 1995 an Atlantic provinces initiative – similar to the Language Arts Consortium in Western Canada – developed a common Language Arts curriculum in which media education figures prominently. It builds on the notion that literacy has moved beyond competency in the written language to the ability to use and under-stand visual and technological means of communications. This curriculum was piloted in 1996 and implemented in 1997. The documents state that media educa-tion is a critical element of the Language Arts curriculum and make it part of every English course.

In the fall of 1992, a group of teachers, parents, librarians, media profession-als, and environmentalists formed the Association of Media Literacy for Nova Scotia (AML-NS). One of the reasons that brought the group of about one hundred people together was the need to stop the Youth News Network (YNN) from selling its commercial news network to Nova Scotia schools. They succeeded in both forming a media education group and in stopping YNN.

AML-NS members publish a newsletter twice yearly, *The Mediator*. Past President Eileen O'Connell has a monthly column on media education issues in the Halifax *Chronicle-Herald*, Nova Scotia's largest circulation daily paper. As well, Gail Lethbridge, editor of *The Mediator*, writes a regular column for *The Teacher*, the newsletter of the Nova Scotia Teachers' Union.

Members of AML-NS have presented workshops to parents and community groups as well at several provincial in-services for teachers. Since 1993, the Atlantic Film Festival has invited teachers to participate with their students in the ScreenScene program and sponsored one event for teachers dealing with media.

The Literacy section of the Nova Scotia Department of Education and Culture together with AML-NS have co-sponsored a media education project for adult learners. Funded by the National Literacy Secretariat and written by AML-NS founding president, Pat Kipping, the kit consists of a workshop manual, a collection of resources, and an annotated guide.

The Nova Scotia College of Art and Design Education Department has built into their courses some components which raise the issue of media education. As well, summer course have been offered by Mount St. Vincent University in media education.

Central Canada – Quebec and Ontario
Over half of Canada's population lives in the two central Canadian provinces of Ontario and Quebec. Quebec's Ministry of Education has developed a reformed curriculum to be implemented in elementary and secondary schools by 1999. Media education will be taught in a cross-curricular pedagogical plan so that it is a basic skill and competence.

In September of 1990, a group of French- and English-speaking secondary teachers, university academics, and others interested in media education formed the Association for Media Education in Quebec (AMEQ), a bilingual grassroots organization composed mainly of teachers. AMEQ is co-chaired by Lee Rother of the Laurenval School Board and Brenda Wilson of Trafalgar School for Girls.

The primary purpose of AMEQ is to provide information, lesson plans and ideas, expertise, and professional development regarding media education. AMEQ contends that media education should be included both in the kindergarten through grade eleven curriculum and in all teacher-training programs. AMEQ actively promotes the idea that parents should also be media educators for their children.

AMEQ has sponsored student media festivals, media education conferences, day-long workshops for teachers and parents, and parent information evenings. AMEQ members regularly lead workshops at provincial education and parent conferences, school board professional development programs, and guest-lecture at McGill University's and Bishop's University's faculties of education. AMEQ executive members have also presented briefs to the Quebec Ministry of Education concerning proposed curricular changes and also to the Canadian Radio-television Telecommunications Commission (CRTC) on violence and the media.

In 1991, the Montreal-based Centre for Literacy, which maintains an open resources collection on every aspect of literacy, began to receive a large number of requests for resources on media education. The Centre has increased the media component of their collection and organizes workshops on media education. A similar development has taken place at the Centre Saint-Pierre, a community-based continuing education centre.

Ontario, where over one-third of Canada's population lives, was the first educational jurisdiction in North America to make media education a mandatory part of the curriculum. In 1987 Ontario's Ministry of Education released new guidelines that emphasized the importance of teaching media education as part of the regular English curriculum. At least one-third of a course in both intermediate and senior division English must be devoted to media study. And in Grades 7 and 8 (twelve- and thirteen-year-olds), 10 per cent of classroom time was dedicated to some form of media studies. In addition students were allowed to choose a complete media studies course as one of the five English credits required for graduation.

At the beginning of April 1995, the Ontario Ministry of Education released two documents: *The Common Curriculum: Policies and Outcomes Grades 1 to 9* clearly outlines what students are expected to know and when they are expected to know it; *Provincial Standards: Language: Grades 1 to 9* provides objective and consistent indicators to determine how well students are learning. From Grades 1 to 9 in Language Arts there are strands which must be: Listening and Speaking, Reading, Writing, Viewing and Representing. The Viewing and Representing strands ensure that media education is now a mandated part of the Language Arts curriculum beginning from Grade 1. There were further revisions to Ontario's Language Arts curricula in 1998 and media education continues to be a strongly mandated part of the English Language Arts curricula in both the elementary and secondary panel.

One group above all is responsible for the continuing successful development of media education in Ontario. This is the Association for Media Literacy (AML). There were seventy people at the AML's founding meeting in Toronto in April of 1978. The founders of the association were Barry Duncan, a secondary school teacher and head of English at Toronto's School of Experiential Education; Arlene Moskovitch, then with the National Film Board of Canada, now a consultant; Linda Schulyer, an elementary teacher, who has since become a principal in Playing With Time, Inc. responsible for the popular *Degrassi* television series; and Jerry McNab, head of the Canadian Filmmakers Distribution Centre, now head of Magic Lantern, a production and distribution centre. By the end of the 1980s, the AML had over one thousand members and a track record of distinguished achievements.

In 1986, the Ontario Ministry of Education and the Ontario Teachers' Federation invited ten AML members to prepare a *Media Education Resource Guide* for teachers. Published by the government in the summer of 1989, the 232-page guide is designed to help teachers of media. It includes teaching strategies and models as well as rationale and aims. This guide is used in many English-speaking countries and has been translated into French, Italian, Japanese, and Spanish.

Prior to the release of the *Resource Guide*, the Ministry seconded the AML authors to give a series of in-service training days to teachers across Ontario in preparation for the introduction of media courses. Since 1987, AML members have presented workshops across Canada, and in Australia, Japan, Europe, Latin America, and the United States. As well, all the media education texts used in Canadian classrooms have been written by members of the AML.

Three times a year, the AML publishes *Mediacy* which updates AML members on what has been happening, lists new publications in the field, announces speakers and topics for quarterly events, and publishes articles on related topics. During the school year, the AML sponsors quarterly events bringing in speakers for workshop presentations to teachers.

From 1987 to 1993, the AML offered three courses for media teachers during summer school in conjunction with the Faculty of Education at the University of Toronto. A steep increase in the cost of summer school courses brought these courses to an end.

In May of 1989, the AML brought together forty-six educators and media professionals for a two-day invitational think tank to discuss future developments of media education in Ontario. This led to two international media education conferences at the University of Guelph in 1990 and 1992. Both conferences were very successful, attracting over five hundred participants from around the world.

After the 1992 conference, representatives from Canadian provincial media education groups met in Toronto to form the Canadian Association of Media Education Organizations (CAMEO). The purpose of the group is to promote media education across Canada and link together Canadian media education organizations. CAMEO member organizations have been involved in a number of Canadian initiatives. Presentations were made by member groups to the CRTC during the national hearings on violence and the media. CAMEO advocated the development of a single national classification system for theatrical release movies and offered its services to develop the called-for media literacy strategies. CAMEO has also petitioned for the inclusion of a fair-use clause in the revised Canadian copyright laws

As well, CAMEO successfully led three struggles in 1996, 1997, and 1998 to keep the Youth News Network out of Canadian classrooms. CAMEO is a strong force in enabling the various provincial media education groups to work together on national issues. This is in contrast to the United States where, as was noted in *The Journal of Communication* (Volume 48/1), whenever media literacy groups gather, ". . . they always circle the wagon – and shoot in."

3. The Canadian Media's Role in Media Education

Having access to good media resources is very important for media teachers. This is especially true in Canada where the current copyright laws complicate the situation. As Canadian media professionals have come to realize that media education does not mean "media bashing," they have been very pleased to work with media educators and to collaborate in the production of a number of excellent audio-visual materials. Here are some examples of this collaboration.

1. For many years Canadian teachers have used films from the National Film Board of Canada (NFB), subscribed to their educational newsletters, and taken part in their workshops. Since 1989, the NFB has issued three video resource packages which are proving very helpful for media teachers:

- *Images and Meaning* is an anthology of nine National Film Board productions to spark discussion and learning in media literacy courses. A small booklet gives a series of discussion guidelines for classes.
- *Media and Society* is especially useful, dealing as it does with media in contemporary society under four main topics: Advertising and Consumerism, Images of Women, Cultural Sovereignty, and Shaping the Truth. Each topic is presented with a short, provocative introduction. The package offers a wide choice of topics in the form of short documentaries, animated films, advertisements, and excerpts. This video package consists of 3 VHS videos containing nineteen NFB films or film excerpts and a 124-page Resource Guide. The Resource Guide includes activities, interviews with filmmakers, backgrounds on the films, student handouts, articles, and quotes.
- *Constructing Reality* deals with truth, fact, objectivity, and the nature of propaganda in the media. The six video cassettes or laserdiscs house an anthology of films, film excerpts, interviews, and original production material for

use in senior media literacy classes. The accompanying Resource Guide raises critical issues around documentary filmmaking and representations of fact and fiction in mainstream media. The package is organized in six sections: The Documentary Process, The Viewing Experience, Documentary Traditions, The Search For Truth, Many Voices, and New Directions.

2. Another resource is the CBC's *Inside the Box*, a series of six packages, each of which include a video and teacher's guide. The subjects dealt with are Television Documentary, Television News, Children's Television, Drama, Television and the Consumer, and Television as an Artistic Medium.

3. Beginning in the autumn of 1991, YTV, the Toronto-based national youth channel, worked with AML executive board member Neil Andersen, to produce media literacy notes for their weekly TV program *Street Noise*. Toronto's Citytv has a weekly program, *Media Television*, which analyzes various aspects of the mass media.

4. The Alliance for Children and Television in collaboration with Health Canada has produced the *Prime Time Parent* kit, which has received an overwhelming response from teachers and parents.

5. The Media Awareness Network has created the *Video for Media Education* catalogue, which offers 115 English and 100 French video titles – all reviewed by media literacy teachers across Canada.

6. Warner Brothers Canada assisted in the publishing of a 1994 media literacy study guide for the animated film *Batman: Mask of the Phantasm*, in *Kids World Magazine*. This guide dealt honestly with the issues of violence in the movie.

7. YTV's series of lesson plans for teachers, written by Neil Andersen and other media literacy teachers – *YTV News in Class* – has dealt with a number of topics including *Television and Violence*. This lesson plan presents ways of discussing such topics as types of media violence, how to report violence on the news without showing it, and other ways children might have learned violent behaviour. It also offers topics for research into the area of media violence as well as suggestions for practical activities.

8. TVOntario has purchased rights to a number of media literacy programs for teachers and has prepared two interactive satellite broadcasts on media literacy. Both of these were done with consultation from media literacy teachers.

9. In the fall of 1995 a majority of Canada's English- and French-language programming services and several U.S. cable services working in partnership with cable operators across Canada came together to form Cable in the Classroom. Today, under executive director Shari Baldwin, Cable in the Classroom is an alliance of some thirty-three networks and the Canadian cable operators in Canada. They are committed to bringing copyright-cleared, commercial-free, educationally relevant programs to elementary and secondary schools across the country. Teachers are free to tape programs of interest and replay them in class. Schedules and support print material are available. Much of this material is used by media teachers in a variety of subjects.

10. Also in 1995 a new service appeared on the Internet – on the World Wide Web – called the *Media Awareness Network*. It is a bilingual, Canadian education web site dedicated to media literacy among young people. The site contains a wide range of copyright-cleared resources to help teachers integrate media literacy and web literacy into their classrooms. Resources include over one hundred and fifty elementary and secondary lesson plans; downloadable games and teacher's guides; an electronic "vertical" file of newspaper articles; current statistics and industry information; and an extensive issues section.

11. The Jesuit Communication Project was set up in 1984 to promote media literacy in Canada. It also serves as a Canadian resource centre for media literacy with a collection of over four thousand books and periodicals on the media, as well as vertical files on media education topics and a large collection of media education teaching materials from around the world. It is used by teachers, researchers, students, and the media from across Canada and around the world. Twice a year, it publishes *Clipboard* – the only international media literacy newsletter – and distributes it to forty-one countries. In 1997, the Jesuit Communication Project, working with Gemini-winning filmmaker Gary Marcuse, CHUM Television Ltd., YTV, TVOntario, Warner Brothers, and the NFB-produced *Scanning Television* – an award-winning collection of some forty excerpts from television for use in media literacy class. The accompanying teacher's guide was written by media

educator Neil Andersen. The guide and the four video kits are published by Harcourt Brace.

12. Two recent releases: a kit for elementary teachers which examines media education elements in the popular children's program *Theodore Tugboat*, and – in a collaboration between Shaw Cable and The Concerned Children's Advertisers – a kit designed for children ages 9 to 12, *TV and Me*. This second kit uses the public service announcements created by the Concerned Children's Advertisers to discuss specific media education concepts.

13. In January 1999, Pacific Cinémathèque in Vancouver issued the first in a series of Film Study Guides developed with the assistance of Alliance Films, Famous Players, the Vancouver Foundation, and the British Columbia Arts Council. The plan is to issue six to eight of these guides for current films free of charge to secondary schools across Canada.

14. CHUM Limited is one of Canada's foremost broadcasting companies and program providers which currently owns and operates twenty-four radio stations, six local independent television stations, and seven specialty channels across Canada. Local television services include Toronto's Citytv, The New VR in Barrie, CFPL, CKNX, and CHWI television stations in South Western Ontario, and CHRO in the National Capital Region. Specialty services include Much Music, MuchMoreMusic, MusiquePlus (50 per cent), Bravo!, Alberta's Access, the Education Station, MusiMax (50 per cent), a new twenty-four-hour French Adult Music Television Station, and Space, the Imagination Station. CHUM Limited was also granted digital specialty channel licences for Star – the Entertainment Information Station and Canadian Learning Television.

CHUM Television has always been a strong supporter of media education through its programming – *Media Television, MovieTelevision, Scanning the Movies, Too Much for Much,* and special editions of *The NewMusic* – as a founding member of Cable in the Classroom, and as a supporter of the Jesuit Communication Project.

Citytv's weekly series *Media Television* provides a critical look at various media. This is an important example of original programming about the media. It has a great potential for use by teachers of media education and is seen in a number of other countries.

Much Music's program *Too Much for Much* brings in media education teachers and students along with station decision-makers and cultural critics to discuss why certain videos are not being aired. As well, as part of Cable in the Classroom, Much Music has developed a number of teacher's guides to accompany the *New Music* programs which appear monthly through Cable in the Classroom.

Scanning the Movies, created and hosted by John J. Pungente, S. J., the award-winning half-hour television program which looks at one current movie a month, began broadcasting across Canada on Bravo! in September 1997. *Scanning the Movies* is for anyone with an interest in the movies. Of special interest to movie buffs as well as to those who teach or study the movies, *Scanning the Movies* is a production of Bravo! in association with Warner Brothers Entertainment Inc.

The first season of the show looked at such films as *L.A. Confidential, Mad City, Contact, Without Limits, The Postman, Conspiracy Theory, Wild America, Sphere, Quest for Camelot*. This show discusses how to "read" movies, to discover how they work and how they communicate through the magic of storytelling on the big screen. The show's study guides and lesson plans can be found on the Cable in the Classroom web site (www.cableducation.ca) and on the Bravo! web site (www.bravo.ca). Neil Andersen, executive member of the Association for Media Literacy, award-winning author, and teacher of English and Media in Scarborough, brings his skills to the preparation of the Internet study guide and lesson plans.

In the fall of 1997, CHUM Television announced the appointment of Sarah Crawford as Director of Media Education, CHUM Television. For a number of years as Director of Communications for Much Music, Sarah has worked closely with the Ontario Association for Media Literacy. She has helped develop media education lesson plans for various aspects of music and popular culture programming. A very vocal public supporter of media education for many years, Sarah has given presentations at media education conferences, promoted various media education projects across the CHUM Television group, and represented CHUM on the Board of Directors for Cable in the Classroom in its start-up years. To the best of my knowledge, CHUM is the first national broadcaster in the world to have a full-time Director of Media Education. This is a historical and important step in media education.

4. And Towards the Millennium

Summit 2000: Children, Youth and the Media – Beyond the Millennium is an international conference to be held in Toronto, Canada, from May 13 to 17, 2000. The conference will draw some 1,500 delegates from around the world. Delegates will be people involved in the production and distribution of screen-based – television, film, computer – media for children and youth, as well as anyone involved in media education, such as teachers, researchers, educators, community and religious groups. This will be a unique opportunity for those who use and teach about the media to meet and talk with those who produce and distribute it.

The program will focus on three content pillars:

- Production and Financing
- Distribution and Access
- Media Education

With keynote speakers in plenary sessions and up to eighty breakout sessions each day, participants will turn the new South Wing of the Metro Toronto Convention Centre into a living laboratory where new solutions to established challenges facing screen-based media can be developed by those who produce, distribute, and teach about the media. The endemic underfunding of children's and youth programming, limits on distribution, impact of globalization and of new, interactive media, marketing, the many issues surrounding media education, regulatory problems, and many other issues will be under the microscope. There will also be time for much informal discussion, bear-pit sessions, screenings and meetings. And there will be time just to meet others and talk. Plenary sessions will be simultaneously translated into English, French, and Spanish.

The Summit is being coordinated by the Alliance for Children and Television, The Jesuit Communication Project, the Ontario Association for Media Literacy, and the American Center for Children's Television. The international steering committee is made up of representatives from each of Canada, Central and South America, the CARICOM countries, Asia, the U.S.A., Europe, the Antipodes, and Africa. The Summit web site has complete information at www.summit2000.net.

5. Making Media Education Work

Over the past thirty years of teaching media education, travelling around the world to see it in action in various countries, in my research, and from talks, e-mails, letters, and phone calls from and with so many media educators from all over, I have found that there are a number of factors which must be in place in order for media education to work properly in any given place – whether that be a country, a province or state, or an individual school district/board. Here is a list of these basic factors:

1. Media education, like other innovative programs, must be a grassroots movement and teachers need to take a major initiative in lobbying for this.

2. Educational authorities must give clear support to such programs by mandating the teaching of media education within the curriculum, establishing guidelines and resource books, and by making certain that curricula are developed and that support materials are available.

3. Faculties of education must offer courses to prepare teachers to teach media education and to this end must hire staff capable of training future teachers in this area. This is the single greatest lack in media education in Canada, where teachers are required to teach it but there is no training in this for teachers. There should also be academic support from tertiary institutions in the writing of curricula and in sustained consultation and research.

4. In-service training at the school district or school board level must be an integral part of program implementation.

5. School districts or school boards must have consultants who have expertise in media education and who will establish communication networks.

6. Suitable textbooks and audiovisual material which are relevant to the country/area must be available.

7. A support organization must be established for the purposes of workshops, conferences, dissemination of newsletters, and the development of curriculum units. Such a professional organization must cut across school boards and districts to involve a cross section of people interested in media education, including parents, teachers, and media professionals.

8. There must be appropriate evaluation instruments which are suitable for the unique quality of media education.

9. Because media education involves such a diversity of skills and expertise, there must be collaboration between teachers, parents, researchers, and media professionals.

Appendix Two: Further Reading and Other Resources

∼

Books

Arthur, Chris (ed.). *Religion and the Media: An Introductory Reader*. Cardiff: University of Wales Press, 1993.

Auletta, Ken. *The Highwaymen: Warriors of the Information Superhighway*. San Diego: Harcourt Brace, 1998.

Bain, George. *Gotcha: How the Media Distort the News*. Toronto: Key Porter, 1994.

Baker, William F. and Dessart, George. *Down the Tube: An Inside Account of the Failure of American Television*. New York: Basic Books, 1998.

Barker, Martin and Petley, Julian (eds.). *Ill Effects: The Media/Violence Debate*. London: Routledge, 1997.

Bazalgette, Cary (ed.). *Primary Media Education*. London: British Film Institute, 1989. (BFI, 21 Stephen Street, London w1p 2ln, England)

Berg, Leah and Wenner, Lawrence (eds.). *Television Criticism*. New York: Longman, 1991.

Bianculli, David. *Dictionary of Teleliteracy: Television's 500 Biggest Hits, Misses and Events*. New York: Continuum, 1996.

Bianculli, David. *Teleliteracy: Taking Television Seriously*. New York: Continuum, 1992.

Bowker, Julian (ed.). *Secondary Media Education*. London: British Film Institute, 1991.

Branston, Gill and Stafford, Roy. *The Media Student's Book*. London: Routledge, 1996.

Buckingham, David. *Cultural Studies Goes to School*. Toronto: Gage, 1994.

Buckingham, David (ed.). *Reading Audiences*. Manchester: Manchester University Press, 1993.

Buckingham, David (ed.). *Watching Media Learning.* London: The Falmer Press, 1990.

Cantor, Muriel and Pingree, Suzanne. *The Soap Opera.* Beverly Hills: Sage, 1983.

Carere, Sharon (ed.). *Responding to Media Violence: Starting Points for Classroom Practice – K–6.* Toronto: The Metropolitan Toronto School Board, Pembroke Publishers, 1998.

Carlsson, Ulla and Von Feilitzen, Cecilia (ed.) *Children and Media Violence.* Sweden: UNESCO, 1998.

Carlsson-Paige, Nancy and Levin, Diane E. *Who's Calling the Shots? How to Respond Effectively to Children's Fascination With War Play and War Toys.* Philadelphia: New Society Publishers, 1990.

Carter, Bill. *The Late Shift.* New York: Hyperion, 1994.

Cooper, Barry. *Sins of Omission: Shaping the News at CBC-TV.* Toronto: University of Toronto Press, 1994.

Copeland, Mary Ann. *Soap Opera History.* Lincolnwood, IL: Publications International, 1991.

CRTC. *Respecting Children: A Canadian Approach to Helping Families Deal with Television Violence.* Ottawa: CRTC, 1996.

Dell Vecchio, Gene. *Creating Ever-Cool: A Marketer's Guide to a Kid's Heart.* New York: Pelican Books, 1997.

Dorland, Michael (ed.). *The Cultural Industries in Canada: Problems, Policies and Prospects.* Toronto: James Lorimer & Company, 1996.

Dornfeld, Barry. *Producing Public Television, Producing Public Culture.* Princeton: Princeton University Press, 1998.

During, Simon (ed.). *Cultural Studies Reader.* London: Routledge, 1993.

Fiske, John. *Media Matters: Everyday Culture and Political Change.* Minneapolis: University of Minnesota Press, 1994.

Fiske, John. *Understanding Popular Culture.* Boston: Unwin Hyman, 1989.

Fore, William F. *Television and Religion: The Shaping of Faith, Values and Culture.* Minneapolis: Augsborg Publishing House, 1989.

Frank, Thomas. *The Conquest of Cool: Business Culture, Counterculture and the Rise of Hip Consumerism.* Chicago: University of Chicago Press, 1997.

Gamson, Joshua. *Freaks Talk Back.* Chicago: University of Chicago Press, 1998.

Giroux, Henry. *Disturbing Pleasures: Learning Popular Culture.* London: Routledge, 1994.

Gitlin, Todd (ed.). *Watching Television.* New York: Pantheon, 1986.

Goldberg, Robert and Goldberg, Gerald Jay. *Anchors*. New York: Birch Lane, 1990.

Goldstein, Jeffrey H. (ed.). *Why We Watch: The Attraction of Violent Entertainment*. New York: Oxford University Press, 1998.

Greenberg, Bradley S. and Gantz, Walter (eds.). *Desert Storm and the Mass Media*. Creskill, NJ: Hampton Press, 1993.

Hart, Andrew (ed.). *Teaching the Media: International Perspectives*. Mahwah, NJ: Lawrence Erlbaum Associates, 1998.

Heaton, Jeanne Albronda and Wilson, Nona Leigh. *Tuning in Trouble: Talk TV's Destructive Impact on Mental Health*. San Francisco: Jossey-Bass, 1995.

Jones, Gerard. *Honey, I'm Home! Sitcoms*. New York: Grove Weidenfeld, 1992.

Kalat, David P. *Homicide: Life on the Street: The Unofficial Companion*. Los Angeles: Renaissance Books, 1998.

Kellner, Douglas. *The Persian Gulf TV War*. Boulder, CO: Westview Press, 1992

Kessler, Judy. *Inside Today*. New York: Villard, 1992.

Kline, Stephen. *Out of the Garden: Toys and Children's Culture in the Age of TV Marketing*. Toronto: Garramond Press, 1994.

Krazicek, David J. *Scooped: Media Miss Real Story on Crime*. New York: Columbia University Press, 1998.

Kurtz, Howard. *Hot Air: All Talk All the Time*. New York: Random House, 1996.

Langer, John. *Tabloid Television: Popular Journalism and the Other News*. London: Routledge, 1998.

Lee, Martin and Solomon, Norman. *Unreliable Sources: Detecting Bias in News Media*. New York: Lyle Stuart Book, 1990.

Leonard, John. *Smoke and Mirrors: Violence, Television and Other American Cultures*. New York: New Press, 1996.

Levine, Michael. *The Princess and the Package*. Los Angeles: Renaissance Books, 1998.

Lichter, S. Robert, Lichter, Linda S., and Rothman, Stanley. *Prime Time: How TV Portrays American Culture*. Washington: Regnery, 1994.

MacArthur, John R. *Second Front: Censorship and Propaganda in the Gulf War*. Berkeley: University of California Press, 1993.

Manoff, Robert Karl and Schudson, Michael (eds.). *Reading the News*. New York: Pantheon, 1986.

Marc, David and Thompson, Robert J. *Prime Time, Prime Movers*. Boston: Little, Brown and Co., 1992.

Masterman, Len. *Teaching the Media*. London: Routledge, 1985.

McDonnell, Kathleen. *Kid Culture: Children & Adults & Popular Culture*. Toronto: Second Story, 1994.

McNeil, Alex. *Total Television: Comprehensive Guide to Programming from 1948 to the Present – 4th Edition*. New York: Penguin, 1997.

Media Literacy Resource Guide. Government of Ontario Book Store.

Miedzian, Myriam. *Boys Will Be Boys: Breaking the Link Between Masculinity and Violence*. New York: Doubleday, 1991.

Moog, Carol. *Are They Selling Her Lips? Advertising and Identity*. New York: William Morrow, 1990.

Mowlana, Hamid, Gerbner, George, and Schiller, Herbert I. *Triumph of the Image: The Media's War in the Persian Gulf – A Global Perspective*. Boulder, CO: Westview Press, 1992.

Munson, Wayne. *All Talk: The Talkshow in Media Culture*. Philadelphia: Temple University Press, 1993.

Nash, Knowlton. *Trivia Pursuit: How Showbiz Values Are Corrupting the News*. Toronto: McClelland and Stewart, 1998.

National Television Violence Study – Volumes 1 and 2. Thousand Oaks, CA: Sage, 1997.

Negroponte, Nicholas. *Being Digital*. New York: Alfred Knopf, 1995.

Nelson, Joyce. *Sultans of Sleaze*. Toronto: Between the Lines Press, 1989.

Nochimson, Martha. *No End to Her: Soap Opera and the Female Subject*. Berkeley: University of California Press, 1992.

O'Brien, Tom. *The Screening of America: Movies and Values from Rocky to Rain Man*. New York: Frederick Ungar, 1990.

Petracca, Michael and Sorapure, Madeleine. *Common Culture: Reading and Writing About American Popular Culture*. Englewood Cliffs, NJ: Prentice Hall, 1995.

Postman, Neil and Powers, Steve. *How to Watch TV News*. New York: Penguin, 1992.

Robertson, Heather-jane. *No More Teachers, No More Books: The Commercialization of Canada's Schools*. Toronto: McClelland and Stewart, 1998.

Rushkoff, Douglas. *Playing the Future: How Kid's Culture Can Teach Us to Thrive in an Age of Chaos*. New York: Harper Collins, 1996.

Schechter, Danny. *The More You Watch, the Less You Know*. New York: Seven Stories Press, 1997.

Schiller, Herber I. *Culture, Inc.: The Corporate Takeover of Public Expression*. New York: Oxford University Press, 1990.

Shattuc, Jane M. *The Talking Cure: TV Talk Shows and Women*. New York: Routledge, 1997.

Shuker, Roy. *Understanding Popular Music*. London: Routledge, 1994.

Solomon, Jack. *The Signs of Our Time*. Los Angeles: Jeremy Tarcher, Inc., 1988.

Stark, Steven D. *Glued to the Set*. New York: The Free Press, 1997.

Thompson, Robert J. *Television's Second Golden Age – From Hill Street Blues to ER*. New York: Continuum, 1996.

Tracy, Kathleen. *The Girl's Got Bite: The Unofficial Guide to Buffy's World*. Los Angeles: Renaissance, 1998.

Turkle, Sherry. *Life on the Screen: Identity in the Age of the Internet*. New York: Simon & Schuster, 1995

Turow, Joseph. *Breaking Up America: Advertisers and the New Media World*. Chicago: University of Chicago Press, 1997.

Twitchell, James B. *Preposterous Violence: Fables of Aggression in Modern Culture*. New York: Oxford University Press, 1990.

Wakin, Edward. *How TV Changed America's Mind*. New York: Lothrop, Lee & Shepard Books, 1996

Whittemore, Hank. *CNN: The Inside Story*. Boston: Little, Brown and Co., 1990.

Winship, Michael. *Television*. New York: Random House, 1988.

Winter, James. *Democracy's Oxygen: How Corporations Control the News*. Montreal: Black Rose Books, 1997.

Media Text Books

Andersen, Neil: *Media Works*. Toronto: Oxford University Press, 1989.

Booth, David, Lewis, Kathy, et al. *Media Sense 4: A Meadow Books Component (Age 8-12)*. Toronto: Harcourt Brace, 1998.

Duncan, Barry, et al. *Mass Media and Popular Culture (2nd Edition)*. Toronto: Harcourt Brace, 1996.

Hone, Rick and Flynn, Liz. *Video in Focus: A Guide to Viewing and Producing Videos*. Toronto: Globe Modern–Prentice Hall, 1992.

Livesley, Jack et al. *Meet the Media*. Toronto: Globe Modern–Prentice Hall, 1990.

Periodicals

Adbusters, 1243 West 7th Ave., Vancouver, BC V6H 1B7, e-mail adbusters@adbusters.org; web site www.adbusters.org

Entertainment Weekly, P.O. Box 60890, Tampa, Florida 33660-0890, U.S.A., phone toll-free 1-800-828-6882; e-mail: letters@ew.com

Metro, Australian Teachers of Media, P.O. Box 2211, St. Kilda West, Victoria 3182, Australia; e-mail: tapp@netspace.net.au; web site: www.cinemdia.net/ATOM

Telemedium, 120 East Wilson Street, Madison, Wisconsin, 53703, U.S.A., e-mail Ntelemedia@aol.com

TV Networks and Government Agencies

ABC, 77 West 66th Street, 9th Floor, New York, NY 10023, phone (212) 456-1725

CBC, Box 500, Station A, Toronto, ON M5W 1E6, phone (416) 205-3351

CBS, 51 West 52nd Street, New York, NY 10019, phone (212) 975-1556

Citytv/Much Music, 299 Queen Street West, Toronto, ON M5V 2Z5, phone (416) 591-5757

CTV, P. O. Box 300, Agincourt Postal Stn., Agincourt, ON M1S 3C6, phone (416) 595-4100

Fox Broadcasting Co., Box 900, Beverly Hills, CA, 90213.

Global, 81 Barber Greene Road, Don Mills, ON M3C 2A2, phone (416) 446-5311

NBC, 30 Rockefeller Plaza, New York, NY 10020, phone (212) 664-2074

PBS, 1320 Braddock Place, Alexandria, VA 22314-1698, phone toll-free 1-800-328-7271

Radio Canada, CP 6000, Montreal, QC H3C 3A8, phone (514) 597-5970

TVOntario, 2180 Yonge Street, Toronto, ON M4S 2B9, phone (416) 484-2600

YTV, 64 Jefferson Avenue, Toronto, ON M6K 3H3, phone (416) 534-1191

CRTC, Public Affairs, Ottawa, ON K1A 0N2, phone (613) 997-0313

Federal Communications Commission, Complaints & Investigations Office, 2025 M Street NW, Room 8210, Washington, DC, U.S.A. 20554.

The Internet
The Media Awareness Network, 1500 Merivale Rd., 3rd Floor, Ottawa, ON K2E 6Z5 phone (613) 224-7721, fax (613) 224-1958. E-mail: info@media-awareness.ca. Check their web site at: www.media-awareness.ca

The University of Oregon web site has links to media literacy sites around the world: interact.uoregon.edu/MediaLit/Homepage

Scanning the Movies:
www.bravo.ca/events/scanningthemovies

Summit 2000 – world media literacy conference in Toronto, May 2000 www.summit2000.net

Canadian Media Education Contacts
Alliance for Children and Television (ACT), 1002–60 St. Clair Avenue East, Toronto, ON M4T 1N5, phone (416) 515-0466, fax (416) 515-0467, e-mail: acttv@interlog.com

Canadian Association for Media Education Organizations (CAMEO)

Cameo Members
   1. Canadian Association for Media Education in British Columbia
   Dan Blake
   Curriculum and Instructional Services Centre (CISC)
   7532–134A Street,
   Surrey, BC V3W 7J1
   phone (604) 590 2255, fax (604) 590 2588
   On-site e-mail: BLAKE_D@dflash.dnet.sd36.surrey.bc.ca
   e-mail: danblake@istar.ca

   2. Alberta Association for Media Awareness
   Sharon McCann
   Film Classification Services
   Alberta Community Development
   Beaver House
   5th Floor, 10158–103 Street
   Edmonton, AB T5J 0X6
   phone (403) 427-2006
   fax (403) 427-0195
   e-mail: SMcCann@mcd.gov.ab.ca
   or: semccann@sas.ab.ca

   3. Media Literacy Saskatchewan
   Bob Pace
   Robert Usher Collegiate
   1414–9th Avenue North
   Regina, SK S4R 8B1
   phone (306) 791-8435
   fax (306) 791-8443
   e-mail: space@cableregina.com

4. Manitoba Association for Media Literacy
Brian Murphy
St. Paul's High School
2200 Grant Avenue
Winnipeg, MB R3P 0P8
phone (204) 831-2300
fax (204) 831-2340
e-mail: brmurphy@minet.gov.mb.ca

5. Association for Media Literacy Ontario
Barry Duncan
2204–1 Aberfoyle Crescent
Toronto, ON M8X 2X8
phone (416) 696-7144
e-mail: baduncan@interlog.com

6. Association for Media Education Quebec
Lee Rother
Lake of Two Mountains School
2105 Deux Montaignes, QC J7R 1W6
phone (514) 491-1000
fax (514) 491-6862
e-mail: irothe@po-box.mcgill.ca

7. Association for Media Literacy Nova Scotia
Trudie Richards
Assistant Professor
Mount St. Vincent University
166 Bedford Highway
Halifax, NS B3M 2J6
phone (902) 457-6210
fax (902) 457-1216
e-mail: Trudie.Richards@MSVU.CA

Cable in the Classroom, 1010–360 Albert Street, Ottawa, ON K1R 7X7, phone (613) 233-3033, fax (613) 233-7650, web site: www.cableducation.ca

Concerned Children's Advertisers, PO Box 2432, Toronto, ON M4P 1E4, phone (416) 484-0871, fax (416) 484-6564, e-mail: concernedchildrens@on.aibn.com

CHUM **Television**, Director of Media Education, Sarah Crawford, 299 Queen Street West, Toronto, ON M5V 2Z5, phone (416) 591-7400, Extension 2900; fax (416) 591-9317; e-mail: sarahc@muchmusic.com – for Citytv, Much Music, MuchMoreMusic, Space, Bravo!, Access.

Jesuit Communication Project, 1002–60 St. Clair Ave. East, Toronto, ON M4T 1N5, phone (416) 515-0466, fax (416) 515-0467, e-mail: pungente@chass.utoronto.ca
    Resource centre and library for Media Literacy, offers workshops and presentations, Newsletter *Clipboard* available for $15 per year.

Pacific Cinémathèque, 200–1131 Howe Street, Vancouver, BC V6Z 2L7, phone (604) 688-8202, fax (604) 688-8204, e-mail: info@cinematheque.bc.ca; web site: www.cinematheque.bc.ca

For other Media Education contacts around the world, please check the Jesuit Communications web site at interact.uoregon.edu/MediaLit/JCP/index.html

Some Media Education Video Resources
The Ad and the Ego. A sixty-minute history and study of advertising, 1996. California Newsreel, 149–9th Street, Suite 420, San Francisco, California, U.S.A. 94103, phone (415) 621-6196.

Beyond Blame: Countering Violence in the Media. A video-based curriculum for children, youth, and adult discussion groups. Center for Media Literacy, 403–4727 Wilshire Blvd., Los Angeles, California 90010, phone 1-800-226-9494, e-mail: cml@medialit.org. For a catalogue of other kits and videos on the media check their web site at www.medialit.org

Buy Me That I, II, III. Three programs that serve as a child's survival guide to TV advertising. Center for Media Literacy, 403–4727 Wilshire Blvd., Los Angeles, California 90010, phone 1-800-226-9494.

Cable in the Classroom offers copyright-cleared, commercial-free, educationally relevant French and English television programs to elementary and secondary schools. Teachers are free to tape programs of interest and replay them in class. Cable in the Classroom, 909–350 Sparks Street, Ottawa, ON K1R 7X7, phone (613) 233-3033.

CBC: *Inside the Box*. Six videos on Documentary, News, Children's TV, Drama, The Consumer, TV as Art. CBC Enterprises, Box 500, Station A, Toronto, ON M5W 1E6.

Consuming Images. Bill Moyers's introduction to the power of the media. TVOntario, P.O. Box 200, Station Q, Toronto, ON M4T 2T1.

Minding the Set. Booklet and video developed by the Alliance for Children and Television and Rogers Cable to help parents and children understand television ($17.20). Lisa Warner, Rogers Cable, 855 York Mills Road, Don Mills, ON M3B 1Z1, phone (416) 446-6795.

NFB: *Constructing Reality; Images and Meaning; Media and Society Live TV*. Four video packages complete with guides which cover varying aspects of the media. NFB Customer Services, P.O. Box 6100, Station A, Montreal, QC H3C 3H5.

Prime Time Parent. A workshop kit for parents and others interested in television and its effect on children. Alliance for Children and Television, 1002–60 St. Clair Avenue East, Toronto, ON M4T 1N5, phone (416) 515-0466, fax (416) 515-0467, e-mail: acttv@interlog.com

Scanning Television. Four hours of video excerpts from Media Television, Citytv, and others for use in Grades 7 to 12 media classes with teaching guide. Toronto: Harcourt Brace, 1997. Phone 1-800-387-7278.

TV and Me. Targeted at students between ages nine and twelve the kit is a combination of video – with PSAs from the Concerned Children's Advertisers – and study guide for classroom use. Concerned Children's Advertisers, 2300 Yonge St., Suite 804, P.O. Box 2432, Toronto, ON M4P 1E4, phone (416) 484-0871, fax (416) 484-6564, e-mail: concernedchildrens@on.aibn.com

Acknowledgements

I am grateful to many people for their help during the writing of this book, among them: Sarah Crawford, Dianne Schwalm, Adrienne Pereira, John Haslett Cuff, Kevin Burns, Paul Sullivan, Geoff Simmonds, Alex Strachan, Neil Andersen, Barry Duncan, Carolyn Wilson, Kathleen Tyner, Len Masterman, Robyn Quin, Barrie McMahon, Maria Way, Cary Bazalgette, Gary Marcuse, Gary Ferrington, Joe Strebinger, Karen McOuat, Cathy Loblaw. I am also indebted to the people at CHUM Television, the Alliance for Children and Television, Sleeping Giant, Media Awareness Network, and TheatreBooks. Thanks to Wil Verheyen; the Association for Media Literacy's executive; Vancouver's The Sylvia; my brother Jesuits, especially Monty Williams, Bill Addley, and Paul Hamill; our editor, Jonathan Webb; and the Whites of the Seattle area.

And I owe a special thanks to Buffy, Giles, Xander, Willow, Cordelia, Oz, Maggie, Joel, Jean-Luc, Cybil, Ally, Drew, Buddy, Fox, and Dana, to name but a few without whom none of this would have been possible.

– J. J. P.